INCENTIVES AND POLITICAL ECONOMY

Laffont provides an incentive-based rationale for the behavior of politicians, both as 'supervisors' in the public goods production process and as residual decision-makers in a regime governed by an incomplete constitution. In doing so he provides theoretical foundations, drawn from industrial organization and information economics, for a political economy of state organization and constitutional governance. For political scientists and economists alike, this is one of the must-read new efforts in positive political economy.

Kenneth A. Shepsle, Harvard University

Jean-Jacques Laffont has been one of the foremost contributors to incentive theory. In this important book he shows by example how valuable the theory is for understanding and evaluating political institutions.

Eric Maskin, Harvard University

Incentives and Political Economy

JEAN-JACQUES LAFFONT

OXFORD
UNIVERSITY PRESS

This book has been printed digitally and produced in a standard specification in order to ensure its continuing availability

OXFORD
UNIVERSITY PRESS

Great Clarendon Street, Oxford OX2 6DP

Oxford University Press is a department of the University of Oxford.
It furthers the University's objective of excellence in research, scholarship,
and education by publishing worldwide in

Oxford New York

Auckland Cape Town Dar es Salaam Hong Kong Karachi
Kuala Lumpur Madrid Melbourne Mexico City Nairobi
New Delhi Shanghai Taipei Toronto

With offices in

Argentina Austria Brazil Chile Czech Republic France Greece
Guatemala Hungary Italy Japan South Korea Poland Portugal
Singapore Switzerland Thailand Turkey Ukraine Vietnam

Published in the United States
by Oxford University Press Inc., New York

Reprinted 2007

ISBN 978-0-19-829424-5

Preface

This book develops the material I used to give the 1997 Clarendon Lectures. I am very grateful to the Economics Department of Oxford University and the Oxford University Press for their invitation to deliver the lectures and for their wonderful hospitality during my visit.

The lectures correspond to an attempt to use principal–agent models and their developments for understanding constitutional design. I view political economy as arising from the need to delegate economic policy to politicians and therefore fundamentally as an incentive problem.

Accordingly this book owes a lot to the many colleagues who helped me over the years to understand the beauty of incentive theory, in particular Jerry Green, Roger Guesnerie, Eric Maskin, Jean-Charles Rochet and Jean Tirole. It draws heavily upon joint work with Marcel Boyer, Antoine Faure-Grimaud, Mathieu Meleu, Tchétché N'Guessan, Jean Tirole and in particular David Martimort. I am grateful to Isabelle Brocas, Avinash Dixit and Yossi Spiegel for their comments on a previous draft. Special thanks are due to Marie-Pierre Boé who has dealt with this manuscript so cheerfully and so professionally.

I would like to make clear at the outset that this book does not claim to provide a comprehensive view of political economy. It only explores some incentive issues raised by the delegation to politicians of various social decisions. Also, it proceeds step by step and each of the models considered incorporates some feature relevant to political economy, everything else being highly stylized. Researchers in political economy will have to embed the elements of theory we provide into their favorite political economy model.

In a nutshell, my view is as follows. From the perspective of contract theory, any realistic political economy model will entail a large number of incomplete contracting features: incomplete constitution, incomplete contract between voters and their representatives, incomplete contracts within the bureaucracy, etc. Consequently, any modeling of the whole picture will require many *ad hoc* assumptions and will leave us with a rather intractable model with non-robust results. At this stage, I find it more instructive to study, at the margin of complete contract theory, pieces of the puzzle to enlighten some major issues of political economy: the capture of politicians by interest groups, the purpose of the separation of powers, the meaning of checks and balances, the extent of discretion left to politicians and its implication for economic policies, the formation of interest groups, the role of delegation, etc.

I do not ignore the limits of this piecemeal approach. Nevertheless, I hope that the reader will find this book useful in considering political economy.

Jean-Jacques Laffont
Toulouse, April 1999

Acknowledgements

In writing this book I have borrowed from a number of papers.

Boyer, M. and J.J. Laffont (1999), 'Toward a Political Theory of the Emergence of Environmental Incentive Regulation', *Rand Journal of Economics*, 30, 137–157.

Faure-Grimaud, A., J.J. Laffont and D. Martimort (1998), 'A Theory of Supervision with Endogenous Transaction Costs', mimeo, IDEI.

Laffont, J.J. (1996), 'Industrial Policy and Politics', *International Journal of Industrial Organization*, 14, 1–27.

Laffont, J.J. (1997), 'Inflexible Rules Against Political Discretion', *Nordic Journal of Political Economy*, 24, 78–87.

Laffont, J.J. (1997), 'Frisch, Hotelling and the Marginal Cost Pricing Controversy', *Econometric Society, Monograph in Honor of R. Frisch*, ed. S. Ström, Cambridge University Press, Cambridge.

Laffont, J.J. and D. Martimort (1999), 'Separation of Regulators against Collusive Behavior', *Rand Journal of Economics*, 30, 232–262.

Laffont, J.J. and D. Martimort (1998), 'Collusion and Delegation', *Rand Journal of Economics*, 29, 280–305.

Laffont, J.J. and D. Martimort (1998), 'Mechanism Design with Collusion and Correlation', to appear in *Econometrica*.

Laffont, J.J. and M. Meleu (1997), 'Reciprocal Supervision, Collusion and Organizational Design', *The Scandinavian Journal of Economics*, 99, 519–540.

Laffont, J.J. and T.T. N'Guessan (1999), 'Competition and Corruption in an Agency Relationship', *Journal of Development Economics*, 60, 271–295.

Laffont, J.J. and J.C. Rochet (1997), 'Collusion in Organizations', *Scandinavian Journal of Economics*, 99, 485–495.

Laffont, J.J. and J. Tirole (1991), 'The Politics of Government Decision Making: A Theory of Regulatory Capture', *Quarterly Journal of Economics*, 106, 1089–1127.

Contents

1

Introduction

'Though I am an economist, and the tools of analysis used in this book are drawn from economic theory, the conclusions of the study are as relevant to the sociologist and the political scientist as they are to the economist.'

Mancur Olson (1965), p. 3

1.1 Political Economy with a Benevolent Monarch

Modern political economy was first developed in countries ruled by monarchs. Economists looked for good policy rules to run the economy of the State. Whatever their beliefs, they could not question the premise that the monarch was a perfectly benevolent agent of the people. They were led to call good rules the ones maximizing social welfare defined in one way or another as the welfare of the people. However, economists could question the benevolence of the administration, the agent of the monarch to implement policies. The dysfunctionings of administrative bodies in charge of the State's economy were indeed a driving force leading to the birth of liberalism as an economic policy which minimizes public intervention in the economy.

Adam Smith (1776) recognized the role of the State in defense, justice, education, public works and institutional design to facilitate private economic activities, with the necessary taxation for financing these public goods. But he was very critical of the public administration of this State intervention. He advocated various policy rules having in mind the design of proper incentives for the various administrative bodies as a main purpose. He recommended decentralization of the administration of local public goods as the best way to accommodate these incentives:

'Public works of a local nature should be maintained by local revenue.' p. 689.

because

> 'The abuses which sometimes creep into the local and provincial administration of a local or provincial revenue, how enormous so ever they may appear, are in reality, however, almost always very trifling, in comparison with those which commonly take place in the administration and expenditure of the revenue of a great empire.' p. 689.

Similarly, he proposed to finance highways, bridges and canals by tolls proportional to the wear and tear, to pay for the expenses and to balance the budget of each public work. Beyond some equity considerations, Smith's main argument for this financing method other than use of the general revenue of the society concerned the incentives of the administration to make the proper investments.

> 'When high roads, bridges, canals, etc are in this manner made and supported by the commerce which is carried on by means of them, they can be made only where that commerce requires them, and consequently where it is proper to make them ... A magnificent high road cannot be made through a desert country where there is little or no commerce, or merely because it happens to lead to the country villa of the intendant of the province, or to that of some great lord to whom the intendant finds it convenient to make his court. A great bridge cannot be thrown over a river at a place where nobody passes, or merely to embellish the view from the windows of a neighbouring palace: things which sometimes happen, in countries where works of this kind are carried on by any other revenue than that which they themselves are capable of affording.' p. 683.

Furthermore, he opposed increasing prices beyond what was needed for balancing the budget because (pp. 685–686) the tolls would be raised and become a great encumbrance to commerce; a tax on carriages in proportion to weights would fall principally on the poor; the roads would be neglected—arguments which mix social welfare considerations with the incentive motives of the administration.

Political economy was already for Adam Smith the design of policies which maximize social welfare under the incentive constraints of the administrative bodies in charge of implementing those policies. We will pursue this paradigm for political economy in the first part of this book using the tools of incentive theory.

1.2 The Design of Democratic Institutions

The advent of democracy eliminated the convenient myth of a monarch maximizing social welfare. Montesquieu and the American Federalists addressed the task of designing more democratic institutions which would favor social welfare. The Constitution founding a given State was supposed to be the mechanism organizing both the representation of the people by elected politicians and the structure of government. The Federalists were well aware of the fact that interest groups would form to influence policy decisions and that appropriate incentives had to be provided for the politicians and the administration.

The monarch was a perfect judge, perfect representative of the people, and perfect decision maker. Now the task was much more difficult. How can society be organized when the judiciary, executive and legislative branches of government must be delegated by the people to agents who have their private interests[1] and when interest groups form to capture those agents? Can we consider the Constitution as a grand contract which would maximize social welfare under incentive constraints just as the monarch was doing? There are several reasons why this cannot be done easily.[2]

[1] The need to take the incentives of politicians into account has not been always recognized. For Rousseau (1948) the government is merely an abstract device for carrying the will of the people. We share Downs' view that information problems are essential to understand why this approach is unrealistic:

> 'Another possible interpretation of Rousseau's theory is that the government consists solely of hired men who carry out the policies ordered by "the will of the people". The argument explains the private motives of the men in government quite simply: they obey the commands of the people with precision in order to keep their jobs, because the slightest disobedience means immediate dismissal. As our whole study shows, this view is incompatible with uncertainty and the division of labor.' Downs (1957), p. 285

[2] 'Dans un Etat populaire, il faut un ressort de plus, qui est la vertu.' Montesquieu (1748), p. 536. Translations of French quotations are provided in the Appendix, beginning on page 228.

The first one is that a contract requires penalties to be enforced and ultimately an outside enforcing mechanism when penalties are resisted. The second one is that a Constitution is necessarily incomplete for bounded rationality reasons and residual decision rights must be allocated to government bodies who then acquire the possibility of discretionary action. The control of the executive and legislative discretionary actions of the politicians and the administrative bodies can only be realized within the general rules of the Constitution, by a judiciary branch with limited power (for incentive reasons) and by reelection mechanisms which affect the private benefits of politicians.

Two degrees of freedom affect the analysis: (a) the choice of the states of nature not contracted for by the Constitution; (b) the limits to judicial power otherwise assumed to be benevolent.

Once these choices have been made, the design of the Constitution could be again conceived as an optimization problem of expected social welfare. The instruments available for optimization are the electoral processes which select the various governmental bodies, the policy instruments made available to them, the allocation of residual decision rights among them, the supervisory activities, i.e. the checks and balances between the various branches of the government, under the individual and collective incentive constraints of the various members of society, namely voters, politicians, bureaucrats, etc.

Such an optimization was the task that the Federalists took upon themselves in the formation of the new American government (Kramnick (1987), p. 48):

> 'Functions of government became arenas for particular social forces to dominate, and the separation and independence of these functions, it would be argued, required a balancing of each against the other, through a sharing and "intermixture" of power . . . in order to produce a moderate, temperate, cooler government.'

At least, this is the task we should assign to a normative theory of constitutional design. I do not ignore the more pessimistic view articulated by John Quincy Adams, according to whom the Constitution was calculated to increase the influence, power and wealth of those who already have these things. Two remarks can be made on this criticism. First, it is useful to understand how the Constitution should theoretically be designed, both in order to evaluate the current institutions and to make citizens aware of an ideal towards which they should strive. This is a wonderful role to be played by intellectuals. Second, the positive problem faced by a ruling group in designing the best Constitution is of a similar nature to the one studied here, except for the objective function to be maximized. The role of intellectuals in helping the ruling class in this design is then more ambiguous.

1.3 Political Economy in Democratic Countries

Given this more complex view of political institutions, what can be the evolution of political economy? First, it should be stressed that most economists have chosen to ignore the interaction between economic policy and politics. Some even believe that it is not 'politically correct' to develop policy recommendations altered by political considerations.

The first Nobel prize winner, R. Frisch, says quite clearly in his Nobel lecture (1970):

> 'It is not the task for us as econometricians and social engineers to go into a detailed discussion of the political system.' p. 228.

Building a purely economic framework available to citizens who can then use it in their political conflicts is a noble task which has the added value of being rather universal and institution-independent. In the long run this might be the best service that economists can provide to society. The role is essentially pedagogical but of limited direct use for policy when providing economic advice to the ruling party because: (a) it is poor advice for this party if the political constraints of its actions are not taken into account; (b) a policy proposal which maximizes social welfare is not what is demanded and will probably be discarded.

Two types of political economy can be practiced: either as an authentic adviser to a ruling party, who looks for the policies which maximize the party's payoff given the economic and political constraints;[3] or as an intellectual who proposes policies which take into account the economic and political constraints in maximizing long-run expected social welfare and which could be adopted as constitutional rules. The latter seems to be the only one available to independent economists who want to have a short-run impact on their society. This is the goal of a real political economy which integrates economics and political science. It is not clear, however, that such economists will be taken seriously by the rest of society, since they claim to be benevolent and thus contradict their whole intellectual approach, which treats all other agents as self-interested.

1.4 The Chicago View of Interest Group Politics

Despite the dominance of the public interest view of public economic intervention, a 'capture' or 'interest group' theory that emphasizes the role of interest groups in the formation of public policy developed. Marx's view that big business controls public institutions is certainly part of this, as well as the work of political scientists at the turn of the century, such as Bentley (1908). The Chicago school started with Stigler's (1971) explanation of the capture of regulatory authorities by the industries they were supposed to regulate. His theory was developed by his colleagues at Chicago, namely Peltzman (1976), Posner (1974) and Becker (1983). The goal of this work was to provide a positive analysis of policy decision making which emphasized the role of interest groups in shaping these policies and showed the lack of empirical relevance of the public interest view of public policy.

Let us consider in some detail Becker's 1983 major piece of work to stress the need to incorporate asymmetric information into the analysis in order to build a convincing positive theory. His general model of competition between political pressure groups is meant to provide a positive explanation of political choices. Politicians, political parties and voters are like a black

[3] 'Otherwise the economists' advice may be as useless as telling a profit-maximizing monopolist to sell his product at marginal cost so as to benefit society.' Downs (1957), p. 283.

box which transmits the pressure of active groups. Competition among the pressure groups which demand favors determines the equilibrium structure of the economic instruments (taxes, subsidies, levels of public goods, etc.) which induce these favors. This is why this positive theory of government has often been said to be only demand-determined.

The supply side of political favors, i.e. why and how politicians and voters offer these favors, is left unmodeled, as Becker (1983), p. 372, acknowledges:

> 'I shall not try to model how different political systems translate the activities of pressure groups into political influence'.

Within this limited scope of demand-determined political equilibrium, Becker implicitly appeals to various assumptions of incomplete information. We will henceforth argue that a more fundamental modeling of information will enable us to develop fruitfully his type of analysis. Furthermore, it will help open the black box of the supply side.

Consider two groups of size n_1 and n_2 who battle over the determination of an economic instrument, say a tax level t, which is favorable to group 1, but unfavorable to group 2. The political system produces a level of t which depends on the political influences of the groups

$$t = T(L_1, L_2), \tag{1.1}$$

with

$$\frac{\partial T}{\partial L_1} > 0 \qquad \frac{\partial T}{\partial L_2} < 0.$$

The influence itself depends on the size of the group n_i and of the resources spent by the group in lobbying:

$$L_i = p_i(n_i, a_i n_i) \qquad i = 1,2, \tag{1.2}$$

where a_i is expenditure per member.

Each group i determines a_i. In so doing, it must solve an eventual free rider problem within the group. Let $U_i(t)$ be the utility derived from t by group i. In the following discussion, if $f(n_i) = n_i$, the free rider problem is completely solved. If $f(n_i) = 1$ free riding is total. Group i then solves

$$\max_{a_i} U_i(t) - f(n_i)a_i; \tag{1.3}$$

hence

$$\frac{\mathrm{d}U_i}{\mathrm{d}t} \cdot \frac{\partial T}{\partial L_i}\frac{\partial p_i}{\partial a_i} = f(n_i) \qquad i = 1,2. \tag{1.4}$$

The equilibrium follows from (1.4).

Becker postulates that there exist deadweight losses, say, associated with taxes. This postulation can be written as

$$\frac{\mathrm{d}U_1}{\mathrm{d}t} + \frac{\mathrm{d}U_2}{\mathrm{d}t} < 0.$$

From the work of Vickrey (1945) and Mirrlees (1971) we know that incomplete information is the explanation of the costly information rents acquired by agents and therefore the fundamental source of these deadweight losses. So, a major inefficiency of political conflicts follows from the inefficiency of redistributive instruments due to asymmetric information. Determining the deadweight losses precisely from a careful modeling of asymmetric information makes it possible to explore (without arbitrary restrictions on instruments) the supply-side effect of political influence. Politics is then a game of redistribution of information rents within the realm of discretion left by the Constitution.

Equation (1.1) is the black box which transforms the demand for influence of the different pressure groups into outcomes. Specifying political institutions in detail is required to open this black box. This is what we can expect from a mature political science. Here also the behavior of voters under incomplete information will be a major building block, for a given set of constitutional rules. Becker was well aware of the role of information and the manipulation of information which affects voters' preferences:

> 'These "preferences" can be manipulated and created through the information and misinformation provided by interested pressure groups . . .
>
> 'The incentive to become well informed about political issues is weaker because each individual has only a minor effect on political outcomes decided by the majority (or by similar rules).' p. 392.

Inside the black box determining the supply of favors, Becker sees a principal–agent problem between pressure groups and politicians or bureaucrats:

> 'A more general analysis would incorporate this principal-agent relation between bureaucrats, politicians and pressure groups into the determination of political equilibrium.' p. 396.

Modern analysis of principal–agent relationships emphasizes information asymmetries. Equation (1.2) stresses two major variables which affect the political influence of a group: the sheer size of the group n_i if only through voting, and the lobbying resources $a_i n_i$, which can represent campaign contributions as well as various bribes to bureaucrats and politicians. Beyond models which can show how campaign contributions may affect the beliefs and the votes of citizens, we also need models of corruption which call for informational foundations. Equation (1.4) specifies how a group determines its lobbying expenses. In particular it embodies the way the group is able (or unable) to mitigate the free rider problem within the group. Absent asymmetric information, a major implication of the Becker analysis is that competition among pressure groups favors efficient methods of taxation (see his Proposition 4, p. 386; see also Stigler (1971), (1982), Becker (1976), (1985), Wittman (1989)). The logic is simple. With rational voters, politicians who make inefficient transfers will be voted out of office.

The Virginia school of political economy claims that, with poorly informed voters, politicians will select inefficient sneaky methods of redistribution (the disguised transfer mechanisms in the Tullock (1983) terminology) over more transparent efficient methods. Becker (1976) and Wittman (1989) criticized the implicit irrationality of voters which seems necessary for such a scheme to last. Recently, Coate and Morris (1995) built a model based on imperfect information with rational voters where inefficient transfer schemes may be selected as follows. There are two types of politicians, good ones and bad ones. They are better informed than citizens. The good ones use a public project that transfers wealth to an interest group only if it is efficient to do so. Bad ones prefer to use the public project to make transfers even when it is inefficient to do so, because in this way they have a chance to protect their (false) reputation of being good. Giving efficient monetary transfers to their favored interest group would reveal immediately that they are bad. The choice of inefficient transfers is for signaling purposes. It remains to understand why we have politicians of two types in equilibrium, why good politicians cannot signal themselves, and why political competition does not provide voters with enough information to identify good and bad politicians. Also, if costless direct transfers are really available, why can't good politicians neutralize the distribution effects of public projects and operate transparent redistributions with these transfers? Implicitly, the reasoning puts restrictions on the instruments available to politicians.

In a world of asymmetric information, any public project creates information rents which cannot be eliminated (or only at extremely high efficiency costs). Costless transfers do not exist. The more general questions are then: How does political decision making distort the allocation of resources away from second-best incentive Pareto efficiency? How can we structure the political game through constitutional rules to avoid large distortions from second best? Why is it not possible to eliminate those distortions?

1.5 The Complete Contracting Approach

One possibility is to introduce the fact that the collective decision maker has socially valuable information which is available at the time of decision making. For example, he is the only one who can acquire relevant information such as the real international situation or the current business conditions. Efficiency requires the use of this information but this opens up the possibility of discretionary behavior.

Nevertheless, the revelation principle tells us that maximization of expected social welfare can be achieved by using the optimal revelation mechanism which extracts in an incentive-compatible way the politician's information and avoids any capture of the politician by interest groups. More generally, one can explore the allocation mechanisms which solve individual and coalitional incentive problems. The politician is then a particular agent of society who has been delegated collective decisions. The emphasis here is on private information and on the necessary distortions required by incentive compatibility.

The outcome of such a political economy would specify both the allocation of tasks, including those of collective decision makers, as well as the rules to be followed. From the revelation principle, such an optimal society would be isomorphic to a vast system of information transmitted from the periphery to the constitutional level which would specify how this information should be used for the allocation of resources.

We will call this approach **the complete Constitution approach**. Politicians are informed supervisors. In Chapter 2 we will describe a simple model of collective decision making based on Tirole's (1986) supervision model, with hard information to illustrate this approach. Chapter 3 will propose a theory of separation of powers within this modeling framework. Chapter 4 will pursue this line of research by considering more complex governments with two or more divisions between which reciprocal favors can occur.

This contractual approach to political economy has several weaknesses. It presumes a perfect benevolent court which enforces contracts. It presumes no complexity cost, and no bounded rationality.

1.6 The Incomplete Contracting Approach

An alternative approach, which we will label **the incomplete Constitution approach**, ignores asymmetric private information. Its point of departure is the non-contractibility assumption about some states of nature which are only known *ex post*.[4] The politician is then the agent who has the residual rights to make collective decisions in cases where the Constitution provides no guidance.

The motivations for this line of thought are both the unavailability of a benevolent court and bounded rationality. It is a

[4] There are other ways to depart from a complete contracting framework by considering limited commitment, renegotiation, multiprincipal governance, and beyond, the transaction costs in the sense of Williamson (1989). North (1990) started the analysis of the politicial process in the transaction cost mode. See Dixit (1996) for a study along those lines.

shortcut to deal with these issues despite the lack of firm foundations. A major problem is that the theory has not been able to provide a satisfactory description of the limits imposed by the non-contractibility problem in the allocation of resources. Either one accepts the Maskin–Tirole (1999) critique and first-best social welfare maximization is achieved (note that this approach still requires a benevolent court) or arbitrary restrictions are put on possible contracts. Three degrees of freedom are then available: first, the game form which selects the decision maker with residual rights of control, e.g. majority voting selects the politician; second, the set of discretionary decisions available to him; third, the non-contractible events. The politician is not controlled here by a contract but by the future decisions of voters. If he wants to remain in control, he must win future elections. Whatever feedback control is provided by elections, and for a given set of non-contractible states of nature, an interesting trade-off still exists: by constitutionally restricting the set of decisions of the politician, one decreases his discretion but one may also destroy *ex post* efficiency. Alternatively, taking as given the set of non-contractible states and with no constraint on the set of decisions, one may look for interesting structures of the political game. They affect how various interest groups influence the politician who redistributes goods among agents.

This is essentially the Chicago approach, which concludes that *ex post* efficiency is achieved since there is no reason why the politician would not maximize the sum to be distributed. Becker's model is of this nature. It is positive in so far as the mapping from group formation to political outcomes is taken as given. Grossman and Helpman (1996) open this black box slightly by modeling the game of bribes between exogenously given interest groups. Persson, Roland and Tabellini (1997), as do most of political science, focus instead on the feedback control of various electoral modes for given sets of decisions. Note that, in all this literature, the motivation that we give here as to why we need politicians in terms of non-contractible states is only implicit.

Rather than a contract, here the outcome of constitutional design defines a particular political game which specifies who has the residual decision rights and the family of instruments available to them. What the analysis can do, beyond the pure positive description of equilibria, is to compare various game forms and various restrictions on instruments.

1.7 Adding Asymmetric Information

By introducing asymmetric information in the above approach, we create a natural mapping from policy instruments to rents which defines the stakes of agents in policy choices even without *ex post* restriction on instruments, except those imposed by individual rationality constraints. Furthermore, this second-best framework convexifies the Pareto frontier even without income effects and creates a potential inefficiency of the political game (as advocated by the rent-seeking literature).

Thus we may combine the informationally based complete constitutional approach with incomplete contracting. Constitutional reforms can strike a balance between efficiency and discretion by restricting politicians' instruments to improve *ex ante* social welfare. They can also change the rules of the political game or the structure of government.

In Chapter 5 we explain the basic trade-off between inflexible rules and political discretion in a random majority voting game. The marginal cost pricing controversy is reviewed in this light in Chapter 6. An application to environmental policy is then developed in Chapter 7.

1.8 Endogenous Coalition Formation

Beyond the individual stakes for policy choices which can be translated into votes, groups form to influence politicians with bribes, campaign contributions, etc.

As Becker (1983), p. 393, has already stressed,

> 'an explicit modeling of coalition formation would surely add to the power of the approach'

and as Persson (1997) notes in his discussion of the recent lobbying models,

> 'One wonders why some regions would have organized interest groups while others would not. This is a difficult question, that still does not have a satisfactory answer, even though Olson (1965) identified the important aspects of the problem.'

In this review of the rent-seeking literature Tollison (1989) also says (p. 521):

> 'The plain truth is that economists know very little about the dynamics of group formation and action.'

We believe that the policy rent mapping provided by asymmetric information is essential for a theory of group behavior. Such a theory should take into account the transaction costs due to asymmetric information within the coalitions. Chapter 8 develops the generalization of the revelation principle for group behavior and shows how a Constitution can be optimized to take into account both individual and coalitional incentive constraints under asymmetric information. Chapter 9 studies a particular type of collusive behavior embodied in delegation. The pros and cons of delegation are then discussed to assess the gains and costs of decentralization. Finally, Chapter 10 concludes.

Part I

Politicians as Informed Supervisors

'You must admit that we shall have found a way to meet your demand for realization, if we can discover how a state might be constituted in the closest accordance with our description. Will not that content you? It would be enough for me.'

Plato (1941), p. 473

2

The Complete Contract Approach to Constitutional Design

'The Constitution is a broad long-term contract between those ruled and the rulers that specifies the conditions on which the agents may exercise power in order to enhance the interests of the principal.'

Lane (1996), p. 180

2.1 Introduction

The principal–agent theory developed in the 1970s and 1980s has produced a large set of insights for understanding how contracts might be established within organizations. This theory explains how a principal who offers a contract to an agent should structure this contract to overcome, at least partially, the asymmetries of information he is facing in order to maximize his expected utility. Optimal contracts with adverse selection, with moral hazard, or with non-verifiability by a third party of some variables are by now relatively well understood.

Despite insightful extensions to multiagent or to multiprincipal organizations, this body of knowledge falls short of a comprehensive theory of organizations. One major reason, beyond the restrictive nature of the organizations studied, lies in the non-cooperative approach generally followed to model multiagent settings. Indeed, in this standard paradigm, if the cooperation of agents is desired by the principal it can be induced by the contracts he offers to the agents, each of whom maximizes his own welfare given the behavior of the other agents. What remains is that the principal is assumed to have complete control over the game played by the agents.[1] Unwanted communication or

[1] See Laffont (1990).

side-contracting between agents can be prevented. This is a rather unrealistic assumption. Contract theory teaches us that the principal structures the contracts so as to minimize, at the lowest possible efficiency cost, the information rents given up to the agents because of their informational advantages. It is quite natural to expect a collective reaction by the agents to protect their rents.

We need to understand how agents can react to the rules of an organization, and, further, to understand how a principal who is aware of the incentives for collusion should design the organization. Modeling coalitional or collusive behavior and characterizing the regulatory responses to such behavior is a major task of any organization theory and in particular of a theory of government.

The empirical relevance of collusion is easy to establish. A clear example is that of auctions, for which the occurrence of cooperative behavior between bidders is well documented. As Porter and Zona (1993) put it: 'Collusion is a very general phenomenon in auctions'. The importance of collusive behavior between economic agents has also been documented in many other contexts. In particular, sociologists of organizations such as Crozier (1963), Dalton (1959), Gouldner (1954) and Mintzberg (1979) have often stressed that economists neglect group behavior. They have distinguished horizontal cliques, such as colluding bidders in an auction, which gather members of the organization at the same hierarchical level, and vertical cliques which gather members of different hierarchical levels (such as a supervisor and a worker, or an auctioneer and a bidder) and which may lead to favoritism and extortion. The capture of regulatory institutions by interest groups was put forward very early in industrial economics by Marx, Stigler (1971) and Olson (1965). It is an important example of what economists call 'vertical collusion'. Let us note also that the corruption inside and outside the organizations of less developed countries appears more and more clearly as a major impediment to economic growth (as documented by Mauro (1995)), and is far from being eradicated in more developed countries.

To put this literature into perspective, it is convenient to go back to the revelation principle. This principle tells us that, in the absence of restrictions on contracts but with decentralized information, any organization is equivalent to a centralized organization in which information must be communicated in an incentive-compatible way to a center which transmits instructions back to the agents about the actions to be implemented (when these actions are verifiable) and recommendations for the (unobservable) effort levels to be exerted (Myerson (1982)). Accordingly, the characterization of feasible incentive-compatible allocations can be easily obtained by characterizing the revelation mechanisms in which all agents truthfully reveal their private information. The best organization from the point of view of a given criterion—for example, social welfare or the center's more narrow objective—is the one which follows from the maximization of the criterion in the set of feasible incentive-compatible allocations. The optimal organization is obtained in the abstract form of revelation mechanisms. What remains then is to find more familiar institutions such as non-linear prices, auctions or managerial incentive schemes which implement these mechanisms.

All along, a non-cooperative behavior of agents has been postulated. Implicitly, the center is assumed to control communication between agents. It is doubtful that the center can completely succeed in this task. Therefore it seems interesting to study the opposite case where communication between agents is perfect and side-contracting between them becomes possible.

The first steps in the literature on coalition formation (such as Green and Laffont (1979) in the study of mechanisms for the provision of public goods; Robinson (1985) in the study of auctions; the sizeable literature on information sharing in oligopolies, etc.) assumed that privately informed agents had access to a technology enabling them, when they formed a coalition, to become fully informed about each other. The foundations of such a technology and the reasons why the principal of the organization had no access to this technology were never discussed.

Tirole (1986) gives a more explicit version of this approach by considering a principal–supervisor–agent hierarchy in which the definition of the supervisor is essentially the definition of an imperfect technology giving verifiable[2] (or hard) information about the agent. Because of the principal's lack of attention or limited expertise, the use of the technology must be delegated to

[2] Here, verifiability has a weaker meaning than usual. We do not mean that the information can be observed by a jury, but only that the principal can be convinced by it of the agent's type.

an intermediary who must be given appropriate incentives[3] to discover the information and transmit it to the principal.

More precisely, suppose that the agent has a cost characteristic θ which is his private information and which can take two values $\underline{\theta}$ or $\bar{\theta}$ with probabilities ν and $1 - \nu$ respectively. With probability $\xi < 1$ (conditionally on the agent being efficient) the technology of the supervisor enables him to discover in a verifiable way the low cost characteristic $\underline{\theta}$. When the supervisor observes (and discloses) that $\theta = \underline{\theta}$, the principal has complete information and can offer a contract leaving no rent to the (efficient) agent. When the supervisor observes nothing, the principal offers a contract which leaves no rent to a $\bar{\theta}$-agent but a positive rent to a $\underline{\theta}$-agent. What are the dimensions of discretion for the supervisor? When he has observed $\underline{\theta}$, he cannot pretend that $\theta = \bar{\theta}$, because the only verifiable information he can obtain is $\theta = \underline{\theta}$, but he can pretend that he has observed nothing and conceal the verifiable information obtained. This opens up the possibility of collusion between the agent and the supervisor.

Tirole (1986) and Laffont and Tirole (1993) then make a number of specific assumptions which enable them to solve the many problems associated with the modeling of collusion and to carry out the whole program of characterizing the optimal organizational response. Two agents only are concerned by the collusion, the supervisor and the agent, and so there is no issue on the formation of subcoalitions.[4] Collusion can only take place when the supervisor has observed that $\theta = \underline{\theta}$ (which occurs with probability $\nu\xi$). In this case, the supervisor and the agent have complete information. The bargaining power in the collusion is allocated to the supervisor. However, alternative assumptions are possible here. The important point is that the principal can anticipate the outcome of bargaining to determine his optimal reaction. The number of collusion constraints is limited by the fact that the agent has only two possible types. The risk-neutral supervisor is assumed to have limited liability so that the principal is obliged to leave him a rent to obtain his information. Finally, and most importantly, a side-contract between the agent and the supervisor

[3] Furthermore the technology is so costly that duplicating it cannot be envisioned.

[4] The other coalitions (principal + agent, principal + supervisor) are ineffective here.

is possible, despite being illegal and not enforceable by a court. This is obviously a shortcut, possibly for an enforcement in the context of a repeated relationship. To capture this limitation of contracting, Laffont and Tirole (1993) introduce some exogenous transaction costs in the side-contracting.

Under these assumptions, it is possible to characterize the optimal organizational response to collusion. This is done in two steps. First, a collusion-proof principle is obtained. This principle states that any allocation of resources induced by the organization can be achieved by a revelation mechanism for the agent and the supervisor which is robust to collusion, i.e. such that the supervisor and the agent do not wish to collude and hide information from the principal. The additional collusion-proof constraint takes a simple but very instructive form: the payment to the supervisor who transmits verifiable information must exceed the stake of collusion discounted by the transaction costs of collusion. The stake of collusion is the information rent which is kept by the agent when the supervisor hides his information. This inequality gives three main ways that can be used by the principal to avoid collusion: to create incentive payments for the supervisor; to decrease the stake of collusion; and to increase the transaction costs of collusion.

The collusion-proof principle is essential because it allows us to extend the constructive methodology of the revelation principle. The usual incentive compatibility conditions and the collusion proof constraint characterize the set of feasible allocations. To obtain the optimal mechanism (i.e. the optimal organization) it is necessary to maximize the objective function of the principal on this set.

This methodology can only be applied in a very particular set of circumstances. However, until recently there was no alternative framework available which would provide insights as to how an organization can adjust to the threat of collusion. As a consequence, a large volume of literature has built up based on this model. For example, the model has been used extensively in Laffont and Tirole (1993) to study such diverse questions as the capture of regulators, favoritism in auctions, or collusion in cost auditing. Let us mention two other examples.

Kofman and Lawarrée (1993) show that it may be desirable for stockholders in the firm to use an external supervisor who is less informed than an internal one if the external supervisor is less easily captured by the manager. Strausz (1997) offers a possible explanation as to why collusion may occur within organizations. He extends Tirole's model by introducing an imperfect technology that allows the principal to detect collusion between the supervisor and the agent (when it occurs). More specifically, after the supervisor has reported to the principal, the latter receives a signal that is imperfectly correlated with the occurrence of collusion. Strausz first shows that when the principal can contract on this signal, and commit not to renegotiate, then no collusion occurs in equilibrium. However, when commitment is not possible, the renegotiation-proof constraint (which is a particular form of contract incompleteness) implies that the principal will not systematically prevent collusion. Intuitively, when collusion can be detected with a high probability, the principal will have no interest in substantially distorting the contract for the small expected benefit of preventing collusion under all circumstances.[5]

In this chapter we use Tirole's methodology in a particular supervision model to study the role of politicians as informed supervisors. This will form a building block for Chapters 3 and 4 which will extend the analysis to construct, respectively, an incentive theory of the separation of powers and a framework for comparing the designs of checks and balances.

2.2 *A Simple Supervision Model*

One reason why we may need politicians is that good social decision making requires information, and acquiring information is a specialized task for which society needs particular agents.[6] Politicians act as informed supervisors. We will study in this chapter how the Constitution[7] should be designed to maxi-

[5] See also Kofman and Lawarrée (1993), Khalil and Lawarrée (1994).

[6] 'Le grand avantage des représentants c'est qu'ils sont capables de discuter les affaires. Le peuple n'y est point du tout propre.' Montesquieu (1748), p. 587.

[7] 'By political constitution, we mean the actual institutional structure of government rather than the documents upon which this structure is based.' Downs (1957), p. 290.

mize expected social welfare, given the need for politicians as supervisors.[8]

2.2.1 *The Optimal Constitution Without Supervision*

Consider the problem of public good provision by a firm which has private information on its cost function. Producing q units of public good has a cost θq. The marginal cost θ can take one of two values $\{\underline{\theta}, \bar{\theta}\}$ with respective probabilities ν and $1-\nu$. Let $\Delta\theta = (\bar{\theta} - \underline{\theta}) > 0$. These probabilities are common knowledge, but only the firm's manager knows the true value of θ. There is a single firm which can produce the public good. Denoting t as the transfer from the government to the firm, to obtain the participation of the firm[9] an individual rationality constraint must be satisfied for all values of the informational parameter θ, i.e.:

$$U \equiv t - \theta q \geq 0. \tag{2.1}$$

Consumers derive a utility $S(q)$, with $S' > 0$, $S'' < 0$, from public good consumption. The funding of public good production requires indirect taxation with a cost of public funds[10] $(1+\lambda) > 1$; hence consumers' welfare is

$$S \equiv S(q) - (1+\lambda)t. \tag{2.2}$$

Public good provision can be organized at the constitutional level. Social welfare is defined as

$$W \equiv S + U = S(q) - (1+\lambda)\theta q - \lambda U. \tag{2.3}$$

The task of the Constitution is to specify the appropriate contract to be offered to the firm in order to maximize expected social

[8] We will maintain the vocabulary of politicians in the whole book. Sometimes the alternative interpretation of bureaucrats will be more appropriate.

[9] We normalize the status quo level of utility for the firm to zero for all types. See Lewis and Sappington (1989), Maggi and Rodriguez (1995), Jullien (1997) and Jeon and Laffont (1999) for analyses of countervailing incentives arising in cases of type-dependent individual rationality levels of utility.

[10] For informational reasons, taxation is almost always distortive and creates deadweight losses which are estimated around 30 percent of tax revenues in developed countries such as the USA and much more in developing countries (see Jones, Tandon and Vogelsang (1990)).

welfare. From the revelation principle,[11] we know that it can be obtained from the optimal revelation mechanism. Such a revelation mechanism here is a pair of contracts $(\underline{q}, \underline{t})$, $(\bar{q}, \bar{t})$ which are incentive-compatible.

For incentive compatibility we must have

$$(\underline{IC}) \quad \underline{t} - \underline{\theta}\underline{q} \geq \bar{t} - \underline{\theta}\bar{q} \tag{2.4}$$

$$(\overline{IC}) \quad \bar{t} - \bar{\theta}\bar{q} \geq \underline{t} - \bar{\theta}\underline{q} \tag{2.5}$$

or, if we use the variables (U,q) instead of (t,q), with $\underline{U} = \underline{t} - \underline{\theta}\underline{q}$ and $\bar{U} = \bar{t} - \bar{\theta}\bar{q}$,

$$(\underline{IC}) \quad \underline{U} \geq \bar{U} + \Delta\theta\bar{q} \tag{2.6}$$

$$(\overline{IC}) \quad \bar{U} \geq \underline{U} - \Delta\theta\underline{q}. \tag{2.7}$$

The individual rationality constraints are now

$$(\underline{IR}) \quad \underline{U} \geq 0 \tag{2.8}$$

$$(\overline{IR}) \quad \bar{U} \geq 0. \tag{2.9}$$

The Constitution should select the pair of contracts which maximizes, under constraints (2.6) to (2.9), expected social welfare, i.e.

$$\nu[S(\underline{q}) - (1+\lambda)\underline{\theta}\underline{q} - \lambda\underline{U}] + (1-\nu)[S(\bar{q}) - (1+\lambda)\bar{\theta}\bar{q} - \lambda\bar{U}]. \tag{2.10}$$

Clearly, (2.8) is implied by (2.6) and (2.9). Indeed, if a contract $(\bar{t},\bar{q})$ provides a non-negative utility level to a type $\bar{\theta}$, a type $\underline{\theta}$, which is more productive, gets a positive utility level if it mimics type $\bar{\theta}$ by selecting the contract $(\bar{t},\bar{q})$. Therefore incentive compatibility requires that the contract $(\underline{t},\underline{q})$ gives a positive utility level to the $\underline{\theta}$-agent. Ignoring (2.7) momentarily, and observing that (2.6) and (2.9) must be binding, we have $\bar{U} = 0$ and $\underline{U} = \Delta\theta\bar{q}$. Substituting into (2.10) and maximizing we obtain:

$$S'(\hat{\underline{q}}) = (1+\lambda)\underline{\theta} \tag{2.11}$$

$$S'(\hat{\bar{q}}) = (1+\lambda)\bar{\theta} + \lambda\frac{\nu}{1-\nu}\Delta\theta \tag{2.12}$$

with

$$\underline{t} = \underline{U} + \underline{\theta}\hat{\underline{q}} = \Delta\theta\hat{\bar{q}} + \underline{\theta}\hat{\underline{q}} \tag{2.13}$$

[11] See Gibbard (1973), Green and Laffont (1977) and Myerson (1979).

$$\bar{t} = \bar{U} + \bar{\theta}\hat{\bar{q}} = \bar{\theta}\hat{\bar{q}}. \tag{2.14}$$

Note that this solution satisfies (2.7) since $\hat{\underline{q}} > \hat{\bar{q}}$.

Under complete information about θ, the Constitution would equate the marginal utility of the public good to its marginal social cost, i.e.

$$S'(\underline{q}^*) = (1 + \lambda)\,\underline{\theta} \tag{2.15}$$

$$S'(\bar{q}^*) = (1 + \lambda)\,\bar{\theta}, \tag{2.16}$$

and would leave no rent to the firm, so that

$$\underline{t}^* = \underline{\theta}\underline{q}^* \qquad \bar{t}^* = \bar{\theta}\bar{q}^*. \tag{2.17}$$

Asymmetric information about θ leads to a trade-off between efficiency and rent extraction. The higher the inefficient type's production level $\bar{q}$, the higher the socially costly rent $\underline{U} = \Delta\theta\bar{q}$ which must be given up to the firm when it is efficient. Equation (2.12) explains how the production level of the inefficient firm must be decreased to optimize this trade-off. The expected marginal efficiency cost $(1 - \nu)\,[S'(\hat{\bar{q}}) - (1 + \lambda)\bar{\theta}]$ must be equated to the expected marginal rent cost $\lambda\nu\Delta\theta$. Note also that no rent is given up to the inefficient type $\bar{\theta}$ and that no production distortion is required from the efficient type.

Let us discuss this essential rent–efficiency trade-off further with the aid of Figure 2.1.

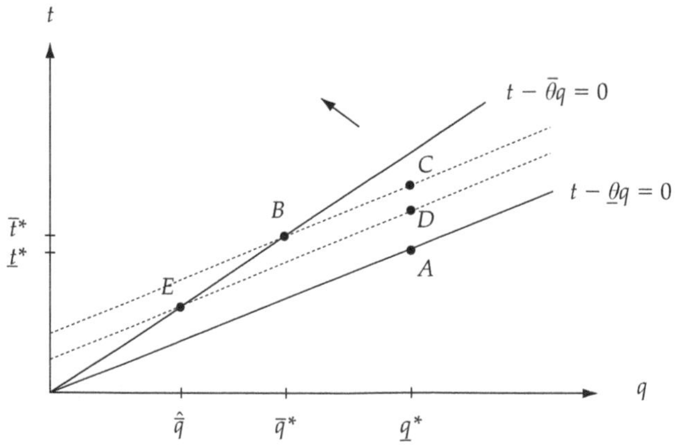

Figure 2.1

A $\underline{\theta}$-firm ($\bar{\theta}$-firm) has indifference curves which are straight lines, $t - \underline{\theta}q$ = constant ($t - \bar{\theta}q$ = constant). We have drawn as solid lines the indifference curves of the two possible types going through 0. A and B correspond to the optimal complete information contracts $(\underline{t}^*, \underline{q}^*)$ and $(\bar{t}^*, \bar{q}^*)$, respectively.

Utilities increase in the north-west direction since firms want more money and less production. So, if under incomplete information we offer A and B, both types select B. (A,B) is not incentive-compatible. One possibility to obtain an incentive-compatible offer is to give a transfer to a firm producing $\underline{q}^*$ which is so high that a $\underline{\theta}$-firm is indifferent between this contract and B. C represents this contract. The pair (C, B) is now incentive-compatible and implements the same quantity allocations as the complete information optimum. However, this is rather costly for social welfare since a rent $\Delta\theta\bar{q}^*$ with a social cost $\lambda\Delta\theta\bar{q}^*$ is given up to a $\underline{\theta}$-firm, i.e. with probability ν.

The best incentive-compatible pair described by the equations (2.11) to (2.14) is obtained by decreasing the quantity requested from type $\bar{\theta}$. This decreases the information rent to $\Delta\theta\hat{\bar{q}}$ but creates an efficiency cost since the marginal utility of production is not equated to the marginal social cost. The optimal trade-off is obtained when the expected marginal social gain of further decreasing the information rent by one unit, i.e. $\lambda\nu\Delta\theta$ (since the rent is given only to type $\underline{\theta}$ with probability ν and is a transfer with a marginal social cost λ), equals the expected marginal social efficiency cost of this decrease, i.e.,

$$(1 - \nu)\frac{\mathrm{d}}{\mathrm{d}\bar{q}}[S(\bar{q}) - (1 + \lambda)\bar{\theta}\bar{q}] = (1 - \nu)[S'(\bar{q}) - (1 + \lambda)\bar{\theta}],$$

since the efficiency cost occurs with probability $(1 - \nu)$. We then obtain equation (2.12), namely

$$(1 - \nu)[S'(\hat{\bar{q}}) - (1 + \lambda)\bar{\theta}] = \lambda\nu\Delta\theta.$$

The best incentive-compatible pair is represented by (D, E) in Figure 2.1. The information rent is now DA instead of CA and the quantity distortion is $\bar{q}^* - \hat{\bar{q}}$ for type $\bar{\theta}$.

It is clear from Figure 2.1 that the incentive constraint of type $\underline{\theta}$ is binding (D and E belong to the same $\underline{\theta}$-indifference curve) and that the participation constraint of type $\bar{\theta}$ is binding (E belongs to the indifference curve characterized by $t - \bar{\theta}q = 0$). The $\bar{\theta}$-agent strictly prefers E to D, i.e. the incentive constraint of type $\bar{\theta}$ is strictly satisfied and D is above the $\bar{\theta}$-indifference curve through A, and so the individual rationality constraint of type $\underline{\theta}$ is strictly satisfied. These qualitative features will be quite general.

As ν increases, the distortion $(\bar{q}^* - \hat{\bar{q}})$ increases and we reach a value ν^* beyond which it is better to give up production when $\theta = \bar{\theta}$. Then, a single contract A is offered. It is accepted by type $\underline{\theta}$ despite the fact that it yields no information rent and is rejected by type $\bar{\theta}$. The critical value ν^* is defined by

$$\nu^*[S(\underline{q}^*) - (1 + \lambda)\underline{\theta}\underline{q}^*] = \nu^* [S(\underline{q}^*) - (1 + \lambda)\, \underline{\theta}\underline{q}^* - \lambda\Delta\theta\hat{\bar{q}}] + (1 - \nu^*)[S(\hat{\bar{q}}) - (1+\lambda)\, \bar{\theta}\hat{\bar{q}}] \quad (2.18)$$

or

$$\lambda\nu^*\Delta\theta\hat{\bar{q}} = (1 - \nu^*)[S(\hat{\bar{q}}) - (1 + \lambda)\hat{\bar{q}}];$$

that is, when the expected cost of rents in the regime with two types equals the expected social utility of having a $\bar{\theta}$-firm in that regime. For ν higher than ν^*, the cost of rents given up to type $\underline{\theta}$ because of the presence of $\bar{\theta}$-firms exceeds the social gain from offering contracts to $\bar{\theta}$-types. We refer to the shut-down regime when only A is offered. In the whole book we will assume that ν is less than ν^*.

2.2.2 *The Supervision Technology*

Let us now introduce a politician who observes a verifiable[12] signal σ equal to θ with probability ξ and observes nothing otherwise ($\sigma = \phi$). The politician is motivated by his income or reward[13] s and has no private wealth, so that his utility function can be written

$$V = s \geq 0.$$

Note that s need not be a monetary income. It can be a private benefit associated with power.

[12] For example, the politician has access to information concerning the real cost of a Franco-German future nuclear power plant before deciding the size of the nuclear program for the twenty-first century.

[13] 'Economic theories of government behavior, in so far as they exist, universally fail to assign any motives to the men in government.' Downs (1957), p. 283.

Consider first the benchmark case where the politician transmits his information truthfully without particular incentives. Then, his report r equates to his signal σ.

If $\sigma = r = \theta$, the Constitution is informed and can implement the complete information allocation with an expected welfare

$$W^{FI} = \nu\left[S(\underline{q}^*) - (1+\lambda)\underline{\theta}\underline{q}^*\right] + (1-\nu)\left[S(\bar{q}^*) - (1+\lambda)\bar{\theta}\bar{q}^*\right].$$

This event happens with probability ξ.

If $\sigma = \phi$, the Constitution is uninformed, and furthermore its posterior beliefs (Pr $(\theta = \underline{\theta}/\sigma = \phi)$) remain equal to the prior beliefs:

$$\Pr(\theta = \underline{\theta}/\sigma = \phi) = \frac{\Pr(\sigma = \phi/\theta = \underline{\theta}) \times \Pr(\theta = \underline{\theta})}{\Pr(\sigma = \phi)}$$

$$= \frac{\nu\,(1-\xi)}{(1-\nu)\,(1-\xi) + \nu\,(1-\xi)} = \nu.$$

Accordingly, the Constitution offers the contract characterized in (2.11)–(2.14) with an expected welfare:

$$W^{AI} = \nu\left[S(\underline{q}^*) - (1+\lambda)\,\underline{\theta}\underline{q}^* - \lambda\Delta\theta\hat{\bar{q}}\right] + (1-\nu)[S(\hat{\bar{q}}) - (1+\lambda)\bar{\theta}\hat{\bar{q}}].$$

This event happens with probability $1 - \xi$.

The expected social welfare with a benevolent politician is

$$\xi W^{FI} + (1-\xi)\,W^{AI}.$$

The social gain provided by the benevolent politician acting as a supervisor is then

$$\Delta W = \xi[W^{FI} - W^{AI}]$$

$$= \xi\left[\lambda\nu\Delta\theta\hat{\bar{q}} + (1-\nu)\{\left[S(\bar{q}^*) - (1+\lambda)\bar{\theta}\bar{q}^*\right] - \left[S(\hat{\bar{q}}) - (1+\lambda)\bar{\theta}\hat{\bar{q}}\right]\}\right]$$

and using a politician is valuable if this gain exceeds the cost of providing the supervision technology to the politician (including his opportunity cost). However, since he is benevolent there is no need to reward him (i.e. $s = 0$ in Figure 2.2).

A reinterpretation of this case described as a benevolent supervisor is that it corresponds to a Nash equilibrium in the behavior of the politician and the firm for contracts offered by the Constitution.

The politician is offered a flat incentive scheme $s = 0$ whatever the report r. He is indifferent to any report and we assume that he

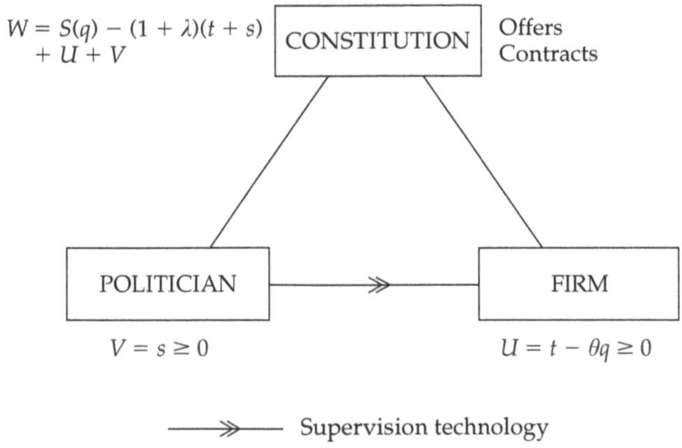

Figure 2.2

reports truthfully. The firm is offered the optimal incomplete information pair (D, E) if $r = \phi$ and the optimal complete information contracts (A or B) if $r = \theta$. More precisely, the firm announces $\tilde{\theta}$.

If $r = \phi$,	it gets D	if $\tilde{\theta} = \underline{\theta}$
	or E	if $\tilde{\theta} = \bar{\theta}$.
If $r = \underline{\theta}$,	it gets A	if $\tilde{\theta} = \underline{\theta}$ or $\tilde{\theta} = \bar{\theta}$.
If $r = \bar{\theta}$,	it gets B	if $\tilde{\theta} = \underline{\theta}$ or $\tilde{\theta} = \bar{\theta}$.

Knowing the politician's strategy, a maximizing behavior of the firm is to report truthfully. The allocation we associated with a benevolent politician is also obtained with a self-interested politician as a Nash equilibrium.

The key for this result is the non-cooperative behavior between the two agents, the politician and the firm. But is it reasonable to expect such behavior?

The politician has some discretion in his activity as a supervisor since, when he receives the signal $\sigma = \underline{\theta}$, he may choose not to report this information.[14] Even though he is indifferent between reporting and not reporting the true signal, he understands that,

[14] Note that there is no stake of collusion when $\theta = \bar{\theta}$ since the firm's utility level is zero whatever the politician's report.

by reporting $r = \phi$ when $\sigma = \underline{\theta}$, and informing the firm of this new strategy (which is costless for the politician), he provides an information rent $\Delta\theta\bar{q}$ to the firm.

Another Nash equilibrium is that the politician always reports $r = \phi$, and we are back to the optimal contract under incomplete information with no politician. However, this equilibrium does not seem very robust. The Constitution can give an infinitesimal wage $\varepsilon > 0$ to the politician if he reports the verifiable information θ. Then, the politician prefers strictly to tell the truth.

If the politician and the firm cannot communicate, then in a static model it is difficult to escape from the conclusion that truthful behavior is the most natural outcome. But the presumption that the Constitution can control communication between the two agents appears highly unrealistic. So, let us consider the extreme opposite case where communication between the agents is costless. The two agents will then understand that there is a common stake for collusion and the self-interested politician will be tempted to propose to hide his signal $\sigma = \underline{\theta}$ if the firm agrees to share with him the information rent which the report $r = \phi$ ensures.

There is, however, a major difficulty in organizing such a collusion, since the two partners do not have access to a jurisdiction which could implement the contract 'I do not reveal $\sigma = \underline{\theta}$ if you pay me b'.

Nevertheless, they have strong incentives to reach an agreement. One case where it seems possible is if the hard signal that the politician has obtained cannot be replicated. Then a quid pro quo, in which the politician gives the firm the unique proof of its type $\underline{\theta}$ in exchange for a monetary payment, does not run the risk that the politician reveals $\sigma = \underline{\theta}$ after having received the payment. Another possibility is that both agents have access to a private third party which has the reputation of enforcing contracts (like the Mafia). It can also correspond to a norm of behavior enforced by repeated relationships, but this setting also offers new instruments to the principal, who can use statistical historical information (remember that he knows the probability ξ). It is then a rough shortcut to a situation where the principal is a short-run player facing long-run players.

In the next section we will assume that the politician makes the collusion offers and that there is a transaction cost in the transfer from the agent to the supervisor as a shortcut to these difficulties.

2.3 Optimal Incentives for the Politician

2.3.1 Optimal Collusion-proof Constitution

From now on in this book we shall consider a simpler supervision technology, which economizes on notation. We assume that the signal can only inform about $\underline{\theta}$. That is, if $\theta = \underline{\theta}$ there is a probability ξ that $\sigma = \underline{\theta}$ and a probability $1 - \xi$ that $\sigma = \phi$. If $\theta = \bar{\theta}$, $\sigma = \phi$ always.[15]

Now, if the politician is benevolent and always transmits signals truthfully when $\sigma = \underline{\theta}$, the constitutional level is completely informed and selects the complete information contract $\underline{q} = \underline{q}^*$, $\underline{U} = 0$. When $\sigma = \phi$, the beliefs of the constitutional level are revised through Bayes's law. The probability of a good type conditionally on $\sigma = \phi$ is

$$\hat{\nu} = \frac{(1 - \xi)\nu}{1 - \xi\nu} < \nu.$$

Maximizing expected social welfare under incentive and individual rationality constraints leads now to

$$S'(\underline{q}^{\phi}) = (1 + \lambda)\underline{\theta}$$

$$S'(\bar{q}^{\phi}) = (1 + \lambda)\bar{\theta} + \frac{\lambda(1 - \xi)\nu}{1 - \nu}\Delta\theta.$$

The politician is useful. His presence leads to a decrease of the information cost of the public good. The expected rent given up to the firm is now $(1 - \xi)\nu\Delta\theta\bar{q}^{\phi}$. The difference with the former supervision technology is that, after receiving $\sigma = \phi$, the Constitution knows that the *ex post* probability it is facing a $\underline{\theta}$-type is lower ($\hat{\nu} < \nu$) because, with probability ξ, some $\underline{\theta}$-types are identified as such. The fear of giving up an information rent is

[15] Another advantage of this technology is the following one. It is difficult to envision cases where the supervisor may sometimes obtain a verifiable proof of the agent's type without assuming that the agent can always provide such a proof. But then the principal can easily oblige the agent to provide this information under the threat of not contracting. With the new technology, the agent can, as the supervisor, only provide verifiable information when $\theta = \underline{\theta}$. Then, the principal cannot require a verifiable proof of the agent's type since for $\theta = \bar{\theta}$ such a proof is impossible. The $\underline{\theta}$-agent can then claim to be a $\bar{\theta}$-agent.

accordingly lower and in the rent–efficiency trade-off one can afford a higher efficiency for a $\bar{\theta}$-type ($\bar{q}^{\phi} > \hat{\bar{q}}$).

However, the politician is self-interested. Unless otherwise motivated he will offer to the firm, when $\sigma = \underline{\theta}$, to conceal his signal with a benefit for the firm of $\Delta\theta\bar{q}^{\phi}$. The maximum amount of money that the firm is willing to offer to the politician is a bribe of $\Delta\theta\bar{q}^{\phi}$ with a value for the politician of

$$\frac{\Delta\theta\bar{q}^{\phi}}{1+\lambda_c}.$$

The positive parameter λ_c models the transaction cost of the side transfer between the politician and the firm. We will denote $k = \dfrac{1}{1+\lambda_c}$. The transaction costs of side transfers reflect the risks of being caught, the inefficiencies of bargaining and the costs incurred to avoid being identified (e.g. bribes in kind rather than in money). They are taken here as exogenous. In Chapter 8 we will provide a theory which endogenizes these transaction costs.

The timing of the collusion game that we choose is described in Figure 2.3.

Providing incentives to the politician can prevent capture by the firm.[16] Suppose that an incentive payment of $\underline{s} = k\Delta\theta\bar{q}^{\phi}$ is given to the politician when he reports the (verifiable) signal $\underline{\theta}$. The expected social cost of this payment is

$$\lambda\nu\xi\underline{s}$$

because it occurs with probability $\nu\xi$ and only has a distributional cost λ since the politician's welfare is included in the social welfare function.

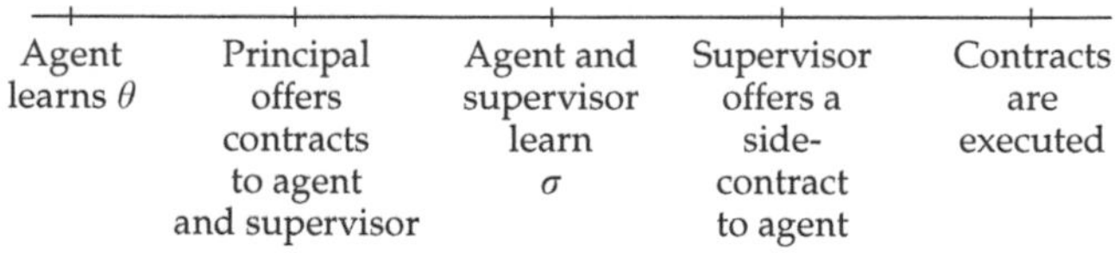
Agent learns θ
Principal offers contracts to agent and supervisor
Agent and supervisor learn σ
Supervisor offers a side-contract to agent
Contracts are executed

Figure 2.3

[16] The question of the desirability of this policy is still open at this stage of the analysis. See also footnote 17.

Expected social welfare can now be written:

$$\nu\xi[S(\underline{q}^*) - (1+\lambda)\underline{\theta}\underline{q}^*] + (1-\nu\xi)\left\{\frac{\nu(1-\xi)}{1-\nu\xi}[S(\hat{\underline{q}}^\phi) - (1+\lambda)\underline{\theta}\hat{\underline{q}}^\phi - \lambda\Delta\theta\hat{\bar{q}}^\phi]\right.$$

$$\left. + \frac{(1-\nu)}{1-\nu\xi}[S(\hat{\bar{q}}^\phi) - (1+\lambda)\bar{\theta}\hat{\bar{q}}^\phi]\right\} - \lambda\nu\xi k\Delta\theta\hat{\bar{q}}^\phi. \quad (2.19)$$

Indeed, with probability $\nu\xi$ the constitutional level is informed that the firm is efficient. With probability $1 - \nu\xi$, it is uniformed. With posterior probability $\frac{\nu(1-\xi)}{1-\nu\xi}$, it will face an efficient firm for which it will have to give up an information rent $\Delta\theta\hat{\bar{q}}^\phi$. With posterior probability $\frac{1-\nu}{1-\nu\xi}$, it will face an inefficient firm. In addition, with probability $\nu\xi$, it will give an incentive payment $k\Delta\theta\hat{\bar{q}}^\phi$ to the politician.

Reoptimizing expected social welfare immediately yields

$$S'(\hat{\underline{q}}^\phi) = (1+\lambda)\,\underline{\theta} \quad (2.20)$$

$$S'(\hat{\bar{q}}^\phi) = (1+\lambda)\bar{\theta} + \frac{\lambda\nu}{1-\nu}\Delta\theta\,[1-(1-k)\xi]. \quad (2.21)$$

The politician is now less useful unless the transaction costs of side transfers go to infinity ($k \to 0$). If $k = 1$, the politician is useless since he costs as much as the decrease of information rent he makes possible.

To avoid corruption the Constitution sets up incentives for politicians. As incentive payments are socially costly, the production level $\hat{\bar{q}}^\phi$ is decreased.[17] This decreases the stake of collusion $\Delta\theta\hat{\bar{q}}^\phi$ and consequently the required incentive payments. The expected rent of the firm $(1-\xi)\nu\Delta\theta\hat{\bar{q}}^\phi$ is now lower ($\hat{\bar{q}}^\phi < \bar{q}^\phi$). The firm suffers from the fear of corruption.

Summarizing, we can state:

> PROPOSITION 2.1 The optimal Constitution creates incentives for politicians to avoid their capture by interest groups, and distorts production downward to decrease the stake of collusion.

[17] We assume here that it is optimal to deter collusion. See Appendix 2 for a proof of this collusion-proof principle.

We have assumed that the supervision technology is costly. Otherwise it would be duplicated by the Constitution to create yardstick competition between several supervisors. Therefore we must note again that politicians as supervisors, studied here, are worth it only if their value exceeds their cost.

Proposition 2.1 emphasizes two constitutional policies in a reduced form and it is worth discussing their practical implementation.

First, one needs to provide rewards to politicians who satisfactorily fulfill their role as informational supervisors. This can be implemented either by judicial power or by the electoral process. Judicial power seems better organized to punish politicians when verifiable proof that they misbehaved is available. A politician is deprived of his salary and of his private benefits in the job in such a case. One reason why judicial power is not given the ability to reward politicians is probably the fear of collusion between this power and politicians. But this is outside the framework of this chapter, which maintains the assumption of a benevolent Constitution. The electoral process may reward politicians who prove that they do the job well. One difficulty is for the electorate to be able to understand when the politicians are doing their jobs properly in the complex informational matters we have in mind here. The need for credible sources of information which publicize the good performances of politicians is essential to implement desirable incentive schemes through the electoral system.

The second policy is the less responsive nature of the contract to the politician's information, the move toward more bureaucratic rules as a constitutional response to capture. It is indeed a well-known feature of administrations and political decision-making mechanisms for them to appear largely unresponsive to information. Proposition 2.1 gives a fundamental appreciation of the role of this bureaucratic bias.

Figure 2.4 summarizes the different distortions according to the type of supervision.

Alternatively, the Constitution could attempt to raise the transaction costs of side-contracts. We can also note:

> PROPOSITION 2.2 The lower the transaction costs of collusion (i.e. the higher k), the lower is expected social welfare, the

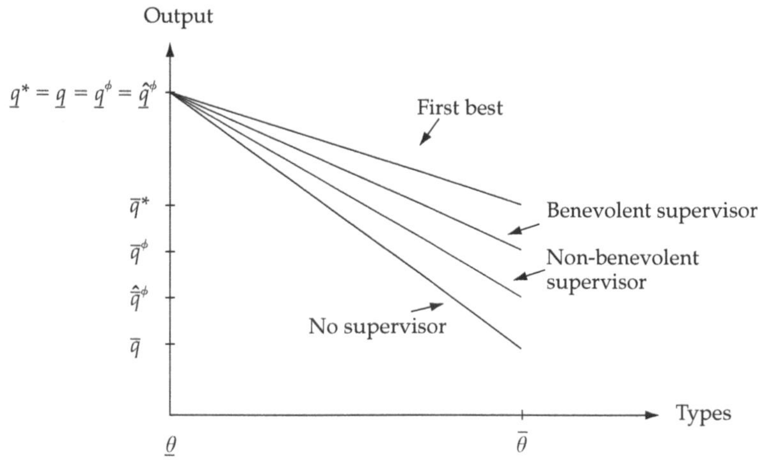

Figure 2.4

higher the downward distortion of the inefficient type's production level, and the lower the expected rent of the firm.

Except for the politician, everybody loses from the prospect of collusion. In particular, the firm would prefer to commit not to enter collusive agreements. This may have strong implications in the following case. Without collusion, the above model is equivalent to a model with contracting between the principal and the agent before the agent discovers his type, as long as the agent is infinitely risk-averse at the zero wealth level (so that the constraint $t - \theta q \geq 0$ still has to hold for any θ). Then, the agent would have incentives to make his information available in exchange for a reasonable payment and the principal's commitment not to hire a supervisor (the payment has to be lower than the expected rent without the supervisor but higher than the expected rent with a corruptible supervisor).

2.3.2 *Equilibrium Collusion*

We now assume that there are two types of politicians. With probability ζ, we have a type-1 politician who (as above) does not engage in collusion if he is rewarded $\underline{s}$ when he reveals that $\theta = \underline{\theta}$ such that

$$\underline{s} \geq k\Delta\theta\bar{q}^{\phi}.$$

With probability $1 - \zeta$, we have a type-2 politician who is more honest or suffers from higher transaction costs of side payments, and a lower payment $\underline{s}$ such that

$$\underline{s} \geq k\Delta\theta\bar{q}^{\phi} - a$$

is enough to prevent collusion.

We have two possible regimes, depending on the values of the parameters.

Regime 1: No collusion.

The payment $\underline{s}$ is chosen so that no politician, whatever his type, wants to engage in collusion, so that

$$\underline{s} = k\Delta\theta\bar{q}^{\phi}.$$

The optimal social welfare is as before and the optimal solution is characterized by (2.20), (2.21).

However, in this solution, there is now some waste of incentive payments since a proportion $1 - \zeta$ of politicians could be made non-corrupted with smaller payments $\underline{s} - a$ instead of $\underline{s}$, but this type of politician cannot be identified. An alternative, which is attractive if ζ is small, is to let the proportion ζ of politicians be corrupted to save on incentive payments. Expected social welfare is then

$$\begin{aligned} \nu\xi(1-\zeta)[S(\underline{q}^*)-(1+\lambda)\underline{\theta}\underline{q}^*]+\nu[1-\xi+\xi\zeta][S(\underline{q}^{\phi})-(1+\lambda)\underline{\theta}\underline{q}^{\phi}-\lambda\Delta\theta\bar{q}^{\phi}] \\ + (1-\nu)[S(\bar{q}^{\phi}) - (1+\lambda)\theta\bar{q}^{\phi}] \\ - \lambda\nu\xi(1-\zeta)(k\Delta\theta\bar{q}^{\phi} - a) \\ - \delta(1-k)\,\xi\zeta\nu\Delta\theta\bar{q}^{\phi}. \qquad (2.22) \end{aligned}$$

Indeed, with probability $\nu\xi(1 - \zeta)$ it is a type-2 politician who discovers that $\theta = \underline{\theta}$ and reveals it (the first term in (2.22)) and he is paid $k\Delta\theta\bar{q}^{\phi} - a$, which has an expected social cost (the fourth term in (2.22)). With probability $\nu(1 - \xi + \xi\zeta)$ it is a $\underline{\theta}$-type firm, but the constitutional level receives the report ϕ either because the politician has observed nothing (with probability $1 - \xi$) or because it is a type-1 politician who is hiding the information (with probability $\xi\zeta$). This corresponds to the second term in (2.22).

Furthermore, we include as a loss the transaction costs of collusion which benefit neither the firm nor the politician (the last term in (2.22)). But to account for the fact that some of this cost could be a revenue for some intermediaries, we introduce the parameter δ in [0, 1].

Optimizing (2.22) we get:

REGIME 2: Partial collusion.

$$S'(\underline{q}^{\phi}) = (1 + \lambda)\underline{\theta} \tag{2.23}$$

$$S'(\bar{q}^{\phi}) = (1 + \lambda)\bar{\theta} + \lambda \frac{\nu}{1 - \nu} \Delta\theta \left\{1 - \xi(1 - k)\left[1 - \zeta\left(1 + \frac{\delta}{\lambda}\right)\right]\right\}. \tag{2.24}$$

This case will be relevant when ζ is small. So, to simplify the exposition we assume that $\zeta(1 + \frac{\delta}{\lambda}) < 1$. Then, as ξ increases, production $\bar{q}^{\phi}$ increases in both regimes. The quality of the supervision technology characterized by ξ and low incentives for the inefficient type, which are both instruments to decrease the firm's rent, are substitute instruments. Note further that, in the corruption case (regime 2), the production level of the inefficient type is lower than in the non-corruption case (regime 1). Indeed, in regime 2 the posterior probability that the principal is facing a $\underline{\theta}$-type firm when he receives the report $r = \phi$ is higher than in regime 1:

$$\left(\frac{\nu[1 - \xi(1 - \zeta)]}{1 - \nu\xi(1 - \zeta)} > \frac{\nu(1 - \xi)}{1 - \nu\xi} \right).$$

Welfare in regime 1 is independent of a while welfare in regime 2 is increasing in a (by the envelope theorem). There is a value a^* such that for a larger than a^* it is better to let corruption happen. It is then so cheap to obtain honest behavior from a proportion $1 - \zeta$ of politicians that letting corruption happen with probability ζ dominates the costly Constitution which ensures absolutely no corruption. Let us index the variables in regime 1 (resp. 2) with C (resp. NC). We then have Figure 2.5.

Let us now consider the effect of an improvement in the supervision technology.

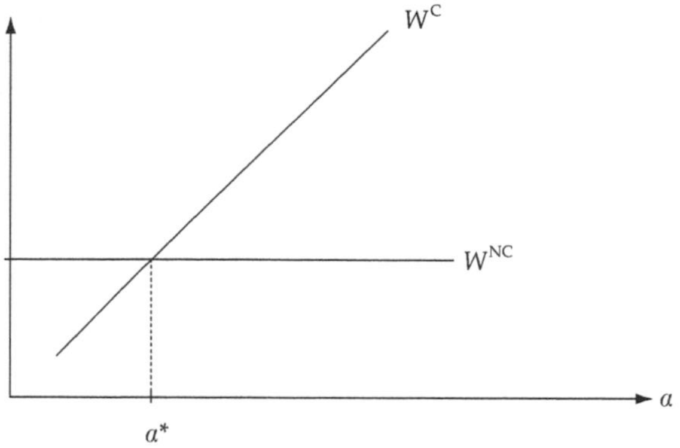

Figure 2.5

PROPOSITION 2.3 A better supervision technology increases welfare and decreases corruption.

PROOF: See Appendix A.2.2.

An increase of information is more favorable in the no-corruption regime because low incentives and better information are substitute instruments. Since $\bar{q}^C < \bar{q}^{NC}$, the instrument of low incentives is used more in the corruption regime. So the marginal value of better information is higher in the no-corruption regime and the set of parameter values for which the corruption regime dominates shrinks as a^* increases.

Furthermore, in both regimes, the probability that the principal is uninformed decreases with ξ and social welfare increases with ξ.

The first part of Proposition 2.3 relies on the fact that low incentives and better supervision are substitute instruments. This may sound natural but the opposite result would hold if they were complements. This would occur with the technology considered at the beginning of this chapter,[18] where both $\underline{\theta}$ and $\bar{\theta}$ are discovered with probability ξ.

It is interesting to discuss the reason why the collusion-proof principle does not hold in this section. When there is asymmetric information for the Constitution about the type of transfers that politicians require to engage in collusion, the revelation principle

[18] See Laffont and N'Guessan (1999) for other cases.

may fail because it rests on the inability of the Constitution to mimic the transfers realized by the colluding partners. We are outside the realm of the revelation principle, as in the case where $\lambda > \lambda_f$ with $k = \frac{1}{1 + \lambda_f}$. Then, too, transfers inside a collusion are less costly than the principal's transfer.

An alternative interpretation is that the Constitution has the same information as the agents about the transaction costs of these transfers, but institutional constraints—the incompleteness of contracts—prevent them from differentiating transfers according to the type of politician. For example, it may be common knowledge that corruption is easier in the South than in the North, but rewards to politicians are identical. It is then a general second-best principle that collusion may help complete incomplete contracts.[19]

2.4 Conclusion

We have presented and discussed in this chapter the main building block of the analysis in Part I. The simple capture or collusion model developed by Tirole (1986) assumes that colluding agents can sign costly contracts. This black box is not completely satisfactory, but the great merit of this model is to provide a framework for characterizing the optimal response to collusive activities within a model with endogenous stakes of collusion. It is a first step, but a useful one to think about the optimal organization of a government facing interest groups. In Chapter 9 we will take some steps toward endogenizing the transaction costs of collusion.

[19] A deeper explanation would require an interpretation of more or less corruptible supervisors in terms of utility functions. Utility functions would depend directly on messages. An honest supervisor would suffer from sending a message different from the truth. A supervisor would then be characterized by two parameters of adverse selection (his signal and his level of corruptibility). Extending the space of actions appropriately to include messages, a collusion-proof principle would hold in this extended framework but it would entail equilibrium collusion in the restricted framework considered here. An extensive discussion of this point is beyond the scope of this book.

Appendix 2

A.2.1 Proof of the Collusion-proof Principle with Hard Supervisory Information

We assume that collusion is organized by the supervisor who holds all the bargaining power in the coalition. Note that in order to use the verifiability of the supervisor's signal it is necessary to consider messages which belong to the space of signals $\{\underline{\theta}, \phi\}$.

If we consider mechanisms with abstract strategy spaces, such verifiability restrictions are meaningless. The collusion-proof principle requires two steps. The first is to characterize what one can implement with general mechanisms and then what one can implement when the supervisor's message space is $\{\underline{\theta}, \phi\}$ with the restriction that

$$\text{if } \sigma = \phi, \quad \text{then} \quad r = \phi;$$

$$\text{if } \sigma = \underline{\theta}, \quad \text{then} \quad r \in \{\underline{\theta}, \phi\}.$$

The first step relies on a collusion-proof principle with soft information that we will establish in Chapter 8. Anything the principal can do with general mechanisms he can realize with revelation mechanisms in which the informed supervisor organizing the collusion has a best strategy, which is to recommend truthful revelation of private information which is considered soft. In this model no gain from supervision can be obtained with soft information. This will also be proved in Chapter 8.

Then we must consider the case where the message space of the supervisor is $M_2 = \{\underline{\theta}, \phi\}$ and let M_1 be the message space of the agent. The principal is the constitutional level, C. The firm is the agent, A, or player 1. The supervisor is the politician, P, or player 2. The grand mechanism G offered by the principal C maps messages (m_1,m_2) belonging to message spaces (M_1, M_2) into a transfer to the firm $t(m_1,m_2)$, a quantity of public good $q(m_1,m_2)$ and a transfer to the politician $s(m_1,m_2)$.

In drawing the game tree of the two-stage game in which C offers the grand contract G and subsequently P offers a side-contract, we take into account the fact that P can only observe a signal if $\theta = \underline{\theta}$ and the fact that it is common knowledge that in this case P has verifiable information that $\theta = \underline{\theta}$.

We want to show that there is no restriction in considering grand contracts G which are revelation mechanisms such that the best strategy of the politician is to reveal his message truthfully.

Two cases must be considered:

CASE 1: Nature chooses $\underline{\theta}$ or $\bar{\theta}$ and $\sigma = \phi$. Then the report of the supervisor is constrained to be ϕ. The game tree reduces to

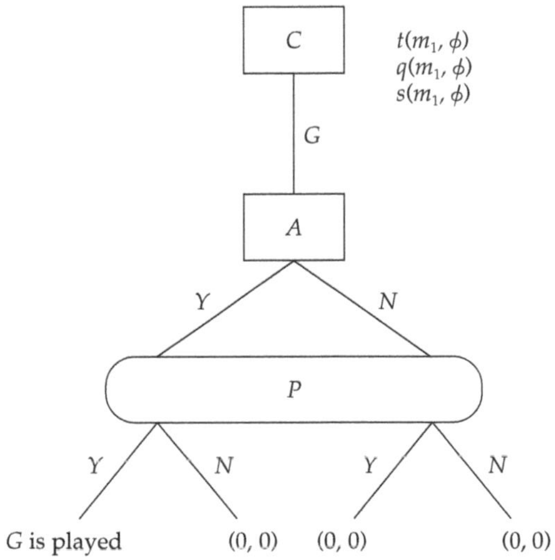

If G is accepted by both players, it is played. Indeed, in this case the politician has no information and this is known by the agent. The politician cannot offer any manipulation of reports which the firm cannot do by itself.

Let $m_1^*(\theta, \phi)$ and ϕ be the optimal strategies of the two players in G. G is then equivalent to the revelation mechanism

$$(\text{I}) \begin{cases} \text{T}(\theta, \phi) = t(m_1^*(\theta, \phi), \phi) \\ \text{Q}(\theta, \phi) = q(m_1^*(\theta, \phi), \phi) \\ S(\theta, \phi) = s(m_1^*(\theta, \phi), \phi) \end{cases}$$

which is truthful by definition of the optimal strategy m_1^*.

CASE 2: Nature chooses $\underline{\theta}$ and $\sigma = \underline{\theta}$:

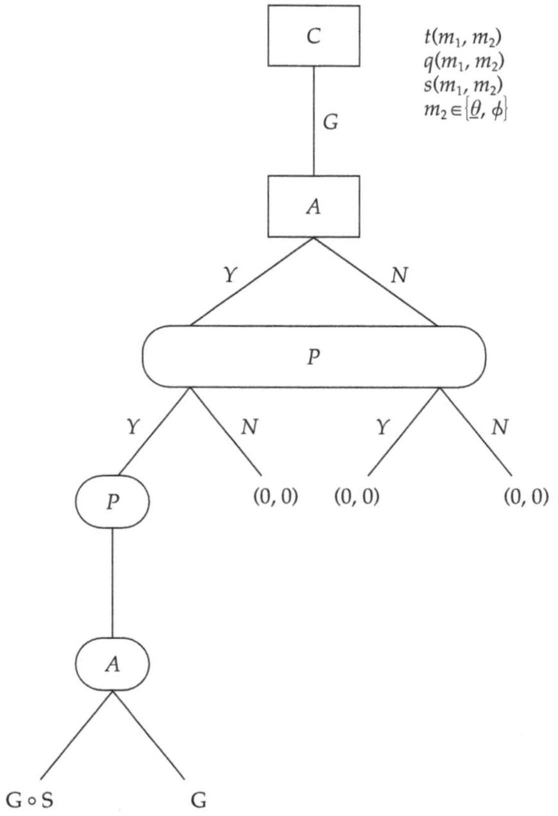

Let $m_1^*(\underline{\theta}, \underline{\theta}) \in M_1$, $m_2^*(\underline{\theta}) \in \{\underline{\theta}, \phi\}$ be the optimal strategies of the two players when G is played non-cooperatively.

If $m_2^*(\underline{\theta}) = \phi$, there is nothing that the politician can offer. If $m_2^*(\underline{\theta}) = \underline{\theta}$, then the politician can offer a side-contract which is not the null contract. He is informed about $\underline{\theta}$ and makes a take-it-or-leave-it offer to the firm which maximizes its welfare under various constraints. The side-contract offered is a manipulation of reports $\phi_1(\underline{\theta}, \underline{\theta}) \in M_1$, $\phi_2(\underline{\theta}, \underline{\theta}) = \phi$ and side payments $y_1(\underline{\theta}, \underline{\theta})$, $y_2(\underline{\theta}, \underline{\theta})$ such that

$$y_2(\underline{\theta}, \underline{\theta}) + k y_1(\underline{\theta}, \underline{\theta}) = 0$$

$$y_1(\underline{\theta}, \underline{\theta}) \leq 0$$

to take into account transaction costs,

$$s(\phi_1(\underline{\theta}, \underline{\theta}), \phi) + y_2(\underline{\theta}, \underline{\theta}) \geq 0$$

to take into account the limited liability constraint, and

$$t(\phi_1(\underline{\theta}, \underline{\theta}), \phi) - \underline{\theta} q(\phi_1(\underline{\theta}, \theta), \phi) + y_1(\underline{\theta}, \underline{\theta}) \geq$$
$$t(m_1^*(\underline{\theta}, \underline{\theta}), m_2^*(\underline{\theta})) - \underline{\theta} q(m_1^*(\underline{\theta}, \underline{\theta}), m_2^*(\underline{\theta}))$$

to take into account the firm's individual rationality constraint.

Define

$$\text{(II)} \begin{cases} T(\underline{\theta}, \underline{\theta}) = t(\phi_1(\underline{\theta}, \underline{\theta}), \phi) + y_1(\underline{\theta}, \underline{\theta}) \\ Q(\underline{\theta}, \underline{\theta}) = q(\phi_1(\underline{\theta}, \underline{\theta}), \phi) \\ S(\underline{\theta}, \underline{\theta}) = s(\phi_1(\underline{\theta}, \underline{\theta}), \phi) + y_2(\underline{\theta}, \underline{\theta}) \\ T(\bar{\theta}, \underline{\theta}) = -\infty \end{cases}$$

and consider the revelation mechanism composed of (I) and (II). It is truth-telling and implements without collusion the allocation reached before with the side-contract, but at a lower cost since $y_1(\underline{\theta}, \underline{\theta}) + y_2(\underline{\theta}, \underline{\theta}) < 0$. Furthermore, the politician cannot offer a new side-contract which improves on this mechanism.

A.2.2: Proof of Proposition 2.3

Let

$$\underline{W}^* = S(\underline{q}^*) - (1 + \lambda)\underline{\theta}\underline{q}^*,$$
$$\underline{W}(q) = S(\underline{q}^*) - (1 + \lambda)\underline{\theta}\underline{q}^* - \lambda\Delta\theta q,$$
$$\bar{W}(q) = S(q) - (1 + \lambda)\,\bar{\theta} q.$$

By definition of α^*:

$$\nu\xi\underline{W}^* + \nu(1 - \xi)\underline{W}(\bar{q}^{NC}) + (1 - \nu)\bar{W}(\bar{q}^{NC}) - \lambda\nu\xi k\Delta\theta\bar{q}^{NC} =$$
$$\nu\xi(1-\zeta)\underline{W}^* + \nu(1-\xi+\xi\zeta)\underline{W}(\bar{q}^{C}) + (1-\nu)\bar{W}(\bar{q}^{C}) - \lambda\nu\xi(1-\zeta)(k\Delta\theta\bar{q}^{C} - \alpha^*)$$
$$-\delta(1 - k)\xi\zeta\nu\Delta\theta\bar{q}^{C}. \tag{2.25}$$

Differentiating with respect to α^* and ξ, we obtain

$$\lambda\nu\xi(1 - \zeta)\mathrm{d}\alpha^* = [\nu\zeta\underline{W}^* - \nu\underline{W}(\bar{q}^{NC}) + \nu(1 - \zeta)\underline{W}(\bar{q}^{C})$$
$$- \lambda\nu k\Delta\theta\bar{q}^{NC} + \lambda\nu(1 - \zeta)(k\Delta\theta\bar{q}^{C} - \alpha^*) + \delta(1 - k)\zeta\nu\Delta\theta\bar{q}^{C})]\mathrm{d}\xi.$$

But from (2.25)

$$\nu\zeta\underline{W}^* - \lambda\nu k\Delta\theta\bar{q}^{NC} + \lambda\nu(1-\zeta)(k\Delta\theta\bar{q}^{C} - a^*) + \delta(1-k)\zeta\nu\Delta\theta\bar{q}^{C}$$

$$-\nu\underline{W}(\bar{q}^{NC}) + \nu(1-\zeta)\underline{W}(\bar{q}^{C}) = \frac{1}{\xi}\{\nu[\underline{W}(\bar{q}^{NC}) - \underline{W}(\bar{q}^{NC})] + (1-\nu)[\overline{W}(\bar{q}^{C})$$

$$-\overline{W}(\bar{q}^{NC})]\}\frac{da^*}{d\xi} \propto [\nu\underline{W}(\bar{q}^{C}) + (1-\nu)\overline{W}(\bar{q}^{C})] - [\nu\underline{W}(\bar{q}^{NC}) + (1-\nu)\overline{W}(\bar{q}^{NC})].$$

The function $\nu\underline{W}(\cdot) + (1-\nu)\overline{W}(\cdot)$ is concave and takes its maximum at $\hat{\bar{q}}$, defined by

$$S'(\hat{\bar{q}}) = (1+\lambda)\bar{\theta} + \lambda\frac{\nu}{1-\nu}\Delta\theta.$$

We have

$$\hat{\bar{q}} < \bar{q}^{C} < \bar{q}^{NC}.$$

Hence

$$\frac{da^*}{d\xi} > 0.$$

Let $W^{NC}(\bar{q})$(resp. $W^{C}(\bar{q})$) be the regime-1 (resp. regime-2) expected social welfare as a function of the inefficient type's production level when the production level of the efficient type is $\underline{q}^*$. Note first that $W^{NC}(\bar{q}^{NC})$ is increasing in ξ. From the envelope theorem, we have that

$$\frac{dW^{NC}}{d\xi}(\bar{q}^{NC}) = \frac{\partial W^{NC}}{\partial\xi}(\bar{q}^{NC})$$
$$= \nu[\underline{W}^* - \underline{W}(\bar{q}^{NC})] - \lambda\nu k\Delta\theta\bar{q}^{NC}$$
$$= \lambda\nu(1-k)\Delta\theta\bar{q}^{NC} > 0.$$

Now we prove that $W^{C}(\bar{q}^{C})$ is increasing in ξ when regime 2 is optimal.

$\Delta(\bar{q}) = W^{NC}(\bar{q}) - W^{C}(\bar{q})$ is proportional to ξ.

If the parameters are such that regime 2 is optimal, we have

$$W^{C}(\bar{q}^{C}) > W^{NC}(\bar{q}^{NC}) > W^{NC}(\bar{q}^{C}).$$

Therefore

$$\Delta(\bar{q}^{C}) < 0 \quad \text{and} \quad \frac{\partial}{\partial \xi}\Delta(\bar{q}^{C}) < 0.$$

Now

$$\frac{dW^{C}}{d\xi}(\bar{q}^{C}) = \frac{\partial W^{NC}}{\partial \xi}(\bar{q}^{C}) - \frac{\partial \Delta}{\partial \xi}(\bar{q}^{C}) + \frac{dW^{C}}{d\bar{q}}(\bar{q}^{C})\frac{d\bar{q}^{C}}{d\xi},$$

$$\frac{\partial W^{NC}}{\partial \xi}(\bar{q}^{C}) = v(1-k)\Delta\theta\bar{q}^{C} > 0; -\frac{\partial \Delta}{\partial \xi}(\bar{q}^{C}) > 0; \frac{dW^{C}}{d\bar{q}}(\bar{q}^{C}) = 0.$$

Hence

$$\frac{\partial W^{NC}}{\partial \xi}(\bar{q}^{C}) > 0.$$

3

An Incentive Theory of the Separation of Powers

'A society in which the guarantee of rights is not assured, nor the separation of powers provided for, has no constitution.'

Article 16 of the French Declaration of the Rights of Man of 1789.

3.1 Introduction

As the quote from the French Declaration of the Rights of Man shows, the separation of powers is viewed as a key question of democracy. It was already in the minds of Montesquieu[1] and the American Federalists, but economists still have little to say about this mythical problem. In this chapter we want to explore this question within the paradigm of a complete Constitution.

A first reason well understood by economists for duplicating regulated agencies is yardstick competition. Using the correlation of signals obtained by these agencies enables the principal to extract their information rent in a costless way. This idea was modeled by Shleifer (1985) in the case of perfect correlation and Crémer and McLean (1988) in the case of an arbitrary degree of non-zero correlation.[2]

In Chapter 8 we will provide a detailed discussion of this idea in relation to collusive behavior. In this chapter we will model a different reason for the separation of powers.[3] We will argue that the

[1] 'Tout serait perdu si le même homme, ou le même corps des principaux, ou des nobles, ou du peuple, exerçaient ces trois pouvoirs: celui de faire des lois, celui d'exécuter des résolutions publiques, et celui de juger les crimes ou les différents des particuliers.' Montesquieu (1748), p. 586.

[2] See also Auriol and Laffont (1992).

[3] As reported in Moe (1986), the separation of powers in a Constitution may also be beneficial when intertemporal commitment is limited. See Tirole (1994), Olsen and Torsvick (1993) and Martimort (1995) for agency models building on this idea.

separation of powers may act as a device against the threat of regulatory capture, and construct an incentive theory of the separation of powers. The general idea has been known for a while among political scientists (Moe (1986), Wilson (1980), Mueller (1997), Chapter 17) but has not been formalized. The public choice school has emphasized the fact that institutional rules may be designed to discourage rent-seeking behavior (see Congleton (1984) and Rose-Ackerman (1978), who argue that increasing the number of individuals who must be bribed before getting an award may be optimal). However, the weakness of this approach is that the rent-seeking activities are only supply-determined.

We define the *power* of a politician as his ability to use his signal on the regulated firm to improve social welfare. When benevolent politicians are in charge of implementing the socially optimal contract, there is no reason for the separation of powers, i.e. for splitting authority among different politicians. They always use their possible discretion, i.e. their power, in order to maximize social welfare. In contrast, as in Chapter 2, non-benevolent politicians may use their power to pursue personal agendas, e.g. by colluding with the regulated firm. Then, there is scope for separation. Separation of agencies or politicians divides the information at their disposal, and consequently limits their discretion in engaging in socially wasteful activities. Instead of having a unique politician implementing the privately efficient collusive offer to the regulated firm, separation introduces a Bayesian Nash behavior between partially informed politicians. When this Bayesian Nash behavior is such that the politicians ask for prudent bribes, which can always be provided by the interest group, the outcome of this collusion game reduces the total collusive offers they make. As a result, the transaction costs of collusive activities increase and preventing collusion becomes easier. Separation improves social welfare.

In Section 3.2 we extend the model of Chapter 2 to make the point. However, this simple extension entails a correlation of signals about the two regulated agencies, which mixes the two ideas of yardstick competition and higher transaction costs of capture. To disentangle the two ideas, we construct in Section 3.3 a model with three types for the regulated firm in order to be able to allocate to the two agencies or politicians supervision technologies which are stochastically independent. Section 3.4 characterizes the optimal collusion-proof Constitution with a single politician who controls both supervision activities. The case of separation of politicians is dealt with in Section 3.5. In particular we discuss in detail the comparative statics of the gains to be expected from the separation of powers. Section 3.6 provides some criticisms of the modeling and some extensions. Finally, Section 3.7 concludes.

3.2 Separation of Powers and Yardstick Competition

In the previous chapter we dismissed the duplication of informed supervisors by appealing to excessive fixed costs. However, the duplication of fixed costs is not always higher than the sampling value offered by two supervision technologies. The first question to ask is whether taking into account the possibilities of collusion affects the choice between one or two technologies. It is a question of the value of duplicating supervision technologies within the control of a single politician. The next question is whether these two technologies should be allocated to two different politicians: the question of the separation of powers. We slightly extend the model of Chapter 2 to explore these issues.

Suppose that, in the model of Chapter 2, we now have two independent signals σ_i such that

$$\Pr(\sigma_i = \underline{\theta}/\theta = \underline{\theta}) = \xi \qquad i = 1,2.$$

The timing is as described in Figure 2.3 with a preliminary decision of having one or two politicians. Consider first the case of one benevolent politician with the two supervision technologies. Either the principal receives at least one informative report (with probability $\xi^2 + 2\xi(1 - \xi)$) and he is fully informed and can implement the efficient allocation for $\theta = \underline{\theta}$. Or he receives no informative report: $r_1 = \phi$; $r_2 = \phi$. His posterior probability that $\theta = \underline{\theta}$ is then given by

$$\Pr(\theta = \underline{\theta} \mid r_1 = \phi, r_2 = \phi) = \frac{\nu(1 - \xi)^2}{(1 - \nu) + \nu(1 - \xi)^2} = \hat{\nu} < \nu.$$

When he receives an informative signal he is more confident now that he is facing an inefficient type. This leads to a trade-off more favorable to efficiency, described by

$$S'(\underline{q}_2^{\phi}) = (1 + \lambda)\underline{\theta}$$
$$S'(\bar{q}_2^{\phi}) = (1 + \lambda)\bar{\theta} + \frac{\lambda(1 - \xi)^2 \nu}{1-\nu}\Delta\theta.$$

Expected social welfare is

$$\nu\xi(2 - \xi)\underline{W}^* + \nu[1 - \xi(2 - \xi)][S(\underline{q}^*) - (1 + \lambda)\underline{\theta}\underline{q}^* - \lambda\Delta\theta\bar{q}_2^{\phi}] + (1 - \nu)[S(\bar{q}_2^{\phi}) - (1+\lambda)\bar{\theta}\bar{q}_2^{\phi}]$$

instead of, with one supervision technology,

$$\nu\xi\underline{W}^* + \nu(1 - \xi)[S(\underline{q}^*) - (1 + \lambda)\underline{\theta}\underline{q}^* - \lambda\Delta\theta\bar{q}^{\phi}] + (1 - \nu)[S(\bar{q}^{\phi}) - (1+\lambda)\bar{\theta}\bar{q}^{\phi}].$$

The improvement of welfare is

$$\Delta W = \{\nu(1 - \xi)\lambda\Delta\theta\bar{q}^{\phi} - \nu[1 - \xi(2 - \xi)]\lambda\Delta\theta\bar{q}_2^{\phi}\} + (1 - \nu)\{[S(\bar{q}_2^{\phi}) - (1+\lambda)\bar{\theta}\bar{q}_2^{\phi}] - [S(\bar{q}^{\phi}) - (1+\lambda)\bar{\theta}\bar{q}^{\phi}]\}$$

The first term represents the expected decrease of the cost of the information rent. Its sign is ambiguous because the rent itself is higher with two technologies since $\bar{q}_2^{\phi} > \bar{q}^{\phi}$ but it is given up less often. The second term is the efficiency gain due to a smaller distortion for the inefficient type's production.

Considered as a function of $\bar{q}$, expected social welfare with two supervision technologies $W_2(\bar{q})$ is always higher than expected social welfare with one supervision technology $W_1(\bar{q})$.

$$W_2(\bar{q}) - W_1(\bar{q}) = \nu\lambda\Delta\theta\bar{q}[\xi - \xi^2].$$

If the politician is not benevolent, collusion-proofness requires expected incentive payments for the politician of

$\nu k\xi\Delta\theta\bar{q}$	with one technology
$\nu k\xi(2 - \xi)\Delta\theta\bar{q}$	with two technologies.[4]

The new difference of welfare levels is

$$\tilde{W}_2(\bar{q}) - \tilde{W}_1(\bar{q}) = \nu\lambda\Delta\theta\bar{q}(1 - k)(\xi - \xi^2).$$

So the gain of double supervision is now smaller because of the cost of collusion-proofness and might not compensate for the

[4] For simplicity we assume that the transaction costs of collusion are identical between supervisors and identical to the case with one supervisor. Neven, Nuttall and Seabright (1993) argue that having sector-specific agencies increases the risks of capture by producers in each sector.

fixed cost of setting up a new supervision technology, as it did with a benevolent politician. We can then ask whether the separation of powers may decrease this cost of collusion-proofness.

Now, we have one politician associated with each supervision technology.[5] The separation of powers is irrelevant if the politicians are benevolent. Let us consider the case of self-interested politicians who may enter collusive agreements with the firm. Clearly the collusion-proof constraints depend on the ways the two politicians and the firm bargain under asymmetric information in the collusion game. To make things as simple as possible, we assume that, when he has observed a favorable signal, a politician makes a take-it-or-leave-it offer only to the firm. This assumption precludes a politician from offering a side-contract to the other politician.[6] Two reasons motivate this choice. First, bribes often take the form of future job opportunities in the private sector for lenient civil servants, the so-called 'revolving door' phenomenon; there does not seem to exist such an equivalent mechanism between two government administrations. More generally, jobs' lengths within administrations can be designed so that those collusive behaviors are less easily enforceable and more easily detected. Second, the Constitution is likely to be able to better control and therefore to prevent monetary transfers between politicians than transfers between the politicians and the regulated firm. The latter assumption is equivalent to saying that side transfers between the politicians incur in fact an infinite transaction cost. Alternatively, Section 3.6.3 explains why considering information sharing between the politicians may not be enough to have them collude when they cannot make monetary transfers between themselves. We distinguish two cases according to the politicians' behavior.

With prudent behavior, politicians make only collusive offers

[5] We assume that these technologies are not transferable between the two politicians. In particular, one politician cannot sell *ex ante*, i.e. before any signal occurs, the value of his technology to the other. Necessarily, such an assumption requires that a benevolent court of justice verifies that the control of each informational technology is the one requested by the Constitution (see also Section 3.6.3).

[6] It also precludes a politician from using a side-contract contingent on the offer of the other politician's side-contract. We assume therefore that such an offer is not observable by the politician who has not made it.

which are accepted with probability 1.[7] Then, at the symmetric Nash equilibrium of those offers, there is no bribe and no cost of collusion-proofness. Indeed, a politician who does not know the other politician's report will not dare to make a collusive offer. The power of competition is fully expressed by this case. If making a collusive offer which is rejected entails a large cost (e.g. being denounced by the firm), dual supervision introduces an uncertainty which is very profitable at the constitutional level.

We obtain a similar but weaker result with the traditional expected utility behavior which ignores those penalties out of equilibrium.

At a non-collusive Nash equilibrium, politician i does not deviate if, when he receives the signal $\sigma_i = \underline{\theta}$, he obtains an incentive payment greater than his expected discounted bribe:[8]

$$s_i \geqslant k(1 - \xi)\Delta\theta\bar{q}.$$

Indeed, with probability ξ the other politician is informed and has truthfully transmitted his message so that the demand for a bribe of $\Delta\theta\bar{q}$ is rejected by the firm which has no rent.

The total expected cost of collusion-proofness is

$$2\nu\xi(1 - \xi)k\Delta\theta\bar{q},$$

instead of

$$\nu\xi(2 - \xi)k\Delta\theta\bar{q},$$

with a single politician.

The presence of the other politician creates a negative externality on the bribe that the informed politician can expect and

[7] This assumption of *prudent behavior* can be motivated along several lines. It can be motivated by appealing to a large degree of risk aversion of the politician. Then he considers only the worst possible state of nature before making his collusive offer. The politician may also be afraid of denunciation by the firm if he makes a bribe offer which cannot be accepted by the firm. Lastly, the one-shot bargaining game between the politician and the firm may be modeled as a sequence of repeated offers by the less informed party (the politician). In this case, when offers are repeated sufficiently often, a politician unable to commit himself to a bribe offer is going to charge the minimum bribe which is consistent with his information (see Gul, Sonnenschein and Wilson (1985)).

[8] We assume here that the politician must make his decision to report his signal to the Constitution before knowing whether his collusive offer will be accepted or not.

therefore a positive externality on the incentive payment required for collusion-proofness. Summarizing the discussion above we have:

> PROPOSITION 3.1: (a) The duplication of supervision technologies is more valuable if the quality of supervision (ξ) is higher and if the transaction costs of collusion are higher (k low).
> (b) The separation of powers decreases the cost of implementing collusion-proofness.

The correlation of the signals σ_1 and σ_2 suggests a yardstick competition effect. Indeed, we have

$$p_{11} = \Pr(\sigma_1 = \underline{\theta} \text{ and } \sigma_2 = \underline{\theta}) = \nu\xi^2$$
$$p_{12} = \Pr(\sigma_1 = \underline{\theta} \text{ and } \sigma_2 = \phi) = p_{21} = \Pr(\sigma_1 = \phi \text{ and } \sigma_2 = \underline{\theta}) = \nu\xi(1-\xi)$$
$$p_{22} = \Pr(\sigma_1 = \phi \text{ and } \sigma_2 = \phi) = 1 - \nu + \nu(1-\xi)^2$$

and

$$\rho = p_{11}p_{22} - p_{12}p_{21} = \xi^2\nu(1-\nu).$$

Proposition 3.1.b could be interpreted as follows. The constitutional level must control a moral hazard behavior which corresponds to collusion. Because of limited liability, it must reward the politicians for honest behavior. The higher is ξ, the higher the correlation of types, and the higher the gain of the dual control in terms of collusion cost ($\xi^2 k\Delta\theta\bar{q}$).

However, there are two forces at work here. The first one is the correlation of signals which creates the possibility of yardstick competition between politicians. But the limited liability constraints considerably restrict this opportunity. The second one is that the competition of politicians introduces an inefficiency in the collusion game which is favorable at the constitutional level. In the next section we isolate the two effects by constructing a model where the signals of the two politicians are independent.

3.3 A Model with Three Types

We consider the same three-tier hierarchy of Constitution–politician–firm as above, but now it is common knowledge that the efficiency parameter θ of the cost function has the following structure:

$$\theta = \bar{\theta} - \theta_1 - \theta_2,$$

where θ_1 and θ_2 are two binary random variables taking their values in $\{0,\Delta\theta\}$.[9] θ_1 and θ_2 may be thought of as improvements in the technology that have been realized or not in the firm. Let us denote $\hat{\theta} = \bar{\theta} - \Delta\theta$ and $\underline{\theta} = \bar{\theta} - 2\Delta\theta$.

The random variables θ_i for $i \in \{1,2\}$ are drawn independently from the same probability distribution on $\{0,\Delta\theta\}$ with respective probabilities $(1 - \nu,\nu)$. The probability distribution of (θ_1,θ_2) induces a discrete distribution $P(.)$ on $\{\underline{\theta},\hat{\theta},\bar{\theta}\}$:

$$P(\underline{\theta}) = \nu^2, \quad P(\hat{\theta}) = 2\nu(1 - \nu), \quad P(\bar{\theta}) = (1 - \nu)^2.$$

The Constitution wishes to maximize under the individual rationality constraints the following social welfare function:

$$SW = S(q) - (1 + \lambda)(t + s) + U + V = S(q) - (1 + \lambda)\theta q - \lambda U - \lambda V.$$

When politicians are benevolent (i.e. transmit their signals truthfully) and *a fortiori* when the Constitution has complete information, the outcome achieved is independent of the supervisory structure.

Two informational technologies are now available. Each informational technology i, $i = 1,2$, generates hard information on the random variable θ_i with probability ξ if this variable is $\Delta\theta$; otherwise nothing is learned. Let σ_i be the signal provided by technology i; then

$$\begin{aligned} \sigma_i &= \Delta\theta \quad \text{with probability } \nu\xi \\ \sigma_i &= \phi \quad \text{with probability } 1 - \nu\xi. \end{aligned}$$

Note that each informational technology is relative to a different piece of private information, contrary to Section 3.2.

If no signal has been observed, i.e. $(\sigma_1 = \phi,\ \sigma_2 = \phi)$, which occurs with probability $(1 - \nu\xi)^2$, the conditional probabilities of each state $(\underline{\theta},\hat{\theta},\bar{\theta})$ are respectively

$$P_0(\underline{\theta}) = \frac{\nu^2(1 - \xi)^2}{(1 - \nu\xi)^2}, \quad P_0(\hat{\theta}) = \frac{2\nu(1 - \nu)(1 - \xi)}{(1 - \nu\xi)^2}, \quad P_0(\bar{\theta}) = \frac{(1 - \nu)^2}{(1 - \nu\xi)^2}.$$

We denote by $W_0(\hat{q}_0,\bar{q}_0)$ the expected social welfare under this full asymmetric information and with a benevolent politician

[9] This model was first developed by Laffont and Martimort (1999).

where, for the next sections, we also make explicit its dependence on the levels of production requested from types $\hat{\theta}$ and $\bar{\theta}$. Denoting $\underline{U}_0$, $\hat{U}_0$, and $\bar{U}_0$, respectively, as the utility level of a firm with characteristic $\underline{\theta}$, $\hat{\theta}$ and $\bar{\theta}$, we have

$$W_0(\hat{q}_0,\bar{q}_0) = P_0(\underline{\theta})[S(\underline{q}_0) - (1 + \lambda)\underline{\theta}\underline{q}_0 - \lambda\underline{U}_0]$$
$$+ P_0(\hat{\theta})[S(\hat{q}_0) - (1 + \lambda)\hat{\theta}\hat{q}_0 - \lambda\hat{U}_0] + P_0(\bar{\theta})[S(\bar{q}_0) - (1+\lambda)\bar{\theta}\bar{q}_0 - \lambda\bar{U}_0].$$

With probability $2\nu\xi(1 - \nu\xi)$, only one signal is observed, i.e. ($\sigma_1 = \Delta\theta, \sigma_2 = \phi$) or ($\sigma_1 = \phi$, $\sigma_2 = \Delta\theta$). The Constitution then suffers from a milder asymmetry of information since it knows that $\theta \in \{\underline{\theta},\hat{\theta}\}$. It updates its beliefs accordingly. The respective probabilities of $\underline{\theta}$ and $\hat{\theta}$ are

$$P_1(\underline{\theta}) = \frac{\nu(1 - \xi)}{1 - \nu\xi}, \qquad P_1(\hat{\theta}) = \frac{1 - \nu}{1 - \nu\xi}.$$

We denote by $W_1(\hat{q}_1)$ the expected social welfare under this milder asymmetry of information with a benevolent politician, where again we make explicit its dependence on the level of production requested from a $\hat{\theta}$-firm. Denoting $\underline{U}_1$ and $\hat{U}_1$ respectively as the utility level of a firm with characteristic $\underline{\theta}$ and $\hat{\theta}$, we have

$$W_1(\hat{q}_1) = P_1(\underline{\theta})[S(\underline{q}_1) - (1 + \lambda)\, \underline{\theta}\underline{q}_1 - \lambda\underline{U}_1] + P_1(\hat{\theta})[S(\hat{q}_1) -$$
$$(1 + \lambda)\hat{\theta}\hat{q}_1 - \lambda\hat{U}_1].$$

When both signals are informative, i.e. with probability $\nu^2\xi^2$, the true state of nature is necessarily $\underline{\theta}$, and complete information regulation is achieved. Let W_2 denote the social welfare in that case. We have

$$W_2 = S(\underline{q}_2) - (1 + \lambda)\underline{\theta}\underline{q}_2 - \lambda\underline{U}_2,$$

where $\underline{q}_2$ is the complete information production and $\underline{U}_2$ is the firm's associated utility level.

As a whole, expected social welfare with a benevolent politician becomes:

$$SW = (1 - \nu\xi)^2 W_0(\hat{q}_0,\bar{q}_0) + 2\nu\xi(1 - \nu\xi)W_1(\hat{q}_1) + \nu^2\xi^2 W_2. \quad (3.1)$$

A contract with a single politician is a triplet $\{t(r_1,r_2,\tilde{\theta}), q(r_1,r_2,\tilde{\theta}), s(r_1,r_2)\}$, where $t(\cdot)$, $q(\cdot)$ and $s(\cdot)$ denote respectively the transfer received by the firm, its production and the politician's reward as a function of both the reports of the politician on the hard information signals (r_1,r_2) he may have observed and the report $\tilde{\theta}$ of the firm on its type. We assume that the politician first reports his signals to the Constitution, and then, if these signals are not fully informative, the principal asks the firm directly for its type. Note that this sequential timing of the game and the fact that the reports of the politician are hard information also imply that the politician's reward does not need to depend on the firm's report. Similarly, the transfer and the output of the firm depend on its report only to the extent that the politician has not already reported hard information on its type.

First, when both pieces of information are discovered, the optimal constitution entails full extraction of the firm's rent $\underline{U}_2 = 0$ and the 'first-best' level of output $S'(\underline{q}_2) = (1 + \lambda)\underline{\theta}$.

Under asymmetric information we can optimize the expected social welfare expressed by (3.1) subject to incentive and participation constraints. Because the single crossing property is satisfied,[10] it will be enough to consider only upward incentive constraints and the inefficient type's individual rationality constraint under both full and partial asymmetric information. The incentive constraints are respectively

$$\underline{U}_0 \geqslant \hat{U}_0 + \Delta\theta\hat{q}_0, \tag{3.2}$$

$$\hat{U}_0 \geqslant \bar{U}_0 + \Delta\theta\bar{q}_0, \tag{3.3}$$

and

$$\underline{U}_1 \geqslant \hat{U}_1 + \Delta\theta\hat{q}_1. \tag{3.4}$$

The relevant individual rationality constraints are:

$$\bar{U}_0 \geqslant 0, \tag{3.5}$$

$$\hat{U}_1 \geqslant 0. \tag{3.6}$$

Optimizing (3.1) under constraints (3.2) to (3.6) yields (with obvious notation) $\underline{q}_0^{AI} = \underline{q}_1^{AI} = \underline{q}_2$ and

$$S'(\hat{q}_0^{AI}) = (1 + \lambda)\hat{\theta} + \lambda \frac{P_0(\underline{\theta})}{P_0(\hat{\theta})} \Delta\theta,$$

[10] If we denote $V(t,q,\theta) = t - \theta q$ as the agent's utility function, the single crossing property (Mirrlees (1971)) says that $\frac{\partial}{\partial\theta}\left[\frac{\partial V}{\partial q} / \frac{\partial V}{\partial t}\right]$ has a constant sign. It is clearly satisfied here. This condition ensures that local incentive constraints imply global incentive constraints.

$$S'(\bar{q}_0^{AI}) = (1 + \lambda)\bar{\theta} + \lambda \frac{P_0(\underline{\theta}) + P_0(\hat{\theta})}{P_0(\bar{\theta})} \Delta\theta,$$

$$S'(\hat{q}_1^{AI}) = (1 + \lambda)\hat{\theta} + \lambda \frac{P_1(\underline{\theta})}{P_1(\hat{\theta})} \Delta\theta.$$

As usual, optimal government entails no distortion for the most efficient type and downward production distortions for the other types.[11]

Since the incentive and the participation constraints (3.2) to (3.6) are binding, we observe that $\hat{U}_0 = \Delta\theta\bar{q}_0^{AI}$, $\underline{U}_0 = \Delta\theta(\hat{q}_0^{AI} + \bar{q}_0^{AI})$ and $\underline{U}_1 = \Delta\theta\hat{q}_1^{AI}$.

With the profile of outputs described above, we have

$$\hat{U}_0 < \underline{U}_0 - \underline{U}_1 \tag{3.7}$$

since $\hat{q}_0^{AI} > \hat{q}_1^{AI}$, and

$$\hat{U}_0 < \underline{U}_1 \tag{3.8}$$

since $\hat{q}_1^{AI} > \bar{q}_0^{AI}$.[12]

When (3.7) and (3.8) hold, an efficient firm loses more than an intermediate firm from the revelation of information. These conditions capture in a simple way the idea that increasingly more favorable information provides an increasingly higher information rent.

[11] Note that the schedule of outputs above is really the solution only if the monotonicity conditions are satisfied, i.e. $\underline{q}_0^{AI} \geqslant \hat{q}_0^{AI} \geqslant \bar{q}_0^{AI}$ under full asymmetry of information and $\underline{q}_1^{AI} \geqslant \hat{q}_1^{AI}$ under partial asymmetry of information. This latter condition is always satisfied. Moreover, since we have

$$\frac{P_0(\underline{\theta})}{P_0(\hat{\theta})} = \frac{\nu(1-\xi)}{2(1-\nu)} \text{ and } \frac{P_0(\underline{\theta}) + P_0(\hat{\theta})}{P_0(\bar{\theta})} = \frac{(1-\xi)\nu(2-\nu(1+\xi))}{(1-\nu)^2},$$

the schedule of outputs under full asymmetric information is strictly decreasing when

$$\frac{\nu}{2(1-\nu)} \leqslant \frac{\nu[2-\nu(1+\xi)]}{(1-\nu)^2},$$

which holds since $3 - (1 + 2\xi)\nu > 0$ is always satisfied.

[12] This latter inequality holds when

$$\frac{P_0(\underline{\theta}) + P_0(\hat{\theta})}{P_0(\bar{\theta})} > \frac{P_1(\underline{\theta})}{P_1(\hat{\theta})},$$

which is satisfied since $\nu\xi < 1$.

3.4 Single Non-benevolent Politician

In this section, we assume that the politician is non-benevolent. Unless he is motivated otherwise by the Constitution, the politician colludes with the firm as follows. When the politician obtains hard information about the firm's type corresponding to either one of $\theta_i = \Delta\theta$, $i \in \{1,2\}$, or $\theta_1 = \theta_2 = \Delta\theta$, he makes a take-it-or-leave-it offer to the firm. In this offer, he asks for the minimal benefit which is consistent with his information and which will be offered to the firm if he does not reveal his signal to the Constitution. This demand is always satisfied, whatever the firm's personal characteristics.

Collusion-proofness[13] is achieved if the principal rewards the politician with a schedule of payments contingent on the messages reported about θ_1 and θ_2, $s(r_1,r_2)$, which is symmetric in (r_1,r_2) and prevents the politician from preferring bribes to honest behavior. We thereafter denote s_2, s_1 and s_0 as the politician's reward when he has reported, respectively, two, one and no pieces of favorable information. From the discussion above, these rewards must satisfy the following collusion-proof conditions:

$$s_2 - s_1 \geqslant k\underline{U}_1 \tag{3.9}$$

$$s_2 - s_0 \geqslant k\underline{U}_0 \tag{3.10}$$

$$s_1 - s_0 \geqslant k\min(\underline{U}_0 - \underline{U}_1, \hat{U}_0). \tag{3.11}$$

Constraint (3.9) says that a fully informed politician prefers to report both signals rather than concealing one of them and extracting only part of an efficient firm's information rent. Constraint (3.10) says that the politician prefers to report both signals rather than hiding both and extracting the whole rent of an efficient agent. When the politician has observed only one signal, collusion is avoided by giving him the benefit he can extract with probability 1 in any collusive offer. Then, he does not know whether the unobserved piece of information yields some rent to an efficient agent $\underline{\theta}$ or whether it yields no rent to an intermediate

[13] There is no loss of generality in restricting the analysis to collusion-proof mechanisms. The collusion-proof principle holds in this context. See Chapter 2.

agent $\hat{\theta}$. He would ask for $\underline{U}_0 - \underline{U}_1$ in the first case and for $\hat{U}_0$ in the second. Hence, constraint (3.11) must be satisfied.

Moreover, the Constitution does not need to compensate the politician for a pair of uninformative signals ($\sigma_1 = \phi$, $\sigma_2 = \phi$); hence $s_0 = 0$. The expected social cost of the politician's rewards is then

$$\lambda[\nu^2\xi^2 s_2 + 2\nu\xi(1 - \nu\xi)s_1].$$

Therefore, the Constitution's objective function with a non-benevolent politician becomes

$$(1 - \nu\xi)^2 W_0(\hat{q}_0, \bar{q}_0) + 2\nu\xi(1 - \nu\xi)W_1(\hat{q}_1) + \nu^2\xi^2 W_2 \\ - \lambda[\nu^2\xi^2 s_2 + 2\,\nu\xi(1 - \nu\xi)s_1].$$

The Constitution maximizes this objective function under the incentive constraints (3.2), (3.3) and (3.4) (taking into account that $\bar{U}_0 = \hat{U}_1 = 0$) and the collusion-proof constraints (3.9) to (3.11). If we assume momentarily that (3.7) and (3.8) hold, we can write (3.11) as $s_1 \geqslant k\hat{U}_0$.

Both (3.10) and (3.11) are binding at the optimum of the Constitution's program since it must minimize the costs of implementing a collusion-proof allocation. Then, (3.7) ensures that (3.9) is slack. Indeed, when (3.10) is binding, the politician is prevented from reporting ($\sigma_1 = \phi$, $\sigma_2 = \phi$) instead of ($\sigma_1 = \Delta\theta$, $\sigma_2 = \Delta\theta$). He has no incentives to conceal only part of his information and to reveal only one of the signals he has learned. Note that, since only (3.10) and (3.11) are binding, $\underline{U}_1$ is irrelevant for collusion purposes and no distortion of $\hat{q}_1$ from the second-best level will be necessary in the constitutional response.

Using the binding collusion-proof constraints, we can rewrite the Constitution's objective function as

$$(1 - \nu\xi)^2 W_0(\hat{q}_0, \bar{q}_0) + 2\nu\xi(1 - \nu\xi)W_1(\hat{q}_1) + \nu^2\xi^2 W_2 \\ - \lambda k[\nu^2\xi^2 \underline{U}_0 + 2\nu\xi(1 - \nu\xi)\hat{U}_0].$$

Optimizing, we find:

PROPOSITION 3.2 The optimal Constitution with a single non-benevolent politician entails:

- Under full asymmetry of information, a schedule of outputs $\underline{q}_0^{\mathrm{I}} = \underline{q}_2$, $\hat{q}_0^{\mathrm{I}}$, and $\bar{q}_0^{\mathrm{I}}$ such that outputs are always lower than with a benevolent politician, $\hat{q}_0^{\mathrm{AI}} > \hat{q}_0^{\mathrm{I}}$ and

$\bar{q}_0^{AI} > \bar{q}_0^{I}$. More precisely, we have

$$S'(\hat{q}_0^{I}) = (1+\lambda)\hat{\theta} + \lambda\left(\frac{P_0(\underline{\theta})}{P_0(\hat{\theta})} + \frac{k\nu^2\xi^2}{(1-\nu\xi)^2 P_0(\hat{\theta})}\right)\Delta\theta \qquad (3.12)$$

$$S'(\bar{q}_0^{I}) = (1+\lambda)\bar{\theta} + \lambda\left(\frac{P_0(\underline{\theta}) + P_0(\hat{\theta})}{P_0(\bar{\theta})} + \frac{k\nu\xi(2-\nu\xi)}{(1-\nu\xi)^2 P_0(\bar{\theta})}\right)\Delta\theta. \qquad (3.13)$$

This schedule of outputs is strictly decreasing when $4 - \xi[5+\nu(1-2\xi)] \geqslant 0$.[14]

- Outputs under the milder asymmetry of information take the same values as for a benevolent politician $\underline{q}_1^{I} = \underline{q}_1^{AI}$ and $\hat{q}_1^{I} = \hat{q}_1^{AI}$.

The Constitution's response to the threat of collusion is, on the one hand, to give incentives to the politician to induce him to reveal information and, on the other hand, to reduce the stakes of collusion in states ($\sigma_1 = \Delta\theta$, $\sigma_2 = \phi$), ($\sigma_1 = \phi$, $\sigma_2 = \Delta\theta$) and ($\sigma_1 = \Delta\theta$, $\sigma_2 = \Delta\theta$). For this purpose, the rents $\hat{U}_0$ and $\underline{U}_0$ must be decreased. Since (3.2) and (3.3) hold as equalities at the optimum, a decrease in $\hat{q}_0$ helps to reduce collusion in state ($\sigma_1 = \Delta\theta$, $\sigma_2 = \Delta\theta$). A decrease in $\bar{q}_0$ also helps to reduce collusion in all those states. Instead, since $\underline{U}_1$ does not enter in any binding collusion-proof constraint, there is no reason to distort $\hat{q}_1$, which keeps the same value as with a benevolent politician.

So far, we have assumed that conditions (3.7) and (3.8), both of which hold for the optimal contract with a benevolent politician, are also satisfied with a non-benevolent politician. It remains to check whether these conditions are also satisfied by the solutions described above to validate our analysis of the collusion-proof binding constraints. In Appendix A.3.1, we prove that these conditions hold when $(1-\xi)^2 > k\xi^2$, i.e., when ξ is small enough.[15]

[14] If this is not the case, one must consider an allocation with bunching.

[15] The particular assumptions we make on the probabilities of the different states of nature, in particular about ξ, are only needed to obtain the precise characterization of the optimal mechanism and to assess the allocative and distributional effects of an organizational choice in the most striking way. Section 3.6.3 shows that the main point concerning the superiority of separation does not require any assumption as long as one insists on prudent behavior.

3.5 Separation of Politicians

3.5.1 Collusion-proof Constraints

The separation of politicians alters the structures of information and therefore the opportunities for collusion. Each politician is now endowed with only one informational technology and therefore monitors only one signal.

In particular, in state $\underline{\theta}$, both politicians may observe a favorable signal. However, none of them knows what the other has observed. For example, one politician, say P_1, is unable to distinguish between state ($\sigma_1 = \Delta\theta$, $\sigma_2 = \phi$) and state ($\sigma_1 = \Delta\theta$, $\sigma_2 = \Delta\theta$).

We look for a Bayesian Nash equilibrium of the collusion game in which both politicians are prevented from colluding. When P_1 has observed a signal, three cases are possible. With probability $\nu\xi$, P_2 has observed a favorable signal and the firm is $\underline{\theta}$; P_1 can ask for the gain obtained by the firm if he does not reveal his information, i.e. $\underline{U}_1$. With probability $\nu(1 - \xi)$, P_2 has observed nothing and the firm is $\underline{\theta}$; P_1 can ask for the gain $\underline{U}_0 - \underline{U}_1$ that the firm can obtain when P_1's piece of information is not revealed. With probability $1 - \nu$, P_2 has observed nothing and the firm is $\hat{\theta}$; P_1 can ask for the gain $\hat{U}_0$. Again, we assume that the politician chooses a prudent offer, i.e., the offer which is always satisfied.

Since each politician is unaware of what has been observed and reported by the other to the Constitution, his behavior in the bribery game is independent of the other politician's report as long as he follows prudent behavior. The bribe that P_1 is asking for is the same whatever P_2's information and the rewards $s_1(\Delta\theta,\Delta\theta)$ and $s_1(\Delta\theta,\phi)$ needed to induce revelation from a politician informed of σ_1 are thus the same. As a consequence, we denote this reward by s_1 when only one signal is reported by the politician.

There is now a single collusion-proof constraint required to make this politician, say P_1, reveal his information:

$$s_1 \geqslant k\min(\hat{U}_0, \underline{U}_0 - \underline{U}_1, \underline{U}_1). \tag{3.14}$$

Suppose that (3.7) and (3.8) still hold (we will check these conditions *ex post*). Then, when each politician receives the signal $\sigma_i = \Delta\theta$, collusion is prevented by giving each of them a reward equal to $k\hat{U}_0$ instead of a total payment $k\underline{U}_0$ in the case of a single politician. The expected cost of the payments to the politicians needed to prevent collusion is thus reduced under separation and becomes

$$2\nu\xi\lambda k\hat{U}_0.$$

3.5.2 *Optimal Constitution under Separation*

Taking this expression into account, we can rewrite the Constitution's objective function:

$$(1-\nu\xi)^2 W_0(\hat{q}_0,\bar{q}_0) + 2\nu\xi(1-\nu\xi)W_1(\hat{q}_1) + \nu^2\xi^2 W_2 - 2\lambda k\nu\xi\hat{U}_0.$$

Optimizing yields the following proposition:

PROPOSITION 3.3

- Under full asymmetry of information, the optimal Constitution under separation decreases the distortion of asymmetric information in state $\hat{\theta}$ and increases it in state $\bar{\theta}$: $\hat{q}_0^S = \hat{q}_0^{AI} > \hat{q}_0^I$ and $\bar{q}_0^S < \bar{q}_0^I < \bar{q}_0^{AI}$.

  More precisely, it entails $\underline{q}_0^S = \underline{q}_2$, $\hat{q}_0^S$ and $\bar{q}_0^S$ such that

$$S'(\hat{q}_0^S) = (1+\lambda)\hat{\theta} + \lambda\frac{P_0(\underline{\theta})}{P_0(\hat{\theta})}\Delta\theta, \tag{3.15}$$

$$S'(\bar{q}_0^S) = (1+\lambda)\bar{\theta} + \lambda\frac{P_0(\underline{\theta}) + P_0(\hat{\theta})}{P_0(\bar{\theta})} + \frac{2k\nu\xi}{(1-\nu\xi)^2 P_0(\bar{\theta})}\Delta\theta. \tag{3.16}$$

  This schedule of outputs is always strictly decreasing.

- Under the milder asymmetry of information, $\underline{q}_1^S$ and $\hat{q}_1^S$ have the same values as with a single politician, $\hat{q}_1^S = \hat{q}_1^I = \hat{q}_1^{AI}$ and $\underline{q}_1^S = \underline{q}_1^I = \underline{q}_1^{AI}$.[16]

The rents asked in the side-contract now depend only on $\bar{q}_0$. As a result there is no further distortion away from the second-best

[16] Again, one can check that conditions (3.7) and (3.8) also apply under separation. Indeed, $P_0(\underline{\theta})/P_0(\hat{\theta}) > P_1(\underline{\theta})/P_1(\hat{\theta})$ implies $\hat{q}_0^S > \hat{q}_1^S$ and therefore that (3.7) holds. Similarly, we have $\hat{q}_1^S = \hat{q}_1^I > \bar{q}_0^I > \bar{q}_0^S$, where the first inequality comes from (3.8) being satisfied with a single politician. Hence, (3.8) is satisfied under separation also.

output of the intermediate agent, so $\hat{q}_0^{S} = \hat{q}_0^{AI}$, and no distortion when one signal has been observed, $\hat{q}_1^{S} = \hat{q}_1^{AI}$. Moreover, since the rent $\hat{U}_0$ is now asked more often, the distortion in state $\bar{\theta}$ must increase as we can read from comparing formulas (3.13) and (3.16). Figure 3.1 illustrates the distortions on the output levels with one or two politicians.

Bureaucratic rules are exacerbated under separation. Each politician receives a single mission, monitoring only one dimension of the agent's performance, and follows rather stringent rules. The amount of discretion left to each politician is captured by the size of the stake $\hat{U}_0$. Since this amount is reduced under separation, the growth in the number of politicians also comes with the choice of more bureaucratic rules to be followed by each politician.

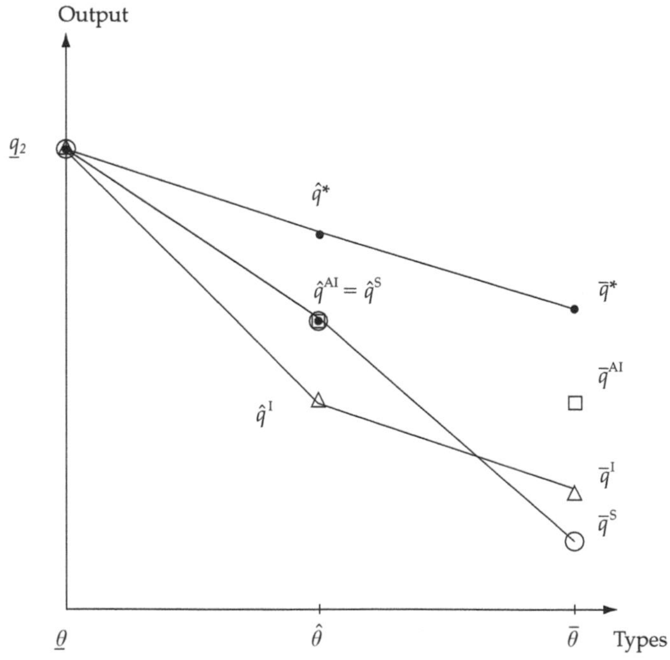

Figure 3.1: Output distortions with one or two politicians

3.5.3 *Comparative Statics: Rent and Welfare*

From Propositions 3.2 and 3.3, it follows that separation decreases the rent of asymmetric information in state $\hat{\theta}$ (since $\hat{U}_0$ is an increasing function of $\bar{q}_0$). The effect seems *a priori* ambiguous in state $\underline{\theta}$. The distributive consequences of separation are indeed more complex. Chapter 2 has shown that an interest group often loses from the institutional response to the threat of capture since the stakes of the relationship are reduced. Here, we allow for heterogeneous interest groups having different pieces of private information. Then, the institutional response to the threat of capture affects the interest groups differently depending on their respective information. Some groups may lose, some may win, but what matters is that globally the principal wins. More precisely, only the efficient firm may win from separation. Hence, everything happens as if the efficient firm has a stronger bargaining power in the collusion game with two politicians rather than one. The efficient firm may be thought to be an intermediate one by both politicians. The gain of the efficient one is made at the expense of the intermediate one. In fact, an efficient firm gets a higher rent under separation when the probability ν is small enough. Indeed, in this case, a rather large distortion of $\hat{q}_0$ (one term on the right-hand side of (3.12) has a denominator which is $(1 - \nu\xi)^2 P_0(\hat{\theta}) = 2\nu(1 - \nu)(1 - \xi)$ and which becomes relatively small when ν is small) and a rather small distortion of $\bar{q}_0$ (one term on the right-hand side of (3.13) has a denominator which is $(1 - \nu\xi)^2 P_0(\bar{\theta}) = (1 - \nu)^2$ and which becomes relatively high when ν is small) must be introduced to reduce the stake of collusion with one politician. Separation increases this first output level more than it reduces the second, resulting in an increase of the overall efficient type's rent.

As separation weakens the collusion-proof constraint in state $(\sigma_1 = \Delta\theta, \sigma_2 = \Delta\theta)$ and does not affect the cost of collusion-proofness in other states, expected social welfare obviously increases with separation. In addition we obtain the following proposition:

> PROPOSITION 3.4 For $\Delta\theta$ small enough whatever $S(\cdot)$ or for $S(\cdot)$ quadratic, i.e. $S(q) = -|S''|q^2/2 + \mu q$ for some μ, whatever $\Delta\theta$, the following results of comparative statics hold:

- Under full asymmetric information, the rent in state $\underline{\theta}$ is larger with separation than with one politician if and only if $1 \geqslant \nu(3 - 2\xi)$. The rent in state $\hat{\theta}$ is always lower with separation.
- The welfare gain from the separation of politicians ΔSW is positive and of second order in $\Delta\theta$:

$$\Delta SW = \frac{\lambda(1+\lambda)k\nu^2\xi^2\Delta\theta^2}{|S''|}\left\{1 + \frac{\lambda}{1+\lambda}\left[\frac{\nu(1-\xi)[3-(1+2\xi)\nu]}{2(1-\nu)^2} + \frac{k\nu\xi}{(1-\nu)^2}\left(2 - \frac{\xi[1+\nu(1-2\xi)]}{4(1-\xi)}\right)\right]\right\}. \qquad (3.17)$$

Proof: See Appendix A.3.2.

Since $3-(1+2\xi)\nu \geq 0$ and $2 - \frac{\xi[1+\nu(1-2\xi)]}{4(1-\xi)} \geq 1$,[17] all terms in (3.17) are non-negative. As expected, welfare increases unambiguously because the separation of politicians increases the transaction costs of collusion. The following reasoning helps to explain the magnitude of this difference in expected welfare. For a given profile of quantities and therefore of rents, one can envision the objective of the Constitution as an implementation problem: to minimize the social loss associated with politicians' rewards subject to a set of collusion-proof constraints. By relaxing one of these constraints, separation improves social welfare by a term which is proportional to the gain on this constraint, i.e. $\underline{U}_0 - 2\hat{U}_0$ if this difference is small, which is the case for $\Delta\theta$ small enough. The next step is to optimize the profile of rents and quantities subject to incentive and participation constraints. When $\Delta\theta$ is small enough, one introduces distortions of the quantities which are of first order in $\Delta\theta$. This makes $\underline{U}_0 - 2\hat{U}_0 = \Delta\theta\,(\hat{q}_0 - \bar{q}_0)$ finally of second order in $\Delta\theta$. Moreover, by direct inspection we find:

Proposition 3.5 ΔSW is increasing in $k, \lambda, \Delta\theta$ and $\frac{1}{|S''|}$

ΔSW increases with the efficiency of the collusive transaction, the cost of public funds, and with the curvature of the

[17] This inequality holds for values of ξ such that the no-bunching condition given in Proposition 3.2 is satisfied.

Constitution's objective function. All these parameters increase the social gain of separation in terms of the politician's rewards, i.e. $\lambda k(\underline{U}_0 - 2\hat{U}_0)$ increases. This is obviously the case for k and λ, which directly increase the benefits of separation by reducing the burden of collusion borne by taxpayers. But a greater curvature of the consumer's utility function also increases the convexity of the rent since it increases the difference between $\hat{q}_0$ and $\bar{q}_0$.

Of particular interest is the dependence of the welfare gain on the efficiency of the side-contracting transaction and on the cost of public funds. First, countries with an inefficient taxation system face high values of λ and are likely to be those which benefit the most from separation. Second, countries where capture and corruption are easier to enforce (k close to unity) are also likely to benefit from an efficient design of their political institutions. It is striking that both features above are present in most developing countries. In particular, provided that transaction costs of side-contracting remain unchanged in the political process, our result suggests that the decentralization of regulatory rights among different bodies is particularly attractive in these countries. A good internal design of the government helps all the more when the government is inefficient in levying taxes and corruption is easily enforced. Montinola, Qian and Weingast (1993) offer some evidence concerning this issue in the case of the implementation of federalism in China.

Separation of powers appears more desirable in developing countries. However, it is likely also to be more difficult to implement there. Low transaction costs of collusion will make it easier for the two regulators to collude.

3.6 *Generalization of the Results*

3.6.1 *Prudent Behavior and Various Preferences*

As we discussed in Sections 3.3 and 3.4, the outcome of the collusive game between the politicians and the firm depends on the relative ranking of $\underline{U}_0 - \underline{U}_1$, $\hat{U}_0$ and $\underline{U}_1$. Focusing on the case of a linear marginal cost has helped us to rank these three quantities. It has also illustrated why being able to get two pieces of favorable information enables a single politician to obtain more bargaining power *vis-à-vis* the firm than what can be achieved by politicians as a pair under separation.

However, the results have a much greater generality and are robust to any specification of the ranking of the information rents that could arise, even if the production technologies do not have constant returns to scale, or if the informational structures were not additive as we have assumed so far.

We generalize our approach as follows. The first step is to compute the minimum rewards s_2 needed to get two pieces of information with a single politician. Since the politician may conceal only one signal even if he has learned both (equation (3.9)), a deviation consisting of hiding only one dimension of the information yields

$$s_1 + k\underline{U}_1 = k(\min(\underline{U}_0 - \underline{U}_1, \hat{U}_0) + \underline{U}_1) = k(\min(\underline{U}_0, \underline{U}_1 + \hat{U}_0)).$$

Since the politician can also hide both signals (equation (3.10)), such a deviation yields $k\underline{U}_0$. The binding collusion-proof conditions (3.9) and (3.10) therefore offer the rewards

$$s_2 = k(\max(\min(\underline{U}_0, \underline{U}_1 + \hat{U}_0); \underline{U}_0)) = k\underline{U}_0$$

whatever the ranking of the different information rents.

Therefore, the social cost of implementing a collusion-proof allocation with one politican is

$$C^{\mathrm{I}} = \lambda k\nu\xi(\nu\xi\underline{U}_0 + 2(1 - \nu\xi)\min(\hat{U}_0, \underline{U}_0 - \underline{U}_1)).$$

Under separation, this cost now becomes (see (3.14))

$$C^{\mathrm{II}} = \lambda k\nu\xi(2\nu\xi\min(\hat{U}_0, \underline{U}_0 - \underline{U}_1, \underline{U}_1) + 2(1 - \nu\xi)\min(\hat{U}_0, \underline{U}_0 - \underline{U}_1, \underline{U}_1)).$$

The difference between these two costs is clear. The term obtained when only one signal has been observed is clearly lower under separation. Moreover, when two signals have been observed, separation is also less costly since we always have

$$2\min(\hat{U}_0, \underline{U}_0 - \underline{U}_1, \underline{U}_1) \leq 2\min(\underline{U}_0 - \underline{U}_1, \underline{U}_1) \leq \underline{U}_0 - \underline{U}_1 + \underline{U}_1 = \underline{U}_0.$$ [18]

Hence, separation always dominates when the politicians play prudently in making their collusive offers to the firm. This shows

[18] The last inequality is strict when $\underline{U}_0 - \underline{U}_1 \neq \underline{U}_1$ and holds generically.

how the prudent behavior that we requested is the only ingredient needed to show the benefit of separation.

However, in contrast to Sections 3.3 and 3.4, the exact writing of the collusion-proof constraints may now also involve $\underline{U}_1$. The corresponding output $\hat{q}_1$ may also possibly be distorted in both cases. Both the allocative efficiency and the distribution of rents are again affected by separation and the allocative and distributive consequences of separation could be derived as in Section 3.4. In particular, social welfare increases with separation, and the new distribution of rents may favor some groups over others.

3.6.2 *Discriminatory Side-contracting Offers*

As we have argued above, the assumption of prudent behavior is quite appealing in the context of side-contracting. We now consider the case where politicians can make side-contract offers that the firm may reject with positive probability. To make comparisons with the case of prudent offers, which we have analyzed in Sections 3.3 and 3.4, we assume also that $\underline{U}_0 - \underline{U}_1 > \underline{U}_1 > \hat{U}_0$.

A single politician who is already aware of one dimension of the firm's type asks for a bribe $\underline{U}_0 - \underline{U}_1$ instead of a prudent one $\hat{U}_0$ when the expected profit of doing so is greater, i.e. when

$$\nu(1 - \xi)(\underline{U}_0 - \underline{U}_1) > (1 - \nu\xi)\hat{U}_0.$$

Under separation, each politician asks for a bribe $\underline{U}_0 - \underline{U}_1$ instead of a prudent one $\hat{U}_0$ or an intermediary one $\underline{U}_1$ when

$$\nu(1 - \xi)(\underline{U}_0 - \underline{U}_1) > \max\{\nu\xi\underline{U}_1, \hat{U}_0\}.$$

Both inequalities above hold in particular when ξ is close to zero and ν close to unity.

The cost of implementing collusion-proofness with a single politician is then

$$C^{\mathrm{I}} = \lambda k[\nu^2\xi^2\underline{U}_0 + 2\nu^2\xi(1 - \xi)(\underline{U}_0 - \underline{U}_1)].$$

Similarly, the cost of implementing collusion-proofness with two politicians is now

$$C^{\mathrm{II}} = \lambda k[2\nu^2\xi^2(\underline{U}_0 - \underline{U}_1) + 2\nu^2\xi(1 - \xi)(\underline{U}_0 - \underline{U}_1)].$$

$C^{\mathrm{II}} > C^{\mathrm{I}}$ since $\underline{U}_0 > 2\underline{U}_1$. The sum of the collusion-proof rewards needed to prevent collusion in state ($\sigma_1 = \Delta\theta$, $\sigma_2 = \Delta\theta$) under separation is larger than what is needed to prevent collusion from a single politician. With discriminatory offers, each politician is ready to run the risk of having his side-contract offer sometimes refused against the high payoff that he may get when this offer is accepted. The optimal contract under separation has to prevent deviations which are mutually inconsistent since a single politician would never ask for a total bribe which would exceed the firm's rent in state ($\sigma_1 = \Delta\theta$, $\sigma_2 = \Delta\theta$), i.e. $\underline{U}_0$.

3.6.3 Collusion Between the Politicians

We now investigate the possibility that the politicians may collude. We again assume that transfers between them are not feasible, but we allow them to report to each other the hard information signal they may have obtained on the firm's type. Then, a three-party bargaining takes place with the firm. Because politicians who share the same information should have equal bargaining power, each of them gets half of the minimal firm's information rent consistent with their pooled information.

Collusive strategies in the politicians' game are as follows: before getting his signal, each politician credibly commits to share or not to share information with the other. We will look at the Nash equilibrium of this game. By both sharing, each politician gets

$$V_{SS} = \nu^2\xi^2\frac{\underline{U}_0}{2} + \nu\xi(1-\nu\xi)\hat{U}_0.$$

When politician 1 shares information but politician 2 does not, politician 1 always asks for $\frac{1}{2}\hat{U}_0$ and his payoff is

$$V_{SN} = \nu^2\xi^2\frac{\hat{U}_0}{2} + \nu\xi(1-\nu\xi)\frac{\hat{U}_0}{2}.$$

When politician 1 does not share information but politician 2 does, politician 1 asks for $\underline{U}_0 - \underline{U}_1$ when he knows for sure that the firm is $\underline{\theta}$. He asks instead for $\frac{\hat{U}_0}{2}$ when only politician 2 has observed a signal and for $\hat{U}_0$ when he is the only one to have observed a signal. His payoff becomes

$$V_{NS} = \nu^2\xi^2(\underline{U}_0 - \underline{U}_1) + \nu\xi(1 - \nu\xi)\frac{3\hat{U}_0}{2}.$$

Lastly, when both politicians refuse to share information, each of them gets

$$V_{NN} = \nu^2\xi^2\hat{U}_0 + \nu\xi(1 - \nu\xi)\hat{U}_0.$$

It is straightforward to check that not sharing is a dominant strategy of this game when (3.7) and (3.8) are satisfied. Indeed, $V_{NN} > V_{SN}$ and $V_{NS} > V_{SS}$. Hence, politicians are caught in a prisoner's dilemma and refuse to share information which would have been beneficial to transfer to improve side-contracting.[19]

3.7 Conclusion

The separation of power among politicians may be an optimal governmental response to the threat of regulatory capture. Separation reduces the non-benevolent politicians' discretion, and the sum of their gains from collusion may be lower than if the politicians were cooperating. Under asymmetric information, the supply of possible bribes always strictly exceeds the total demand of the politicians when their collusive offers are satisfied, whatever the firm's personal characteristics. This result is robust to changes in the regulated firm's preferences and the timing of the collusion game. It shows how important it is to have structural foundations for the collusive activities, since the organization of government affects those activities. Shleifer and Vishny (1993) propose a positive theory of government organization, and argue that complementary permits should be offered by the same agency. The reason is that an agency does not take into account the demand for bribes of other regulatory bodies when it makes its own bribe proposal. A standard model of oligopoly competition is used to show that an equilibrium with excessive bribery takes place under separation. The difference with our normative approach is twofold. First, because information plays no role in

[19] However, as we suggested already in Section 3.5, more research on the difficulties of implementing the separation of powers is required.

the Shleifer and Vishny (1993) analysis, it is hard to see why bribes are in fact offered in the first place: the supply side of the market for bribes is exogenous. Here, the foundations of corruption are explicit. Second, in our model, competition between competing agencies is optimally organized by the Constitution itself and not an exogenous starting point. We can take into account how the organizational response affects the cost of the threat of corruption.

We have also assumed that the transaction costs of side-contracts were the same with one or two regulators. In fact, these transaction costs are lacking theoretical foundations in the current literature.[20] They may depend on several factors, including the frequency of the relationship between the politician and the firm, the importance of their future gains of cooperation, their information on each other, and the level of trust that has been developed between them. All these quantities are likely to differ when one considers separation and, consequently, transaction costs may change. Neven, Nuttall and Seabright (1993) have suggested that the transaction costs of collusion decrease when politicians have more specialized tasks. In the same vein, we have assumed so far that the collusion technology has constant marginal returns. For obvious psychological reasons a politician may not like to engage in collusive activities without being promised a high enough return. Clearly, those increasing return technologies also favor the choice of separation.

The basic message of this chapter is that monopoly in information acquisition may be a curse for the government when collusion is a concern. Information *per se* introduces increasing returns in the benefits of side-contracts. The argument is robust to a broad set of assumptions, both on the ranking of rents and on the timing of the side-contracting game. Therefore, it might be considered as a general principle in governmental design. The framers of the Constitution may decide to divide powers between various politicians and administrators to limit the social costs of side-contracting. However, implementing this separation of powers may prove to be difficult.

[20] See Part III for a way of endogenizing these transaction costs.

Appendix 3

A.3.1 Profiles of rents

We want to check that the conditions (3.7) and (3.8) are satisfied by the optimal contract with a single non-benevolent politician. To prove $\underline{U}_0 < \underline{U}_0 - \hat{U}_0$ is equivalent to checking that $\hat{q}_1^{AI} < \hat{q}_0^{I}$. This occurs when

$$\frac{\nu}{2(1-\nu)}(1-\xi) > \frac{\nu\xi^2}{2(1-\nu)(1-\xi)}k.$$

This holds when $k\xi^2 < (1-\xi)^2$.

We also observe that $\underline{U}_1 > \hat{U}_0$ whenever $\hat{q}_1^{AI} > \bar{q}_0^{I}$. This latter inequality occurs when

$$0 < 1 + \frac{\lambda}{1+\lambda}\left(\frac{(1-\xi)\nu(1-\xi\,\nu)}{(1-\nu)^2} + \frac{k\nu\xi(2-\nu\xi)}{(1-\nu)^2}\right).$$

Since $1 \geq \xi\nu$, the condition above is always satisfied.

A.3.2 Proof of Proposition 3.4

We compare rents with one or two politicians for $\Delta\theta$ small enough:

$$\Delta\hat{U}_0 = \Delta\theta(\bar{q}_0^{S} - \bar{q}_0^{I}) = \frac{\Delta\theta^2\lambda k\nu^2\xi^2}{(1-\nu)^2 S''}.$$

Second

$$\Delta\underline{U}_0 = \Delta\theta(\hat{q}_0^{S} - \hat{q}_0^{I}) + \Delta\hat{U}_0,$$

and

$$\Delta\underline{U}_0 = \frac{\Delta\theta^2\, k\,\lambda\,\nu\xi^2\,[1-(3-2\xi)\nu]}{2\,|S''|\,(1-\nu)^2(1-\xi)}.$$

We denote

$$SW^{I}(\hat{q}_0^{I}, \bar{q}_0^{I}, \hat{q}_1^{I}) = (1-\nu\xi)^2 W_0(\hat{q}_0^{I}, \bar{q}_0^{I}) + \nu^2\xi^2 W_2$$

$$+\, 2\nu\xi(1-\nu\xi)W_1(\hat{q}_1^{I}) - \nu^2\xi^2 k\lambda\underline{U}_0 - 2\nu\xi(1-\nu\xi)k\lambda\hat{U}_0,$$

and

$$SW^S(\hat{q}_0^S, \bar{q}_0^S, \hat{q}_1^S) = (1 - \nu\xi)^2 W_0(\hat{q}_0^S, \bar{q}_0^S) + \nu^2\xi^2 W_2$$

$$+ 2\nu\xi(1 - \nu\xi)W_1(\hat{q}_1^S) - 2\nu\xi k\lambda\hat{U}_0.$$

We observe that the difference in expected welfare under both organizations can be written as

$$\begin{aligned}\Delta SW &= SW^S(\hat{q}_0^S, \bar{q}_0^S, \hat{q}_1^S) - SW^I(\hat{q}_0^I, \bar{q}_0^I, \hat{q}_1^I)\\ &= SW^I(\hat{q}_0^S, \bar{q}_0^S, \hat{q}_1^I) - SW^I(\hat{q}_0^I, \bar{q}_0^I, \hat{q}_1^I) + \nu^2\xi^2\lambda k\,(\underline{U}_0^S - 2\hat{U}_0^S).\end{aligned}$$

We denote the first term by A and the second by B. A is the difference in expected welfare with one politician computed with the quantities corresponding to the cases with two or one politicians. It is therefore of second order in $\Delta\theta$ when $\Delta\theta$ is small.

B is the gain of separation in terms of the politician's wage. It is a positive number (since $\hat{q}_0^S > \bar{q}_0^S$) and of second order in $\Delta\theta$. After computation, we find

$$A = \frac{\nu^3\xi^4k^2\lambda^2\Delta\theta^2[1+(1-2\xi)\nu]}{4S''(1-\nu)^2(1-\xi)} \leq 0$$

$$B = \frac{\nu^2\xi^2k\lambda(1+\lambda)\Delta\theta^2}{|S''|}\left[1 + \frac{\lambda}{1+\lambda}(1-\xi)\left(\frac{\nu[2-\nu(1+\xi)]}{(1-\nu)^2} - \frac{\nu}{2(1-\nu)}\right) + \frac{\lambda}{1+\lambda}\,\frac{2\nu\,\xi\,k}{(1-\nu)^2}\right].$$

Adding A and B yields formula (3.18).

Moreover, these Taylor expansions are exact in the case of a quadratic utility function $S(q) = -\dfrac{|S''|q^2}{2} + \mu q$. Variable μ is large enough to ensure that outputs are positive.

4

Checks and Balances

'A little attention to the subject will convince us, that these three powers ought to be in different hands, and independent of one another, and so ballanced, and each having that check upon the other, that their independence shall be preserved.'

Essex Result of 1778 in Handlin and Handlin (1996).[1]

4.1 Introduction

In Chapters 2 and 3 we studied the supervisory role of governmental bodies or politicians with respect to regulated sectors of the economy. Chapter 3 provided some foundations for the separation of this supervision function among several bodies. Indeed, we see that governments are organized with several ministries, and that the Constitution sets up executive, legislative and judiciary branches. In this chapter, we study the design of reciprocal supervision between governmental bodies of the same hierarchical level, very much like the two politicians of Chapter 3. It is a way to explore the model of checks and balances launched by James Madison in The Federalist Papers of 1787.

First we will study how the Constitutional level, which has two politicians to run two sectors, can design reciprocal supervision between the politicians. We assume that each politician is also a supervisor of the other politician and study how the Constitution can deter collusion between politicians. We will argue that such a design creates opportunities for reciprocal favors between politicians which are very costly for the Constitution and which may

[1] As emphasized by Casper (1997), the Essex Result considerably complicated the debate over separation of powers by invoking the notion of checks and balances. The Essex Result was a critique by the towns of Essex County in the 1778 draft of the Constitution of Massachusetts which was rejected.

justify the limitation of these horizontal supervision activities either in the form of relatively inefficient supervision technologies or in the form of asymmetric supervision. We will also investigate under which circumstances it may be better to let politicians collude.

Reciprocal favors have been documented mainly in the organization literature but are highly relevant for analyzing governments. When the manager of a firm cannot monitor his employees directly, he must use a supervisor. Among the several functions of a supervisor is his role for partially bridging the informational gap between the manager and his employees. In a code of ethics for a foreman, Deb (1963) notes:

> 'the foreman must control cost in his shop ... the foreman will not take recourse to passive supervision by mainly avoiding disputes or differences with his men or dodging troubles; will not attempt to attain cheap popularity with workers at the cost of duties'.

An interpretation of this code of conduct is that the foreman must achieve low cost if indeed the technology is a low-cost technology, even when the manager does not know it. In so doing he will hurt the employees, who will see their work level increased or their information rent decreased; hence the second rule saying that he should not collude with the workers.

Also, Dalton (1959) mentions in his discussion of the relationships between foremen and workmen (the line):

> 'toleration of minor rule-breaking by the line in exchange for aid from the line in crises', p. 104.

Actually, this chapter was motivated by the observed practice in some universities of an exchange of favors between the chair of a department who tolerates that professors do not fulfill their service obligations (such as the number of hours they teach) and the favor of not reporting that the chair himself is not accomplishing all of his duties. But such exchanges of favors are very common both in the administration and in firms. Also we know the dangers of using teacher evaluations by students as inputs to the compensation of professors, which may induce demagogical behavior.

The peer-monitoring literature has emphasized the virtues of reciprocal monitoring to alleviate limited liability constraints (see Banerjee, Besley and Guinnane (1992), Besley and Coate (1995), Stiglitz (1990), Laffont and N'Guessan (1999)). Similarly, the literature on teams (Holmström and Milgrom (1989), Itoh (1993)) has claimed the benefits of collusion of agents when it is based on superior information. Here, we stress some dangers of peer supervision.

The separation of powers advocated by Locke and Montesquieu is only one aspect of the organization of governments, firms or regulatory bodies. It can be rationalized either as an instrument of information extraction through yardstick competition (see Neven, Nuttall and Seabright (1993), Chapter 3) or an instrument to discourage rent seeking and corruption (Congleton (1984), Chapter 3) or to improve the accountability of elected officials (Persson, Roland and Tabellini (1997)). Even Locke and Montesquieu[2] had in mind a more complex design by giving the executive a share in legislative power and by acknowledging the judicial role of the House of Lords. Similarly, when the US Constitution was drafted, as emphasized by Kramnick (1987) in his introduction to the Federalist Papers:

> 'the Anti-federalists still have a valid point in insisting that the Constitution created was much more a mixed government of shared powers, much more a government of checks and balances, than a separation of powers', p. 53.
>
> 'The President was given legislative power by the Constitution through his veto power.' p. 50.
>
> 'the state judiciary came to be regarded by Federalists not only as needing separation and independence, but also as a potential check on the social forces dominating the state legislature', p. 49.

[2] 'Mais, si dans un Etat libre, la puissance législative ne doit pas avoir le droit d'arrêter la puissance exécutrice, elle a droit, et doit avoir la faculté d'examiner de quelle manière les lois qu'elle a faites ont été exécutées . . .'

'Quoiqu'en général la puissance de juger ne doive être unie à aucune partie de la législative, cela est sujet à trois exceptions . . .'

'La puissance exécutrice doit prendre part à la législation par sa faculté d'empêcher.' Montesquieu (1748), p. 589.

And, through section II article 4, the Senate was given control of the President by the impeachment procedure. Furthermore, the US Constitution requires Senate approval in the appointment of Supreme Court judges and a few other key federal offices as well as ratification of foreign treaties, congressional approval of a declaration of war and judicial review of federal legislation and administrative acts.

Taking as given the separation of powers or tasks, we analyze in this chapter the design of checks or controls that the framers of the Constitution might want to set up as a complement to the incentive schemes imposed on each power.

Section 4.2 presents a model in which two politicians supervise each other. The optimal symmetric Constitution is characterized in Section 4.3. An asymmetric Constitution is studied in Section 4.4, where it is shown in what circumstances it can dominate the optimal symmetric one. Another kind of manipulation of information is considered in Section 4.5 which exploits the design of Section 4.3. Then, it is shown that letting collusion happen is sometimes an optimal strategy. Section 4.6 extends the analysis to the case of three politicians and Section 4.7 compares various systems of checks and balances. Section 4.8 concludes.

4.2 The Model

We slightly extend the model of Chapter 2 to include two activities, each one controlled by a politician. Politician 1 runs the production of public good 1 with a cost function

$$C_1 = \theta_1 q_1,$$

where q_1 is the production level and θ_1 in $\{\underline{\theta}, \bar{\theta}\}$ is a productivity parameter representing the private information of politician 1. Let $\nu = \Pr(\theta_1 = \underline{\theta})$. Politician 1's utility level is

$$U_1 = t_1 - \theta_1 q_1,$$

with a utility level for the rest of society given by

$$S(q_1) - (1 + \lambda)t_1.$$

Similarly, politician 2 has a cost function

$$C_2 = \theta_2 q_2,$$

with θ_2 in $\{\underline{\theta}, \bar{\theta}\}$, $\nu = \Pr(\theta_2 = \underline{\theta})$,

$$U_2 = t_2 - \theta_2 q_2,$$

$$S(q_2) - (1 + \lambda)t_2.$$

The random variables θ_1 and θ_2 are independent. Social welfare is given by

$$\begin{aligned} W &= S(q_1) + S(q_2) - (1 + \lambda)(t_1 + t_2) + U_1 + U_2 \\ &= S(q_1) + S(q_2) - (1 + \lambda)(\theta_1 q_1 + \theta_2 q_2) - \lambda(U_1 + U_2). \end{aligned}$$

To simplify the analysis of reciprocal supervision we have integrated vertically each politician with the sector he supervises. There is no asymmetry of information left between the politician and the firm he controls. The results of this chapter could be easily extended to a more general setup by bringing together Chapters 3 and 4. The complete information benchmarks are defined by

$$\begin{aligned} S'(q_1^*) &= (1 + \lambda)\,\theta_1, \quad t_1^* = \theta_1 q_1^*, \\ S'(q_2^*) &= (1 + \lambda)\,\theta_2, \quad t_2^* = \theta_2 q_2^*. \end{aligned}$$

Each politician i will behave strategically with respect to his private information θ_i, just like the firm in Chapter 2. In addition, politician 1 exerts a costless supervision of politician 2 which is modeled as follows. Politician 1 observes a signal σ_1 about politician 2's efficiency θ_2. The supervision technology is as in Chapter 2 such that

$$\begin{aligned} \sigma_1 &= \underline{\theta} \quad \text{with probability } \xi \text{ if } \theta_2 = \underline{\theta}, \\ &= \phi \quad \text{otherwise.} \end{aligned}$$

When $\sigma_1 = \underline{\theta}$, politician 2 is aware of it. Symmetrically, politician 2 observes σ_2 in $\{\underline{\theta}, \phi\}$ about θ_1. The timing of contracting is as follows:

1	2	3	4	5
Constitution selects politicians and offers contracts	Politicians learn their type θ_i and their signal σ_i	Politicians report their signal	Politicians announce their type if necessary	Contracts are executed

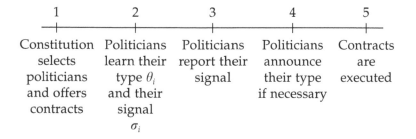

When collusion between politicians happens, it takes place between time 2 and 3. All politicians are *ex ante* identical and are selected randomly by the Constitution.[3] We also assume that politicians are infinitely risk-averse at the zero profit level so that *ex post* individual rationality constraints must be satisfied.

Consider as a second benchmark the case where politicians behave strategically with respect to their private information concerning their sector, but perform benevolently their supervisory function of the other politician.

Consider politician 1 for example. Two cases are possible. Either the Constitution is informed about θ_1 (by politician 2). In this case, which happens with probability $\nu\xi$, the complete information allocation is achieved, i.e.

$$S'(\underline{q}^*) = (1 + \lambda)\,\underline{\theta}, \quad t_1 = \underline{\theta}\underline{q}^*.$$

Or the Constitution remains uninformed but has new beliefs following the signal $\sigma_2 = \phi$ which are characterized by

$$\hat{\nu} = \frac{(1 - \xi)\nu}{1 - \nu\xi} < \nu.$$

The control problems concerning the two politicians are separable. For politician 1, with the signal $\sigma_2 = \phi$, the optimal contract is characterized as in Chapter 2 with new beliefs $\hat{\nu}$. We obtain

$$S'(\hat{\underline{q}}) = (1 + \lambda)\underline{\theta}$$

$$S'(\hat{\bar{q}}) = (1 + \lambda)\bar{\theta} + \frac{\lambda(1 - \xi)\nu}{1 - \nu}\Delta\theta$$

$$\underline{U}_1 = (1 - \xi)\nu\Delta\theta\hat{\bar{q}}$$

$$\bar{U}_1 = 0.$$

The situation for politician 2 is similar.

Let us denote $\underline{W}^* = S(\underline{q}^*) - (1+\lambda)\,\underline{\theta}\,\underline{q}^*$ as the complete information welfare for an efficient type, and

$$W^{AI} = \hat{\nu}\,[S(\hat{\underline{q}}) - (1 + \lambda)\underline{\theta}\hat{\underline{q}} - \lambda\Delta\theta\hat{\bar{q}}] + (1 - \hat{\nu})\,[S(\hat{\bar{q}}) - (1 + \lambda)\bar{\theta}\hat{\bar{q}}]$$

[3] 'Le suffrage par le sort est de la nature de la démocratie.' Montesquieu (1748), p. 533.

as the expected social welfare with beliefs $\hat{\nu}$. The global expected welfare is then

$$2\nu\xi\underline{W}^* + 2(1-\nu\xi)\,W^{AI}.$$

4.3 Optimal Symmetric Constitution

Suppose now that politician *i* can be captured by politician *j* in his supervisory task, as the politician could be captured by the firm in Chapter 2. Consider for example politician 1 who has observed $\sigma_1 = \underline{\theta}$. If he sends the (verifiable) report $r_1 = \underline{\theta}$ to the Constitution, the complete information allocation with no rent for politician 2 is achieved. He can instead hide his signal to the benefit of politician 2. And similarly for politician 2's supervisory activity. The incentive constraints of the politician concerning his message about himself and about the other politician are separable. (See Appendix A.4.1.)

Invoking the collusion-proof principle we can specify the collusion-proof constraints in the various states of nature. Consider first the two symmetric states of nature $\{\sigma_1 = \underline{\theta}, \sigma_2 = \phi\}$ and $\{\sigma_1 = \phi, \sigma_2 = \underline{\theta}\}$. Let $\underline{s}_2$ (resp. $\underline{s}_1$) be the reward to politician 2 (resp. 1) from the Constitution when politician 2 (resp. 1) makes the report $r_2 = \underline{\theta}$ (resp. $r_1 = \underline{\theta}$) and politician 1 (resp. 2) makes the report $r_1 = \phi$ (resp. $r_2 = \phi$).

Collusion-proofness requires

$$\underline{s}_1 \geq k\,\Delta\theta\bar{q}_2$$
$$\underline{s}_2 \geq k\,\Delta\theta\bar{q}_1$$

with an expected cost for symmetric solutions of

$$2\nu\xi(1-\nu\xi)k\Delta\theta\bar{q}.$$

The most interesting case occurs in the state of nature $\{\sigma_1 = \underline{\theta}, \sigma_2 = \underline{\theta}\}$. Then, the two politicians can exchange the favors of not reporting their true signal. We argue that this type of collusion is easier than the previous (asymmetric) ones which required a transfer between the politicians which is potentially dangerous. Here it is enough that the two politicians exchange phone calls to implement their collusion.

More precisely, we make a non-linearity assumption in the transaction costs of side transfers by postulating a discount factor k' larger than k in the case of reciprocal favors. Let $\underline{\underline{s}}_1$ and $\underline{\underline{s}}_2$ be the rewards to politicians 1 and 2 for the reports $\{r_1 = \underline{\theta}, r_2 = \underline{\theta}\}$. Collusion-proofness requires

$$\underline{\underline{s}}_1 + \underline{\underline{s}}_2 \geq k'\Delta\theta(\bar{q}_1 + \bar{q}_2),$$

i.e. an additional expected cost for the Constitution at a symmetric solution

$$2(\nu\xi)^2 k'\Delta\theta\bar{q}.$$

The Constitution must select optimal contracts taking into account these supervision costs and the usual incentive and individual rationality constraints. Solving these constraints as usual and inserting the solution into the social welfare we can decompose the Constitution's objective function into six different states, as follows.

With probability $(1 - \nu)^2$, both politicians are inefficient. No rent and no supervision payment needs to be given up; hence a contribution to the objective function of

$$2(1 - \nu)^2 [S(\bar{q}) - (1 + \lambda)\bar{\theta}\bar{q}].$$

With probability $(1 - \nu)\,\nu\,(1 - \xi)$ one politician is inefficient and the other is efficient but not identified as such. A rent $\Delta\theta\bar{q}$ must be given up to the efficient politician; hence a contribution (since there are two such cases) of

$$2(1 - \nu)\nu(1 - \xi)\,[S(\bar{q}) - (1 + \lambda)\bar{\theta}\bar{q} + S(\underline{q}) - (1 + \lambda)\,\underline{\theta}\,\underline{q} - \lambda\Delta\theta\bar{q}].$$

With probability $(1 - \nu)\nu\xi$ a politician is inefficient; the other one is efficient and identified as such by the supervisor. A supervisory payment $k\Delta\theta\bar{q}$ must be paid; hence a contribution (there are two such cases) of

$$2(1 - \nu)\nu\xi\,[S(\bar{q}) - (1 + \lambda)\bar{\theta}\bar{q} + S(\underline{q}^*) - (1 + \lambda)\,\underline{\theta}\,\underline{q}^* - \lambda k\Delta\theta\bar{q}].$$

With probability $\nu^2\xi^2$ both politicians are efficient and have been identified. The high supervisory payments needed to avoid reciprocal favors must be paid; hence a contribution of

$$2\nu^2\xi^2\,[S(\underline{q}^*) - (1 + \lambda)\,\underline{\theta}\,\underline{q}^* - \lambda k'\Delta\theta\,\bar{q}].$$

With probability $\nu^2(1 - \xi)^2$ both politicians are efficient and have not been identified as such. Information rents must be given up; hence a contribution of

$$2v^2(1-\xi)^2\,[S(\underline{q}) - (1+\lambda)\,\underline{\theta}\,\underline{q} - \lambda\Delta\theta\bar{q}].$$

Finally, with probability $v^2\xi\,(1-\xi)$ both politicians are efficient and only one has been identified. The informed politician now receives both a rent for his own firm and a supervisory payment; hence (there are two such cases) a contribution of

$$2v^2\xi\,(1-\xi)\,[S(\underline{q}) - (1+\lambda)\,\underline{\theta}\,\underline{q} - \lambda k\Delta\theta\bar{q} - \lambda\Delta\theta\,\bar{q} + S(\underline{q}^*) - (1+\lambda)\,\underline{\theta}\,\underline{q}^*].$$

Collecting all these terms to form expected social welfare W^I and maximizing with respect to $\bar{q}$, $\underline{q}$ yields

$$S'\,(\underline{q}) = (1+\lambda)\underline{\theta} \tag{4.1}$$

$$S'\,(\bar{q}) = (1+\lambda)\bar{\theta} + \frac{\lambda\Delta\theta v}{1-v}\,[1 - \xi + k\xi\,(1 - v\xi) + k'v\xi^2]. \tag{4.2}$$

The downward distortion of production is greater than under benevolent supervision since more payments have to be made to acquire information. The two additional terms $k\xi(1 - v\xi) + k'v\xi^2$ in (4.2) reflect this incentive cost. When $k' = k$ we are back to the classical formula (2.12) of Chapter 2. The new insights will come from the different transaction costs of side-contracting.

When $\xi = 0$, the supervision technology is useless and we find the same result as in the case without collusion. As ξ increases from 0 to 1, the distortion is reduced for $v \leq 1/2$. However, for $v > 1/2$ the optimal quality ξ of supervision may be less than unity. Actually it is

$$\xi = \min\left(1, \frac{1}{2v}\,\frac{1-k}{k'-k}\right)$$

or

$$\xi = \frac{1}{2v} \quad \text{for} \quad k' = 1.$$

The intuition for this result stems from the non-linearity of the transaction costs in the side transfers. A high value of ξ increases the probability of extracting the rents, but also increases the probability of the state of nature in which rent extraction is very costly, namely the case of reciprocal favors. Better mutual information between politicians may hurt society, which has an incentive of not providing them with the best information structures even if they are costless.

When $k = k' = 1$ the supervision technology is useless because it is as expensive to pay politicians for their supervisory activity as it is to give up information rents. As k or k' decreases (with $k \leq k'$) the distortion decreases, since the transaction costs of side-contracting are increasing. Summing up we have:

> PROPOSITION 4.1 (a) The optimal collusion-proof symmetric Constitution provides incentive payments for supervisory functions to both agents and decreases the incentives for production of the inefficient type with respect to the first-best and with respect to the benchmark case of benevolent supervision.
> (b) The Constitution may prefer to endow the politicians with imperfect supervisory technologies even when they are costless.

Proposition 4.1.a is in line with our former results. The optimal constitutional response to collusion is the creation of incentives for politicians and a reduction in the stakes of collusion. Proposition 4.1.b is more novel. It shows that the control of communication—here in the form of supervision—is an essential part of the design of governments and organizations. It must be arranged in a way which minimizes the fulfillment of collusion-proof constraints and this can take the form of restricting communication between politicians.

To obtain the optimal Constitution, we have made the incentive payments for supervision functions of both politicians' messages. Suppose that the reward to a politician is only allowed to be a function of his own message. Collusion-proofness now requires

$$\underline{s}_1 + \underline{s}_2 \geq k'\Delta\theta(\bar{q}_1 + \bar{q}_2)$$

$$\underline{s}_1 \geq k\,\Delta\theta\bar{q}_2$$

$$\underline{s}_2 \geq k\,\Delta\theta\bar{q}_1,$$

i.e. for a symmetric solution it imposes the cost

$$[2\nu(1-\nu)\xi + 2\nu^2\xi(1-\xi) + 2\nu^2\xi^2]\,k'\Delta\theta\bar{q}$$

in addition to the expected cost of rents

$$[2\nu(1-\nu)(1-\xi) + 2\nu^2(1-\xi)^2 + 2\nu^2\xi(1-\xi)]\Delta\theta\bar{q}.$$

Suppose instead that the Constitution stops preventing collusion in state $\{\sigma_1 = \underline{\theta}, \sigma_2 = \underline{\theta}\}$. Collusion is prevented in the other cases with expected incentive payments of only

$$[2\nu(1-\nu)\xi + 2\nu^2(1-\xi)\xi]k\Delta\theta\bar{q},$$

but an expected cost of rents

$$[2\nu(1-\nu)(1-\xi) + 2\nu^2\xi^2 + 2\nu^2(1-\xi)^2 + 2\nu^2\xi(1-\xi)]\,\Delta\theta\bar{q}.$$

Comparing expected costs, we see immediately that it is better to let collusion happen if and only if

$$\nu\,\xi < \frac{k' - k}{1 - k}.$$

Such a condition can hold only if there is a non-linearity in transaction costs, i.e. $k' > k$. Full collusion-proofness is more desirable if the quality of auditing (ξ) and the probability of an efficient type (ν) are high enough. The cost of collusion-proofness in the case of reciprocal favors is then particularly high. We obtain:

> PROPOSITION 4.2 If the reward of the supervisory activity of each politician can depend only on his own report, it is better to let collusion happen in the state of nature $\{\sigma_1 = \underline{\theta}, \sigma_2 = \underline{\theta}\}$ if $\nu\xi < (k' - k)/(1 - k)$.

Contractual incompleteness makes collusion a second-best response. If the rewards were provided through private benefits generated by successful elections and if politicians were running in different elections, we would have such a case.

4.4 Supervision and Division of Tasks

So far we have restricted the analysis to symmetric supervisory structures which give rise to the possibility of exchanges of favors. A natural idea is to break this opportunity by suppressing (for example) the messages that politician 2 might send to the

Constitution about politician 1's efficiency. This can be achieved by providing politician 2 with an inefficient supervision technology or by committing not to listen to politician 2's report about politician 1.

The Constitution's objective function can now be written

$$
\begin{aligned}
W^{\mathrm{II}} = {} & (1 - \nu)^2[S(\bar{q}_1) - (1 + \lambda)\bar{\theta}\bar{q}_1 + S(\bar{q}_2) - (1 + \lambda)\bar{\theta}\bar{q}_2] \\
& + (1 - \nu)\nu(1 - \xi)[S(\bar{q}_1) - (1 + \lambda)\bar{\theta}\bar{q}_1 + S(\underline{q}_2) - (1 + \lambda)\underline{\theta}\underline{q}_2 \\
& \qquad - \lambda\Delta\theta\bar{q}_2] \\
& + (1 - \nu)\nu\xi[S(\bar{q}_1) - (1 + \lambda)\bar{\theta}\bar{q}_1 + S(\underline{q}^*) - (1 + \lambda)\,\underline{\theta}\underline{q}^* \\
& \qquad - \lambda\, k\Delta\theta\bar{q}_2] \\
& + \nu(1 - \nu)[S(\underline{q}_1) - (1 + \lambda)\underline{\theta}\underline{q}_1 - \lambda\Delta\theta\bar{q}_1 + S(\bar{q}_2) - (1 + \lambda)\bar{\theta}\bar{q}_2] \\
& + \nu^2(1 - \xi)[S(\underline{q}_1) - (1 + \lambda)\underline{\theta}\underline{q}_1 - \lambda\Delta\theta\bar{q}_1 + S(\underline{q}_2) - (1+\lambda)\underline{\theta}\underline{q}_2 \\
& \qquad - \lambda\Delta\theta\bar{q}_2] \\
& + \nu^2\xi[S(\underline{q}_1) - (1 + \lambda)\underline{\theta}\underline{q}_1 - \lambda\Delta\theta\bar{q}_1 - \lambda k\Delta\theta\bar{q}_2 + S(\underline{q}^*) - (1 + \lambda)\underline{\theta}\underline{q}^*].
\end{aligned}
$$

Optimizing, we obtain:

$$S'(\underline{q}_1) = S'(\underline{q}_2) = (1 + \lambda)\underline{\theta}$$

$$S'(\bar{q}_1) = (1 + \lambda)\bar{\theta} + \frac{\lambda\nu}{1 - \nu}\Delta\theta$$

$$S'(\bar{q}_2) = (1 + \lambda)\bar{\theta} + \lambda\frac{\nu}{1 - \nu}[1 - (1 - k)\xi]\Delta\theta.$$

More production is required from politician 2 because he can protect his rent less often than politician 1. To show simply the possible superiority of asymmetric regulation over symmetric regulation, we restrict the possibilities in the asymmetric case by imposing equality of production levels. Then it is easy to compute the difference of objective functions, which is such that

$$\Delta = \frac{W^{\mathrm{II}} - W^{\mathrm{I}}}{\lambda\Delta\theta\,\bar{q}} = -\,\nu\xi(1 - k) + 2\nu^2\xi^2(k' - k).$$

The additional cost of asymmetric supervision is that with probability $\nu(1 - \nu\xi)\xi$ the rent of politician 1, $\Delta\theta\bar{q}$, is given up instead of the lower supervision payment $k\Delta\theta\bar{q}$, since no message is now sent by politician 2. The (possible) gain from asymmetric regulation is that, with probability $\nu^2\xi^2$, a supervision payment

$k\Delta\theta\bar{q}$ and a rent $\Delta\theta\bar{q}$ to politician 2 are paid instead of the more costly supervision payments $2k'\Delta\theta\bar{q}$. Hence we have:

PROPOSITION 4.3 If

$$\nu\xi \geq \frac{1}{2}\frac{1-k}{k'-k},$$

it is optimal to create a partial division of tasks by assigning the supervisory activity to a single politician.

Note that such a dominance requires the non-linearity of transaction costs ($k < k'$) and that the condition for the superiority of asymmetric control can be interpreted as a minimal quality of supervision (in particular, $\xi > \frac{1}{2\nu}$ if $k' = 1$).

A more complete comparison calls for simultaneously optimizing supervision technologies and structural control. For each type of Constitution, we optimize the (costless) supervision technologies. For $\nu < 1/2$, it is optimal in both cases to have the best-technology ($\xi = 1$) and, as above, a complete comparison would require computing the optimal (different) production levels in the asymmetric case. However, for $\nu > 1/2$ and $k' = 1$, the optimal supervision technology corresponds to $\xi = \frac{1}{2\nu}$ in the case of symmetric supervision and $\xi = 1$ in the case of asymmetric control. Then, we obtain:

PROPOSITION 4.4 If

$$\nu > \frac{1}{2} \quad \text{and} \quad k' = 1,$$

asymmetric control with the optimal supervision technology ($\xi = 1$) always dominates symmetric supervision with the optimal supervision technology ($\xi = \frac{1}{2\nu}$).

PROOF: Constrain production levels to be equal in the asymmetric case for $k' = 1$ and specialize welfare for the relevant supervision technology. Then

$$W^{\mathrm{I}}\left(\xi = \frac{1}{2\nu}\right) - W^{\mathrm{II}}(\xi = 1) = -\left(\nu - \frac{1}{2}\right)(1-k)\Delta\theta\bar{q} < 0.$$

4.5 Multidimensional Collusion Activities

So far we have implicitly assumed that an efficient politician, when undetected by the other politician, was unable to provide the other politician with a verifiable proof of his efficiency. Then, collusion-proofness is desirable as proved along the lines of Chapter 2. Suppose now that each politician, when efficient, has a verifiable proof of his type that of course he can hide from the Constitution.

This opens up a new dimension of collusion which is not independent of the way the Constitution structures transfers to elicit supervisory messages. Because of the low transaction costs of reciprocal favors in the state ($\sigma_1 = \underline{\theta}, \sigma_2 = \underline{\theta}$), the Constitution must provide, to avoid collusion, higher transfers in this state than in the other states. This instrument to deter collusion triggers another type of collusion by creating an incentive, for an efficient politician who has identified the other politician as efficient but has not himself been identified, to identify himself to the other politician by showing his verifiable proof of efficiency.[4] Then, they can both transmit the informative signals $r_1 = \underline{\theta}, r_2 = \underline{\theta}$ and benefit from the high transfers $\underline{\underline{s}}$.

Suppose that this illicit identification strategy can sometimes be detected and punished by the Constitution. The gain for the colluding partners is then only

$$2\delta k' \lambda \Delta\theta \, \bar{q} \quad \text{with} \quad \delta < 1$$

when they follow this strategy, and therefore the expected cost for the Constitution is then only (there are two such cases)

$$2\nu^2 \xi(1 - \xi) 2\delta k' \lambda \Delta\theta \bar{q}.$$

The Constitution's program can now be written:

$$\max_{\{\underline{q}, \bar{q}\}} W^{\text{III}} \equiv \{2(1 - \nu)^2 [S(\bar{q}) - (1 + \lambda)\bar{\theta}\bar{q}]$$

$$+2(1 - \nu)\nu(1 - \xi) \, [S(\bar{q}) - (1 + \lambda)\bar{\theta}\bar{q} + S(\underline{q}) - (1 + \lambda)\underline{\theta}\underline{q} - \lambda\Delta\theta\bar{q}]$$

[4] We assume that a politician can provide information about his own type which enables the other politician to obtain a verifiable proof of his true type, but that the constitutional level would not be able to do so.

$$+ 2(1 - \nu)\nu\xi \, [S(\bar{q}) - (1 + \lambda)\bar{\theta}\bar{q} + S(\underline{q}^*) - (1 + \lambda)\underline{\theta}\underline{q}^* - \lambda k \Delta\theta\bar{q}]$$

$$+ 2\nu^2\xi^2 \, [S(\underline{q}^*) - (1 + \lambda)\underline{\theta}\underline{q}^* - \lambda k' \Delta\theta\bar{q}]$$

$$+ 2\nu^2(1 - \xi)^2 \, [S(\underline{q}) - (1 + \lambda)\underline{\theta}\underline{q} - \lambda\Delta\theta\bar{q}]$$

$$+ 2\nu^2\xi(1 - \xi) \, [S(\underline{q}) - (1 + \lambda)\underline{\theta}\underline{q} - 2\delta\lambda k' \Delta\theta \, \bar{q} + S(\underline{q}^*) - (1 + \lambda)\underline{\theta}\underline{q}^*]\}$$

with a solution

$$S'(\underline{q}) = (1 + \lambda)\,\underline{\theta}$$

$$S'(\bar{q}) = (1 + \lambda)\bar{\theta} + \frac{\lambda\Delta\theta\nu}{1 - \nu}[1 - \xi(1 - \nu)(1 - k) - 2\xi(1 - \xi)\nu(1 - \delta k') - \xi^2\nu(1 - k')]. \tag{4.3}$$

Note that such a communication pattern between politicians occurs only if they gain from the lower costs of collusion ($k' > k$) despite the risk of penalty if identification is observed by the Constitution. This happens if and only if

$$1 + k < 2\delta k', \tag{4.4}$$

which is also the condition under which the distortion in (4.3) is larger than in (4.2). The reason for this greater distortion is that the Constitution must fight this additional dimension of collusion.

We will now assume that if the Constitution allows collusion in the state $\{\sigma_1 = \underline{\theta}, \sigma_2 = \underline{\theta}\}$, it alters the transaction costs of using the identification strategy. The probability of being detected when the illicit identification occurs is higher, inducing a transaction cost δ' which discourages this activity,[5] i.e.

$$2\delta' k' < 1 + k < 2\delta k'. \tag{4.5}$$

Allowing collusion in the state $\{\sigma_1 = \underline{\theta}, \sigma_2 = \underline{\theta}\}$ is more costly for the Constitution since a rent $\Delta\theta\bar{q}$ is given up for each politician instead of a supervisory payment $k'\Delta\theta\bar{q}$. However, by deterring

[5] This can be justified by the fact that the required policing of collusion is more limited and more attention can be focused on the illegal identification.

the other dimension of collusion, it can improve upon the collusion-proof contract.

When collusion is allowed, the Constitution's program is

$$\max_{\{\underline{q},\bar{q}\}} W^{IV} \equiv \{2(1-\nu)^2[S(\bar{q}) - (1+\lambda)\bar{\theta}\bar{q}]$$
$$+ 2(1-\nu)\nu(1-\xi)\,[S(\bar{q}) - (1+\lambda)\bar{\theta}\bar{q} + S(\underline{q}) - (1+\lambda)\underline{\theta}\underline{q} - \lambda\Delta\theta\bar{q}]$$
$$+ 2(1-\nu)\nu\xi\,[S(\bar{q}) - (1+\lambda)\bar{\theta}\bar{q} + S(\underline{q}^*) - (1+\lambda)\underline{\theta}\underline{q}^* - \lambda k\Delta\theta\bar{q}]$$
$$+ 2\nu^2[\xi^2 + (1-\xi)^2]\,[S(\underline{q}) - (1+\lambda)\underline{\theta}\underline{q} - \lambda\Delta\theta\bar{q}]$$
$$+ 2\nu^2\xi\,(1-\xi)\,[(S(\underline{q}) - (1+\lambda)\underline{\theta}\underline{q} - \lambda k\Delta\theta\bar{q} - \lambda\Delta\theta\bar{q} + S(\underline{q}^*) - (1+\lambda)\underline{\theta}\underline{q}^*]\}$$

yielding

$$S'(\underline{q}) = (1+\lambda)\,\underline{\theta}$$

$$S'(\bar{q}) = (1+\lambda)\bar{\theta} + \frac{\lambda\Delta\theta\nu}{1-\nu}\,[1 - \xi(1-\nu\xi)(1-k)]\,\Delta\theta\bar{q}.$$

Comparing W^{III} and W^{IV}, we obtain:

PROPOSITION 4.5 If transaction costs are such that (4.4) and (4.5) hold, then letting collusion happen dominates symmetric control in a neighborhood of $\nu = 0$, for ξ small enough or k' close enough to unity.

PROOF: Using the envelope theorem, we note first that

$$\frac{d}{d\nu}(W^{IV} - W^{III})\bigg|_{\nu=0} = 0$$

since the welfare levels differ only by terms in ν^2. To compare the second derivatives at $\nu = 0$, it is sufficient to look at the partial second derivatives since

$$\left(\frac{\partial^2}{\partial\nu\partial\bar{q}}(W^{IV} - W^{III})\bigg|_{\nu=0} = 0\right).$$

Then

$$\frac{\partial^2}{\partial\nu^2}(W^{IV} - W^{III}) = 4\xi\lambda\Delta\theta\bar{q}^*\,[-\xi(1-k') + (1-\xi)(2\delta k' - 1 - k)].$$

Under (4.4), $2\delta k' - 1 - k > 0$. So for ξ small enough or k' close enough to unity,

$$\frac{\partial^2}{\partial v^2}(W^{IV} - W^{III}) > 0;$$

and hence the superiority of collusion over symmetric control in a neighborhood of $v = 0$.

When there are multiple collusive activities and when there are externalities between the transaction costs of preventing these various activities, it may happen, as above, that allowing collusion in one activity decreases the cost of preventing the other collusive activity so much that it dominates full collusion-proof mechanisms. It occurs when there are negative externalities in the costs of controlling various collusive activities.

With the additional collusion activity, social welfare differs from W^I only with probability $2v^2\xi(1 - \xi)$. For the same production level of the inefficient type,

$$W^I - W^{III} = 2v^2\xi(1 - \xi)[2\delta k' - (1 + k)]\lambda\Delta\theta\bar{q}.$$

Symmetric control with both types of collusion is dominated by asymmetric control if and only if

$$-v\xi(1 - k) + 2v^2\xi^2(k' - k) + 2v^2(1 - \xi)\xi[2\delta k' - (1 + k)] > 0$$

or

$$v > \frac{1 - k}{2\,[\xi(k' - k) + (1 - \xi)(2\delta k' - 1 - k)]}. \tag{4.6}$$

We obtain:

Proposition 4.6 If δ' is such that (4.5) fails and therefore collusion is dominated by symmetric control and if (4.6) holds, it is optimal to create a division of tasks by assigning the supervisory authority to a single politician.

Finally, note that there is a range of parameters for which allowing collusion in the state $\{\sigma_1 = \underline{\theta}, \sigma_2 = \underline{\theta}\}$ is the best policy. For v small enough, collusion dominates symmetric control from Proposition 4.5 and, furthermore,

$$\frac{d}{dv}[W^{II} - W^{IV}]_{v=0} = -\xi\frac{1 - k}{k}\lambda\Delta\theta\bar{q} < 0.$$

This is due to the fact that collusion avoids the transmission of information between politicians as asymmetric control does, but at a negligible cost of the order of ν^2 for ν small, instead of a cost of the order of ν for asymmetric control.

4.6 A Model with Three Politicians

We consider the straightforward extension of the model to the case of three politicians to pursue the analysis of checks and balances. The third politician controls the production of public good 3 with a cost function

$$C_3 = \theta_3 q_3,$$

where q_3 is the production level and θ_3 in $\{\underline{\theta}, \bar{\theta}\}$ is a productivity parameter representing the private information of politician 3. Again, let $\nu = \Pr(\theta_3 = \underline{\theta})$. Politician 3's utility level is

$$U_3 = t_3 - \theta_3 q_3.$$

Now, social welfare is

$$W = \sum_{i=1}^{3} [S(q_i) - (1 + \lambda)\, \theta_i\, q_i - \lambda U_i].$$

Politician i may observe a signal σ_i^j on politician j's efficiency characteristic θ_j which either is uninformative or provides (with probability ξ) a verifiable proof that $\theta_j = \underline{\theta}$ when it is indeed the case. We will study the design by the Constitution of supervisory activities and the design of incentive contracts for the politicians. The timing is as described in Section 4.3.

To limit the number of cases to consider we will assume that the costs of supervision are such that three signals only can be afforded. Furthermore, we assume that duplicating the supervision of politician j by the same politician i has no value. Given the symmetry of the problem, we are left with two types of supervisory structures: those which involve a reciprocal supervision such as

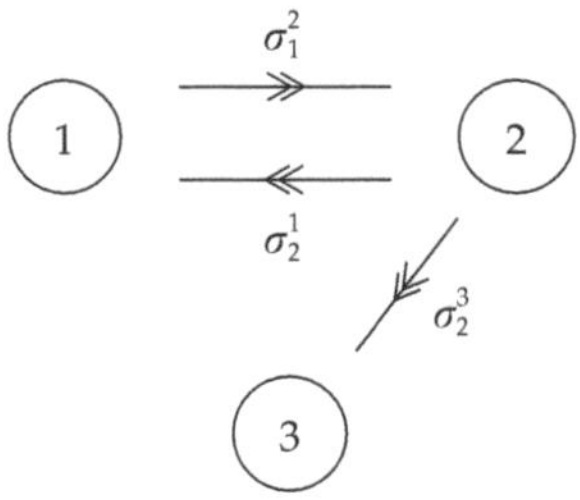

or

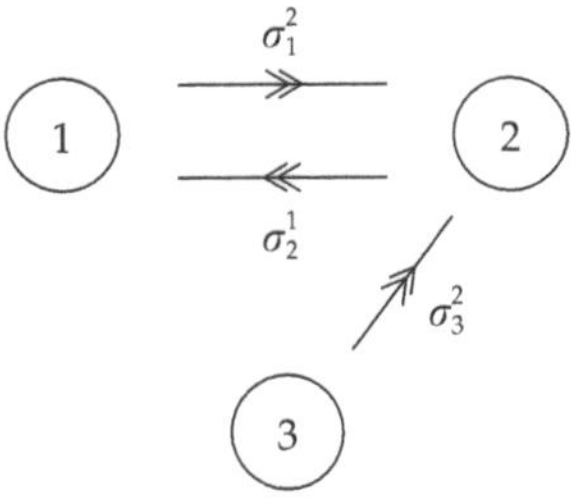

Case a

Case b

or those which avoid reciprocal supervision:

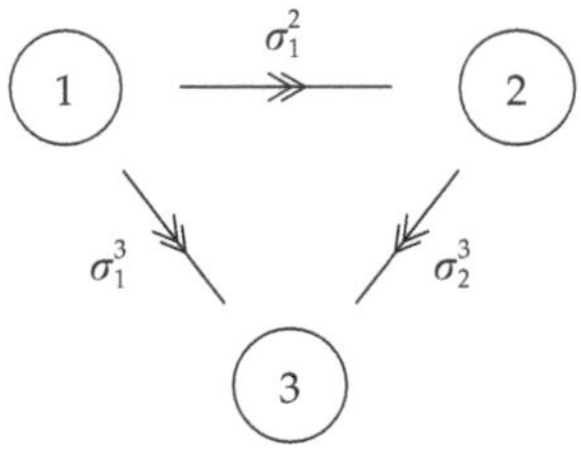

or

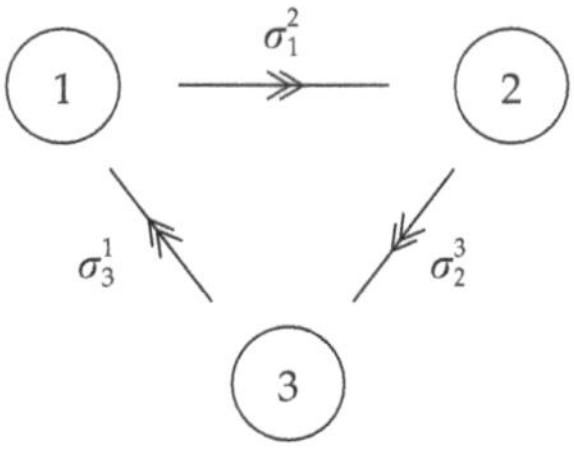

Case c

Case d

In the previous sections, we have shown that reciprocal supervision creates the opportunity of exchanges of favors between politicians which are very costly for the principal. Below, we will discard the structures with reciprocal supervision and concentrate the analysis on the comparison between case c and case d. In case d, each politician supervises and is supervised but no reciprocal supervision takes place. We will call this case 'checks and balances' (CB). Case c is asymmetric, with the characteristic that politician 1 is not supervised, but exerts two supervisions, and politician 3 is supervised twice. We will call this case 'specialized supervision' (SS).

4.7 *Optimal Supervisory Structures*

In the case of benevolent supervision for case d (CB structure) we obtain the global expected welfare

$$W_{CB} = 3\nu\xi \underline{W}^* + 3(1 - \nu\xi)W^{AI}.$$

In case c (SS structure) we must treat each politician separately. Politician 1 is never supervised. So the optimal contract corresponds to $\xi = 0$, i.e.

$$S'(\underline{q}_1^+) = (1 + \lambda)\underline{\theta}$$

$$S'(\bar{q}_1^+) = (1 + \lambda)\bar{\theta} + \frac{\lambda\nu}{1 - \nu}\Delta\theta$$

and an expected social welfare

$$W_{1+}^{AI} = \nu\,[S(\underline{q}_1^*) - (1 + \lambda)\underline{\theta}\underline{q}_1^* - \lambda\Delta\theta\bar{q}_1^+] + (1 - \nu)\,[S(\bar{q}_1^+) - (1 + \lambda)\bar{\theta}\,\bar{q}_1^+].$$

Politician 2 is supervised once, as in the CB structure; hence

$$S'(\underline{q}_2^+) = (1 + \lambda)\underline{\theta}$$

$$S'(\bar{q}_2^+) = (1 + \lambda)\bar{\theta} + \lambda\frac{(1 - \xi)\nu}{1 - \nu}\Delta\theta$$

and an expected welfare

$$W_{2+}^{AI} = \nu\xi\underline{W}^* + (1 - \nu\xi)W^{AI}.$$

For politician 3,

$$\Pr(\theta_3 = \underline{\theta}/\sigma_1^3 = \phi \text{ and } \sigma_2^3 = \phi) = \frac{\nu(1 - \xi)^2}{1 - \nu + \nu(1 - \xi)^2} = \hat{\nu};$$

hence the solution

$$S'(\underline{q}_3^+) = (1 + \lambda)\underline{\theta}$$

$$S'(\bar{q}_3^+) = (1 + \lambda)\bar{\theta} + \lambda\frac{\nu(1 - \xi)^2}{1 - \nu}\Delta\theta$$

with an expected welfare

$$W_{3+}^{AI} = \nu[1 - (1 - \xi)^2]\underline{W}^* + \nu(1 - \xi)^2[S(\underline{q}_3^*) - (1 + \lambda)\underline{\theta}\underline{q}_3^* - \lambda\Delta\theta\bar{q}_3^+] + (1 - \nu)[S(\bar{q}_3^+) - (1 + \lambda)\bar{\theta}\bar{q}_3^+].$$

The global expected utility is

$$W_{SS} = W_{1+}^{AI} + W_{2+}^{AI} + W_{3+}^{AI}.$$

The comparison of the two supervisory structures is as follows:

for $\xi = 0$, they are equivalent, and for $\xi = 1$, CB dominates SS since CB corresponds to complete information while SS has incomplete information about politician 1.

Let us consider a neighborhood of $\xi = 0$ to compare the two informational structures in the case where $S(q) = q - \frac{q^2}{2}$. Appendix A.4.2 shows that

$$\left.\frac{dW_{CB}}{d\xi}\right|_{\xi=0} = \left.\frac{dW_{SS}}{d\xi}\right|_{\xi=0}$$

and that

$$\left.\frac{d^2W_{CB}}{d\xi^2}\right|_{\xi=0} > \left.\frac{d^2W_{SS}}{d\xi^2}\right|_{\xi=0} \quad \text{if } \lambda \text{ is small enough.}$$

Therefore, CB dominates SS in the neighborhood of $\xi = 0$. This is expected since the gains from supervising politician 3 twice are proportional to ξ^2, which is negligible for ξ small. The CB structure corresponds to a better allocation of the scarce supervision resources.

Suppose collusions by pairs of two politicians are now possible. This will decrease the value of each structure without changing the ordering in a neighborhood of $\xi = 0$ since the incentive costs of collusion-proofness are linear in ξ and identical between the two structures at $\xi = 0$.[6]

However, the picture changes when collusions of three agents are taken into account. To simplify the exposition of the main point, suppose that the transaction costs of collusion when a politician must be compensated for hiding his message are very high, say $k = 0$.

In the SS structure, a collusion of three politicians requires compensation for politician 1 and therefore will not occur. On the contrary, in the CB structure, reciprocal favors with low transaction costs $k' > 0$ can occur when all politicians are efficient. If all politicians have observed an informative signal (which happens with probability ξ^3), they can organize the suppression of the information without any compensation; hence a cost for the Constitution to avoid collusion of

[6] Hence, the first derivatives of welfare with respect to ξ remain identical at $\xi = 0$ and second derivatives are unchanged.

$$3\lambda k' v^3 \xi^3 \Delta\theta \hat{\hat{q}}$$

where $\hat{\hat{q}}$ is defined in the optimal collusion-proof mechanism, i.e.

$$\hat{\hat{q}} = 1 - (1 + \lambda)\bar{\theta} - \frac{\lambda \Delta\theta v(1 - \xi)}{1 - v} - \frac{\lambda k' v^3 \xi^3 \Delta\theta}{1 - v}.$$

In a neighborhood of $\xi = 0$, the first and second derivatives of W_{CB} are unchanged; then the ranking of structures is unchanged since in SS collusion is not possible.

However, SS may dominate CB for ξ high enough. Indeed, for ξ close to unity, only politician 1's regulation entails a significant distortion. But for $k' v^2$ close enough to unity, the distortion in SS is similar but happens for the three politicians.

For SS to dominate, the transaction costs of reciprocal favors must be small enough (k' high) and must happen often enough (ξ close to unity and v close to unity). This last condition is due to the fact that the reciprocal favor effect is proportional to v^3, the probability that they are all efficient, whereas the informational advantage of the CB structure is proportional to v.

4.8 Conclusion

When a principal designs an organization to his best advantage, he tries to set up a system of supervision of his agents to reduce the informational gap he suffers from. Similarly, a well-designed Constitution must organize the supervision of the various governmental bodies. We have presented some pitfalls which exist in this design. Reciprocal supervision may trigger a type of collusion which is very costly to fight and which may justify asymmetric design whereby only one agent is allowed to monitor his peers. We have provided an example where allowing collusion may be an optimal strategy because transaction costs in some states of nature are affected by collusion in some other states of nature.

We hope that this chapter and this part of the book have convinced the reader that interesting insights into the design of governments can be derived from the theory of collusion developed by economists for studying organizations. Much remains to be done to develop this line of research and extend the foundations of the theory of collusion. Part III of the book will make some progress in the latter direction. Concerning checks and balances, we will conclude in similar fashion to Montesquieu (1748), Livre XI, p. 598.

> 'Je voudrais rechercher, dans tous les gouvernements modérés que nous connaissons, quelle est la distribution des trois pouvoirs, et calculer par là les degrés de liberté dont chacun d'eux peut jouir. Mais il ne faut pas toujours tellement épuiser un sujet, qu'on ne laisse rien à faire au lecteur. Il ne s'agit pas de faire lire, mais de faire penser.'

Appendix 4

A.4.1 *Separability of incentive constraints*

We can distinguish nine cases:

1. $\theta_1 = \bar{\theta}, \theta_2 = \bar{\theta}$ with probability $(1 - \nu)^2$
2. $\theta_1 = \bar{\theta}, \theta_2 = \underline{\theta}, \sigma_1 = \phi$ with probability $(1 - \nu)\nu(1 - \xi)$
3. $\theta_1 = \underline{\theta}, \theta_2 = \bar{\theta}, \sigma_2 = \phi$ with probability $(1 - \nu)\nu(1 - \xi)$
4. $\theta_1 = \underline{\theta}, \theta_2 = \underline{\theta}, \sigma_1 = \phi, \sigma_2 = \phi$ with probability $\nu^2 (1 - \xi)^2$
5. $\theta_1 = \bar{\theta}, \theta_2 = \underline{\theta}, \sigma_1 = \underline{\theta}$ with probability $(1 - \nu)\nu\xi$
6. $\theta_1 = \underline{\theta}, \theta_2 = \bar{\theta}, \sigma_2 = \underline{\theta}$ with probability $(1 - \nu)\nu\xi$
7. $\theta_1 = \underline{\theta}, \theta_2 = \underline{\theta}, \sigma_1 = \underline{\theta}, \sigma_2 = \phi$ with probability $\nu^2\xi(1 - \xi)$
8. $\theta_1 = \underline{\theta}, \theta_2 = \underline{\theta}, \sigma_1 = \phi, \sigma_2 = \underline{\theta}$ with probability $\nu^2\xi(1 - \xi)$
9. $\theta_1 = \underline{\theta}, \theta_2 = \underline{\theta}, \sigma_1 = \underline{\theta}, \sigma_2 = \underline{\theta}$ with probability $\nu^2\xi^2$.

In the first four cases, the Constitution receives from the politicians only messages about themselves. There is no loss of generality in considering only revelation mechanisms

$$(\underline{t}, \bar{t})\ (\underline{q}, \bar{q})$$

with the (binding) incentive and individual rationality constraints

$$\bar{t} = \bar{\theta}\bar{q}$$
$$\underline{t} = \underline{\theta}\underline{q} + \Delta\theta\bar{q}.$$

In case 5, we must avoid the deviation $r_1 = \phi$, $\tilde{\theta}_2 = \bar{\theta}$, which requires (with $\underline{t}_5 = \underline{\theta}\underline{q}^*$)

$$\bar{t}_5 \geq \bar{\theta}\bar{q} + k\Delta\theta\bar{q} \equiv \bar{t} + \underline{s},$$

and similarly in case 6.

In case 7 we must avoid two deviations:

$$\tilde{\theta}_1 = \bar{\theta} \text{ and}$$
$$\tilde{\theta}_2 = \bar{\theta} \text{ with } r_1 = \phi,$$

which requires

$$t_7^1 \geq \bar{\theta}\bar{q} + \Delta\theta\bar{q} = \underline{t}$$
$$t_7^2 \geq \bar{\theta}\bar{q} + k\Delta\theta\bar{q} \equiv \bar{t} + \underline{s},$$

and similarly in case 8.

In case 9 we must avoid the simultaneous deviations

$$t_9^1 \geq \bar{\theta}\bar{q} + k'\Delta\theta\bar{q} \equiv \bar{t} + \underline{\underline{s}}$$
$$t_9^2 \geq \bar{\theta}\bar{q} + k'\Delta\theta\bar{q} \equiv \bar{t} + \underline{\underline{s}}.$$

So, it appears that the transfers for truthful revelation of the soft information, $\tilde{\theta}_1 = \theta_1$, $\tilde{\theta}_2 = \theta_2$, and the transfers for truthful revelation of the hard information, $r_1 = \underline{\theta}$, $r_2 = \underline{\theta}$, can be treated separately as we have done in the text.

A.4.2 Comparison between CB and SS

- $W_{CB} = 3\nu\xi\underline{W}^* + 3[(1-\xi)\nu\underline{W}(\xi) + (1-\nu)\bar{W}(\xi)]$

with

$$\underline{W}(\xi) = S(\underline{q}^*) - (1+\lambda)\underline{\theta}\underline{q}^* - \lambda\Delta\theta\hat{\bar{q}}$$
$$\bar{W}(\xi) = S(\hat{\bar{q}}) - (1+\lambda)\bar{\theta}\hat{\bar{q}}$$

and

$$S'(\hat{\bar{q}}) = (1+\lambda)\bar{\theta} + \frac{\lambda(1-\xi)\nu}{1-\nu}\Delta\theta.$$

For

$$S(q) = q - \frac{q^2}{2}, \qquad \frac{d\hat{q}}{d\xi} = \frac{\lambda\nu}{1-\nu}\Delta\theta$$

$$\frac{d}{d\xi} W_{CB} = 3\nu\underline{W}^* - 3\nu\underline{W}(\xi)$$

$$\left.\frac{d^2}{d\xi^2} W_{CB}\right|_{\xi=0} = -3\nu \frac{d\underline{W}}{d\hat{q}} \frac{d\hat{q}}{d\xi} = \frac{3(\lambda\nu\Delta\theta)^2}{1-\nu}.$$

- $W_{SS} = W_{1+}^{AI} + W_{2+}^{AI} + W_{3+}^{AI}$

$$\frac{dW_{1+}^{AI}}{d\xi} \equiv 0, \quad \frac{dW_{2+}^{AI}}{d\xi} = \nu(\underline{W}^* - \underline{W}(\xi)), \quad \left.\frac{d^2 W_{2+}^{AI}}{d\xi^2}\right|_{\xi=0} = \frac{(\lambda\nu\Delta\theta)^2}{1-\nu}$$

$$W_{3+}^{AI} = \nu[1-(1-\xi)^2]\underline{W}^* + \nu(1-\xi)^2\underline{\underline{W}}(\xi) + (1-\nu)\bar{\bar{W}}(\xi)$$

with

$$\underline{\underline{W}}(\xi) = S(\underline{q}^*) - (1+\lambda)\underline{\theta}\underline{q}^* - \lambda\Delta\theta\bar{q}_3^+$$
$$\bar{\bar{W}}(\xi) = S(\bar{q}_3^+) - (1+\lambda)\bar{\theta}\bar{q}_3^+$$

and

$$S'(\bar{q}_3^+) = (1+\lambda)\bar{\theta} + \lambda\frac{\nu(1-\xi)^2}{1-\nu}\Delta\theta$$

$$\frac{dW_{3+}^{AI}}{d\xi} = 2\nu(1-\xi)(\underline{W}^* - \underline{\underline{W}}(\xi))$$

$$\frac{d^2 W_3^{AI}}{d\xi^2} = -2\nu(\underline{W}^* - \underline{\underline{W}}(\xi)) + \frac{4(\lambda\nu(1-\xi)\Delta\theta)^2}{1-\nu}.$$

At $\xi = 0$

$$\left.\frac{dW_{SS}}{d\xi}\right|_{\xi=0} = 3\nu(\underline{W}^* - \underline{W}(0))$$

because $\underline{W}(0) = \underline{\underline{W}}(0)$.

$$\left.\frac{d^2 W_{SS}}{d\xi^2}\right|_{\xi=0} = 5\frac{(\lambda\nu\Delta\theta)^2}{1-\nu} - 2\nu(\underline{W}^* - \underline{W}(0));$$

hence

$$\left.\frac{\mathrm{d}W_{SS}}{\mathrm{d}\xi^2}\right|_{\xi=0} = \left.\frac{\mathrm{d}W_{CB}}{\mathrm{d}\xi}\right|_{\xi=0} = 0$$

$$\left.\frac{\mathrm{d}^2W_{SS}}{\mathrm{d}\xi^2}\right|_{\xi=0} < \left.\frac{\mathrm{d}^2W_{CB}}{\mathrm{d}\xi^2}\right|_{\xi=0} \Leftrightarrow \frac{(\lambda\nu\Delta\theta)^2}{1-\nu} < \nu(\underline{W}^* - W(0)).$$

But

$$\bar{q} = 1 - (1+\lambda)\bar{\theta} - \frac{\lambda\nu}{1-\nu}\Delta\theta$$

and

$$\underline{W}^* - \underline{W}(0) = \lambda\Delta\theta\bar{q}.$$

Comparing second derivatives we have

$$\left.\frac{\mathrm{d}^2W_{SS}}{\mathrm{d}\xi^2}\right|_{\xi=0} < \left.\frac{\mathrm{d}^2W_{CB}}{\mathrm{d}\,\xi^2}\right|_{\xi=0} \Leftrightarrow \frac{2\lambda\nu\Delta\theta}{1-\nu} < 1 - (1+\lambda)\bar{\theta}.$$

Part II

Flexibility Versus Discretion in Constitutional Design

'Stripped to its essentials, Wicksell's message was clear, elementary and self-evident. Economists should cease proffering policy advice as if they were employed by a benevolent despot, and they should look to the structure within which political decisions are made. Armed with Wicksell, I, too, could dare to challenge the still-dominant orthodoxy in public finance and welfare economics.'

Buchanan (1987), Nobel lecture.

5

Political Economy and Industrial Policy

'Side payments will insure that the orthodox Pareto optimality surface will be reached, but the redistribution that will take place through the collective-choice process will not represent the "optimal" shifting among positions on this orthodox optimality surface.'

Buchanan and Tullock (1965), p. 195.

5.1 Introduction

A major task of political economy is to explain the pattern of government intervention in industries, that is to say industrial policy. The 'public interest' approach views the government or the regulatory agencies as benevolent maximizers of social welfare. It derives policies which correct market imperfections such as monopoly pricing or environmental externalities. In the last ten years this paradigm has been substantially improved by taking into account the various informational asymmetries faced by the social maximizers. Industrial policy can then be viewed as resulting from an optimal trade-off between efficiency distortions and information rents. For example, in the case of natural monopolies, industrial policy selects cost-reimbursement rules of regulated firms in a family of rules which arbitrate differently between the efficiency of production and the size of the information rents captured by the firms. Price-cap regulation favors efficiency; cost-plus regulation favors rent extraction. A public-interest approach under incomplete information can explain why such a choice matters and how the optimal choice depends on cost–demand informational characteristics and on the industrial structure.[1]

This approach has been challenged in various ways. In political

[1] See Laffont and Tirole (1993), Chapter 2.

science, authors as diverse as Montesquieu, the American Federalists, Marx, Truman (1951) and Bernstein (1955) have been concerned by the potential for capture. Governments may favor special interest groups. By taking a more disaggregated view of government, distinguishing regulatory agencies from political executives, by recognizing the multiprincipal nature of governments, the political science literature has emphasized the rents that can be captured by various intermediaries who are needed in the implementation of industrial policies (Niskanen (1971), Kaufman (1961), Wilson (1980)).

This point of view can be formalized as we did in Part I by recognizing the hierarchical structure of government still maintaining, at the constitutional or governmental level, the public interest paradigm. Then we can ask questions such as: How should industrial policy be designed at the constitutional level to deal with the capture problems—capture of regulatory commissions by firms or interest groups such as environmentalists, capture by firms of politicians who can influence regulatory commissions, etc? How should the government or agencies be structured to mitigate the costs of capture?

The public interest approach has also been challenged by economists—the Chicago school and the Virginia school—who take the political system as given and essentially uncontrollable. These authors study how the various interest groups influence the democratic process or the elected politicians to extract rents. Implicitly these politicians control the various agencies in charge of implementing policies. For example, Peltzman (1976) and Becker (1983, 1985) develop models of political influence of interest groups. The Virginia school emphasizes how politicians and bureaucrats compete for the rents associated with bribes and kickbacks. The deadweight losses generated by the rent-seeking activities must be added to the original deadweight loss associated with the original rent, e.g. due to monopoly pricing, in order to obtain a complete assessment of social cost.

These positive approaches suffer from methodological limitations. By ignoring informational asymmetries, these theories are unable to explain the rents and discretions which are so essential in their theories.[2] In the absence of informational asymmetries,

[2] We have discussed the incomplete contract approach in Chapter 1, Section 1.6.

regulated firms would be unable to extract rents and therefore would have no incentive to influence industrial policy. Similarly, voters and legislators would be able to control their agents (governments or commissions), who could not get away with policies favoring interest groups over the common good. By blackboxing the supply side of influence activities, they have ignored a crucial agency relationship between the people and the politicians, or between politicians and bureaucrats, a relationship that has been analyzed in the political science literature.

There exists a large volume of literature attempting to test interest-group theories of industrial policy. However, dissatisfaction remains. For example, in his 1989 survey for the *Handbook of Industrial Organization*, R. Noll says:

> 'While the findings of the studies of the economic effects of regulation are consistent with interest group theories, their scope is too narrow to constitute a test of them. The reason is that they do not link the effects of regulation to the causal variables that are the focus of the political theories—the elements of transactions costs and information imperfections that would permit an inefficient political equilibrium that delivered distributive benefits in ways that are predicted by the nature and sources of these factors.'[3]

Recognizing the uncontrollable nature of the political system in a fine-tuning way in view of communication costs and inefficient judicial systems, we can attempt to derive simple constitutional rules for industrial policies which simultaneously take into account the inefficiencies of the political system and informational asymmetries.[4] Section 5.2 shows how, under incomplete information, the political inefficiencies of a majority system affect the regulatory rules and the incentives of the regulatory institutions. Section 5.3 proves that ownership of firms matters in such a setup. In Section 5.4 we explore the opportunity of introducing incentives against the capture of regulatory agencies as a

[3] Similarly, Neven (1994) shows that a few variables describing political institutions and regimes suffice to account for 90 percent of the variance of state aids in the European Community. He then calls for a structural approach.

[4] A similar approach, which stresses both informational asymmetries and political inefficiencies, is being pursued at a formal level in macroeconomics by Persson and Tabellini (1996) and Aghion and Bolton (1994).

constitutional rule. Pricing is the topic of Section 5.5, where the distortions of second-degree price discrimination due to political factors are examined. Then, the pros and cons of the constitutional constraint of no discrimination in pricing are studied. Section 5.6 extends the analysis when lump-sum transfers are available. Section 5.7 concludes.

5.2 Political Interference in the Rent–Efficiency Trade-off

We consider the public good provision model of Chapter 2. Now, we distinguish two types of consumers. There is a proportion a of type-1 consumers with utility function $S(q)$ and a proportion $(1 - a)$ of type-2 consumers with utility function $\beta S(q)$, $\beta > 1$.

From a normative point of view we must simply substitute $S(q)$ in Chapter 2 with

$$aS(q) + (1 - a)\beta S(q) \equiv [a + (1 - a)\beta]S(q).$$

A complete Constitution would maximize, for each value of λ, expected social welfare under the incentive and individual rationality constraints of the firm; hence

$$[a + (1 - a)\beta]S'(\underline{q}^{\mathrm{Opt}}) = (1 + \lambda)\underline{\theta} \tag{5.1}$$

$$[a + (1 - a)\beta]S'(\bar{q}^{\mathrm{Opt}}) = (1 + \lambda)\bar{\theta} + \frac{\lambda \nu}{1 - \nu}\Delta\theta. \tag{5.2}$$

We assume now that the Constitution cannot be made contingent on the value of λ which we view here as a shortcut for the non-verifiable business conditions. Let var (λ) denote the variance of λ. If it is desirable to make industrial policy conditional on λ, the Constitution must delegate its design to a third party informed *ex post* of the value of λ. Politicians are leading candidates for this role of residual decision makers.

To pursue the analysis we need a political model which explains how politicians are selected and what their incentives are. For this purpose we consider a simple random majority model.[5] The proportion a of type-1 consumers is supposed to

[5] We could consider more general supermajority rules (see Aghion and Bolton (1997)).

fluctuate randomly each period. With probability $\frac{1}{2}$, α equals α^* $> \frac{1}{2}$; then type 1 has the majority. With probability $\frac{1}{2}$, α equals $1 - \alpha^* < \frac{1}{2}$; then type 2 has the majority. Each majority delegates to a politician the role of residual decision maker for industrial policy and we assume that the politician faithfully represents the interests of the majority which has chosen him.

We consider first the case where the public good is produced by a publicly owned firm. When type i consumers have the majority, they can appropriate the rent of asymmetric information. For example, they can organize an auction among themselves to choose the politician who is willing to pay *ex ante* the expected information rent he will capture. The transfers paid to the firm are still financed by indirect taxes with a deadweight loss of λ, and the Constitution imposes non-discriminating indirect taxes.

Accordingly, majority 1, say, maximizes type-1 consumers' expected welfare under incentive and individual rationality constraints or

$$\max \nu\{\alpha^*[S(\underline{q}) - (1 + \lambda)\underline{t}] + \underline{U}\} + (1 - \nu)\{\alpha^*[S(\bar{q}) - (1 + \lambda)\bar{t}] + \bar{U}\}$$

with

$$\begin{aligned} \bar{U} &\geq 0 \\ \underline{U} &\geq \bar{U} + \Delta\theta\bar{q} \\ \bar{t} &= \bar{U} + \bar{\theta}\bar{q} \\ \underline{t} &= \underline{U} + \underline{\theta}\underline{q}, \end{aligned}$$

or

$$\max \nu\{\alpha^*[S(\underline{q}) - (1+\lambda)\underline{\theta}\underline{q}] - [(1+\lambda)\alpha^* - 1]\Delta\theta\bar{q}\} + (1-\nu)\alpha^*[S(\bar{q}) - (1+\lambda)\bar{\theta}\bar{q}],$$

yielding

$$S'(\underline{q}^{M1}) = (1 + \lambda)\underline{\theta} \tag{5.3}$$

$$S'(\bar{q}^{M1}) = (1 + \lambda)\bar{\theta} + \frac{[(1 + \lambda)\alpha^* - 1]\nu}{\alpha^* (1 - \nu)}\Delta\theta. \tag{5.4}$$

We assume $(1 + \lambda)\alpha^* > 1$ to simplify the analysis. Otherwise majority 1 would like to maximize the information rent and we would have to take into account type-2 consumers' individual rationality constraints.

Similarly, for majority 2 we obtain

$$\beta S'(\underline{q}^{M2}) = (1 + \lambda)\underline{\theta} \qquad (5.5)$$

$$\beta S'(\bar{q}^{M2}) = (1 + \lambda)\bar{\theta} + \frac{[(1 + \lambda)\, a^* - 1]\nu}{a^*\,(1 - \nu)}\,\Delta\theta. \qquad (5.6)$$

We must distinguish two effects of the delegation of public policy to politicians.

When $\beta = 1$, public good production is higher than the optimal production when $\theta = \bar{\theta}$ (compare (5.4) and (5.6) with (5.2)). The reason is that majority i fully appropriates the information rent; hence a per capita rent of $\frac{\underline{U}}{a^*}$ exists which is higher than in the expected social welfare. Therefore each majority in turn will overvalue the information rent in the rent–efficiency trade-off. Note that the lower a^* is, the higher the distortion. When $a^* = 1$, there is no distortion since each majority in turn represents the whole population. When $a^* = 1$ and $\beta > 1$, relative to the social optimum, majority 1 produces too little public good in both states of nature $\underline{\theta}$ and $\bar{\theta}$ while majority 2 produces too much. In general, the two effects described above combine.

We can now ask the following question. When should the Constitution prefer to delegate industrial policy to politicians rather than impose an *ex ante* optimal industrial policy on the basis of the expectation of λ? This latter policy is characterized by:

$$[a + (1 - a)\beta]S'(\underline{q}) = (1 + E\lambda)\underline{\theta} \qquad (5.7)$$

$$[a + (1 - a)\beta]S'(\bar{q}) = (1 + E\lambda)\bar{\theta} + \frac{E\lambda\, \nu}{1 - \nu}\,\Delta\theta. \qquad (5.8)$$

We immediately have:

> PROPOSITION 5.1 For any $a^* < 1$ and $\beta > 1$, delegation is dominated by the inflexible Constitution for var (λ) small enough. For any var$(\lambda) > 0$, delegation dominates the inflexible Constitution for β close enough to 1 and a^* close enough to 1.

An inflexible Constitution cannot take advantage of the variability of business conditions in the trade-off between rent extraction and efficiency but always maximizes expected social welfare. When industrial policy is delegated to politicians, this trade-off is performed under complete information about business conditions, but with a biased view of the value of the regulated firm's information rent. When the uncertainty about business conditions is large, the politicial inefficiency in decision making is worth it—at least if the political conflicts are not too large (β close to unity and α^* also).[6]

5.3 Ownership Matters

In this section, we ask whether public ownership or private ownership should be chosen as a constitutional rule. Suppose now that the firm is private and belongs to type 2 consumers. If type 2 has the majority, it appropriates the information rent just as under public ownership. We get the same outcome as described by (5.5), (5.6). If type 1 has the majority, it does not value the rent and solves

$$\max \nu\alpha^* [S(\underline{q}) - (1+\lambda)\underline{\theta}\underline{q} - (1+\lambda)\Delta\theta\bar{q}] + (1-\nu)\alpha^*[S(\bar{q}) - (1+\lambda)\bar{\theta}\bar{q}];$$

hence

$$S'(\underline{q}_p^{M1}) = (1+\lambda)\underline{\theta} \tag{5.9}$$

$$S'(\bar{q}_p^{M1}) = (1+\lambda)\bar{\theta} + \frac{(1+\lambda)\,\nu}{1-\nu}\Delta\theta. \tag{5.10}$$

Comparing (5.10) and (5.4), we see that public good provision is smaller than under public ownership because the information rent is undervalued by majority 1.

We see that, contrary to the Coase theorem, the type of ownership affects the allocation of resources. Ownership matters as it does in any incomplete contract model.[7]

One may ask whether public ownership or private ownership dominates as a constitutional rule. For this purpose, let us compare expected social welfare in the two cases.

PROPOSITION 5.2 For $\Delta\theta$ small, public ownership always dominates private ownership.

[6] Cukierman and Spiegel (1998) compare direct democracy (which is poorly informed) with representative democracy (which is better informed but is influenced by particular constituencies).

[7] It is an incomplete contract model since the Constitution does not impose a complete contract on the politicians.

PROOF: Let $V(q)$ denote $S(q) - (1 + \lambda)\bar{\theta}q$. Since decisions under public or private ownership coincide under majority 2, the difference of expected social welfare between the private and the public ownership cases reduces to

$$\Delta W = \frac{1}{2}\{[\alpha^* + (1-\alpha^*)\beta](1-\nu)[V(\bar{q}_p^{M1}) - V(\bar{q}^{M1})] - \lambda\nu\Delta\theta(\bar{q}_p^{M1} - \bar{q}^{M1})\}.$$

We note that $\Delta W = 0$ at $\Delta\theta = 0$.

Also we have

$$\frac{d\Delta W}{d\Delta\theta} \propto (1-\nu)[\alpha^* + (1-\alpha^*)\beta]\frac{\nu}{1-\nu}\Delta\theta\left[(1+\lambda)\frac{d\bar{q}_p^{M1}}{d\Delta\theta} - \left(1+\lambda-\frac{1}{\alpha^*}\right)\frac{d\bar{q}^{M1}}{d\Delta\theta}\right] - \lambda\nu[\bar{q}_p^{M1} - \bar{q}^{M1}] - \lambda\nu\Delta\theta\left(\frac{d\bar{q}_p^{M1}}{d\Delta\theta} - \frac{d\bar{q}^{M1}}{d\Delta\theta}\right).$$

Again we note that

$$\frac{d\Delta W}{d\Delta\theta} = 0 \quad \text{at} \quad \Delta\theta = 0$$

$$\left.\frac{d^2\Delta W}{d\Delta\theta^2}\right|_{\Delta\theta=0} = \nu\{[\alpha^* + (1-\alpha^*)\beta](1+\lambda) - 2\lambda\}\left[\left.\frac{d\bar{q}_p^{M1}}{d\Delta\theta}\right|_{\Delta\theta=0} - \left.\frac{d\bar{q}^{M1}}{d\Delta\theta}\right|_{\Delta\theta=0}\right] + \frac{\nu}{\alpha^*}[\alpha^* + (1-\alpha^*)\beta]\left.\frac{d\bar{q}^{M1}}{d\Delta\theta}\right|_{\Delta\theta=0}$$

$$= \frac{\nu^2}{\alpha^* S''(1-\nu)}\left[[\alpha^* + (1-\alpha^*)\beta]\left(2 + 2\lambda - \frac{1}{\alpha^*}\right) - 2\lambda\right]$$

$$< 0 \quad \text{for any} \quad \beta \geq 1, \quad \alpha^* \geq \frac{1}{2}, \ \lambda \geq 0.$$

So in a neighborhood of $\Delta\theta = 0$, the comparison is driven by the second derivative, which is always negative. Public ownership always dominates.

The intuition for this result is as follows. The two cases differ only when majority 1 is in charge. Take the case $\beta = 1$ first. Under majority 1, with public ownership, there is excessive production while there is underproduction with private ownership. For $\Delta\theta$, small social welfare behaves as a quadratic function in $\Delta\theta$ and underproduction is always greater than overproduction. Indeed, we have

$$\frac{1-\nu}{\nu} V'(\bar{q}^{\text{Opt}}) = \lambda\Delta\theta$$

$$\frac{1-\nu}{\nu} V'(\bar{q}^{\text{M1}}) = \left[\lambda - \left(\frac{1}{\alpha^*} - 1\right)\right]\Delta\theta$$

$$\frac{1-\nu}{\nu} V'(\bar{q}_p^{\text{M1}}) = (\lambda + 1)\Delta\theta.$$

For any $\alpha^* > \frac{1}{2}$, the deviation is greater for q_p^{M1} than for q^{M1}.

When $\beta > 1$ the quantity $\bar{q}^{\text{Opt}}$ of the social optimum increases and this can only favor public production which was excessive before.

However, for large $\Delta\theta$ and a social value of the public good which is such that $S''' < 0$, for β close to unity and α^* close to $1/2$, the excessive production of public ownership may be more damaging than the underproduction of private ownership. Then, private ownership may be preferable.[8]

5.4 *Incentives against Capture as a Constitutional Rule*

Let us pursue the analysis under private ownership by type-2 consumers, when $\beta = 1$ and when there is a regulatory agency that we model as the supervising politician of Chapter 2. The agency receives a signal $\sigma = \underline{\theta}$ when $\theta = \underline{\theta}$ with probability ξ. Otherwise, it receives signal $\sigma = \phi$.

The agency can be potentially captured by the firm as in Chapter 2. However, if majority 2 has control, one may argue that the firm will not enter a collusive agreement with the agency since the political principal coincides with the owner of the firm.[9] We will compare two regimes. In regime 1 no incentives for the

[8] Note also that if type-1 consumers have the ownership, a β greater than unity may favor private ownership since, when majority 2 has the majority, the underproduction effect due to the non-internalization of the information rent is partially compensated for by the fact that type 2 consumers value the public good more than the average consumer does.

[9] The argument is a little loose since the manager may have different incentives than the majority. However, the members of the majority should be able to design a contract which gives up no surplus to a third party such as the regulatory commission.

agency are created. In regime 2 incentives to avoid any capture of the agency are put in place.

REGIME 1: Then, under majority 2 there is no capture of the agency even without incentives. Social welfare is

$$W = \nu\xi \, \underline{W}^* + (1 - \nu\xi)W^{M2},$$

where $\underline{W}^*$ is the complete information welfare when $\theta = \underline{\theta}$ and where W^{M2} denotes the conditional welfare when the agency gets no informative signal.

$$W^{M2} = \frac{\nu(1-\xi)}{1-\nu\xi}[S(\underline{q}^{M2}) - (1+\lambda)\underline{\theta}\underline{q}^{M2} - \lambda\Delta\theta\bar{q}^{M2}]$$

$$+ \frac{1-\nu}{1-\nu\xi}[S(\bar{q}^{M2}) - (1+\lambda)\bar{\theta}\bar{q}^{M2}]$$

with $\underline{q}^{M2}$ and $\bar{q}^{M2}$ defined by

$$S'(\underline{q}^{M2}) = (1+\lambda)\underline{\theta}$$

$$S'(\bar{q}^{M2}) = (1+\lambda)\bar{\theta} + \frac{[(1+\lambda)\alpha^* - 1]\nu(1-\xi)}{1-\nu}\Delta\theta,$$

since majority 2 appropriates the information rent.

On the contrary, under majority 1, the firm will capture the agency to protect its rent. The transaction costs of capture are for the society

$$(1 - k)\xi\nu\Delta\theta\bar{q}^{M1}.$$

since they occur only for an efficient firm which is identified by the agency.

Majority 1 maximizes its own welfare without any information from the agency.

Social welfare is then

$$\nu[S(\underline{q}^{M1}) - (1+\lambda)\underline{\theta}\underline{q}^{M1} - \lambda\Delta\theta\tilde{\bar{q}}^{M1}] + (1-\nu)[S(\tilde{\bar{q}}^{M1}) - (1+\lambda)\bar{\theta}\tilde{\bar{q}}^{M1}]$$
$$- (1-k)\xi\nu\Delta\theta\tilde{\bar{q}}^{M1} \equiv W(\tilde{\bar{q}}^{M1}) - (1-k)\xi\nu\Delta\theta\tilde{\bar{q}}^{M1},$$

where $\tilde{\bar{q}}^{M1}$ is here the solution[10] of

[10] We take into account the facts that the transaction costs of collusion are supported only by the members of majority 2 and that majority 1 does not appropriate the information rent.

$$S'(\tilde{\bar{q}}^{M1}) = (1+\lambda)\theta + \frac{(1+\lambda)\nu\Delta\theta}{1-\nu}.$$

Without an incentive scheme for the agency we get an expected welfare of

$$\frac{1}{2}[\nu\xi\underline{W}^* + (1-\nu\xi)W^{M2} + W(\tilde{\bar{q}}^{M1}) - (1-k)\xi\nu\Delta\theta\tilde{\bar{q}}^{M1}]. \quad (5.11)$$

REGIME 2: Alternatively, one can decide constitutionally to design incentives for the agency so that it never accepts bribes, at a social cost[11]

$$\lambda\nu\xi k\Delta\theta\bar{q}^{M1}.$$

Social welfare is then

$$\nu\xi\underline{W}^* + (1-\nu\xi)\hat{W}(\bar{q}^{M}) - \lambda\nu\xi k\Delta\theta\bar{q}^{M1}$$

where $\hat{W}(\bar{q}^{M})$ is social welfare when majority M chooses its policy after message ϕ. Majority 1 solves

$$\max \nu(1-\xi)\{\alpha^*[S(\underline{q}^{M1}) - (1+\lambda)\underline{\theta}\underline{q}^{M1} - (1+\lambda)\Delta\theta\bar{q}^{M1}]\}$$
$$+ (1-\nu)\alpha^*[S(\bar{q}^{M1}) - (1+\lambda)\bar{\theta}\bar{q}^{M1}] - \alpha^*\nu\xi\lambda k\Delta\theta\bar{q}^{M1};$$

hence

$$S'(\hat{\bar{q}}^{M1}) = (1+\lambda)\bar{\theta} + \left[\frac{(1+\lambda)\nu(1-\xi)}{(1-\nu)} + \frac{k\xi\lambda\nu}{(1-\nu)}\right]\Delta\theta.$$

Similarly, majority 2 solves[12]

$$\max \nu(1-\xi)\alpha^*\{S(\underline{q}^{M2}) - (1+\lambda)\underline{\theta}\underline{q}^{M2} - [(1+\lambda)\alpha^* - 1]\Delta\theta\bar{q}^{M2}\}$$
$$+ (1-\nu)\alpha^*[S(\bar{q}^{M2}) - (1+\lambda)\bar{\theta}\bar{q}^{M2}] - \alpha^*\nu\xi\lambda k\Delta\theta\bar{q}^{M1};$$

hence

$$S'(\hat{\bar{q}}^{M2}) = (1+\lambda)\bar{\theta} + \frac{[(1+\lambda)\alpha^* - 1]\nu(1-\xi)}{(1-\nu)}\Delta\theta.$$

[11] Incentive payments to avoid collusion are calibrated to avoid capture when majority 1 has the majority (which is the case when it matters), but are always paid. These payments are shared by all consumers.

[12] Here the incentive payments for the agency are taken as given.

Note that $W^{\mathrm{M2}} = \hat{W}(\bar{q}^{\mathrm{M2}})$ as $\hat{\bar{q}}^{\mathrm{M2}} = \bar{q}^{\mathrm{M2}}$.
We obtain an expected welfare of

$$\nu\xi\underline{W}^* + (1 - \nu\xi)\frac{1}{2}[\hat{W}(\hat{\bar{q}}^{\mathrm{M1}}) + \hat{W}(\hat{\bar{q}}^{\mathrm{M2}})] - \lambda\nu k\xi\Delta\theta\hat{\bar{q}}^{\mathrm{M1}}. \quad (5.12)$$

Comparing (5.11) and (5.12), it is better to set up incentives for the regulatory agency if (with $V(q) = S(q) - (1 + \lambda)\bar{\theta}q$),

$$\frac{1}{2}\{[(1 - \nu)V(\hat{\bar{q}}^{\mathrm{M1}}) - \lambda\nu(1 - \xi)\Delta\theta\hat{\bar{q}}^{\mathrm{M1}}] - [(1 - \nu)V(\tilde{\bar{q}}^{\mathrm{M1}}) - \lambda\nu\Delta\theta\tilde{\bar{q}}^{\mathrm{M1}}]\}$$
$$+ \frac{1}{2}(1 - k)\xi\nu\Delta\theta\tilde{\bar{q}}^{\mathrm{M1}} \geq \lambda\nu\xi k\Delta\theta\hat{\bar{q}}^{\mathrm{M1}}; \quad (5.13)$$

that is, if

EXPECTED SUPERVISION GAINS + EXPECTED TRANSACTION COSTS OF CAPTURE

$\geq$

COST OF INCENTIVES FOR AGENCY.

The expected supervision gains are double: first, with probability $\nu\xi$ one saves on information rents; and, second and relatedly, one can afford a higher level of production for the inefficient type.[13]

5.5 Political Price Discrimination Versus Uniform Pricing

We return to the general preferences of Section 5.1 and we assume that the good is now a private good, but that the Constitution cannot differentiate between the two types of consumers in pricing. We assume that θ is known and that the public firm which produces the private good is controlled by the majority in power. In this section we assume that λ is certain.

If α, the size of the majority, was contractible, the Constitution

[13] See Faure-Grimaud and Martimort (1999) for a study of the relationship between political principals and their bureaucracy, in which they show that a more independent bureaucracy plays a stabilization role with respect to the excessive fluctuations which political majorities would implement.

could design the non-linear tariff which maximizes expected social welfare, i.e. it would solve

$$\max \alpha[S(q_1) - T_1] + (1 - \alpha)[\beta S(q_2) - T_2]$$
$$- (1 + \lambda)\{\theta[\alpha q_1 + (1 - \alpha)q_2] - \alpha T_1 - (1 - \alpha)T_2\}$$

s.t.

$$S(q_1) - T_1 \geq S(q_2) - T_2 \tag{5.14}$$
$$\beta S(q_2) - T_2 \geq \beta S(q_1) - T_1 \tag{5.15}$$
$$S(q_1) - T_1 \geq 0 \tag{5.16}$$
$$\beta S(q_2) - T_2 \geq 0. \tag{5.17}$$

In this case of two types only, a general non-linear tariff is represented by the pair (q_1, T_1), (q_2, T_2), where T_i is the payment required to obtain the quantity q_i; (5.15) and (5.16) are the self-selection constraints and (5.17) and (5.18) the consumers' individual rationality constraints. The solution to this program is

$$\beta S'(q_2^*) = \theta \tag{5.18}$$

$$S'(q_1^*) = \frac{\theta}{1 - (\beta - 1)\dfrac{\lambda}{1 + \lambda}\dfrac{1-\alpha}{\alpha}}, \tag{5.19}$$

$$T_1 = S(q_1^*), \quad T_2 = S(q_1^*) + \beta[S(q_2^*) - S(q_1^*)].$$

This is the usual optimal second-degree price discrimination. However, if α is not contractible, we can either design this tariff on the basis of the expectation of α (here $\frac{1}{2}$) or delegate to political majorities the choice of a tariff. If type 1 has the majority, it solves

$$\max \alpha^* [S(q_1) - T_1 - (1 + \lambda)\{\theta[\alpha^* q_1 + (1 - \alpha^*)q_2] - \alpha^* T_1 - (1 - \alpha^*)T_2\}]$$

under the constraints (5.14) to (5.17). If we assume that $(1 + \lambda)\,\alpha^* < 1$, a type-1 majority still wants to extract rents from type 1 consumers[14] and the usual incentive and individual rationality constraints are binding such that

$$T_1 = S(q_1), \quad T_2 = S(q_1) + \beta[S(q_2) - S(q_1)]$$

[14] In the opposite case, we would have to take individual rationality constraints into account.

and

$$\beta S'(q_2^{M1}) = \theta \tag{5.20}$$

$$S'(q_1^{M1}) = \frac{\alpha^* \theta}{1 - \beta(1 - \alpha^*)}. \tag{5.21}$$

If type 2 has the majority it solves

$$\max \alpha^* [\beta S(q_2) - T_2 - (1 + \lambda)\{\theta[(1-\alpha^*)q_1 + \alpha^* q_2] - (1 - \alpha^*)T_1 - \alpha^* T_2\}]$$

under constraints (5.14) to (5.17). Hence

$$\beta S'(q_2^{M2}) = \theta \tag{5.22}$$

$$S'(q_1^{M2}) = \frac{\theta}{1 - \dfrac{[(1+\lambda)\alpha^* - 1](\beta - 1)}{(1 + \lambda)(1 - \alpha^*)}}. \tag{5.23}$$

The intuition of the results (see Figure 5.1) is quite clear. A type-1 majority undervalues the information rent that only type 2 consumers can capture because they value the good more than type 1 consumers. Since this information rent is $(\beta - 1)S(q_1)$, a type-1 majority decreases q_1 too much. There is excessive price discrimination to decrease the rent of type 2. Similarly, a type-2 majority overvalues the information rent and increases q_1 too much to obtain a higher rent. Political discrimination is excessively volatile. One may be tempted to impose instead a policy which is non-contingent on α, e.g. an optimal non-linear price on the basis of $E\alpha$ or more simply a pooling (non-discriminating) contract (q, T) on the basis of $E\alpha$.

Suppose first that α is known. Then the optimal pooling contract solves

$$\max \alpha S(q) + (1 - \alpha)\beta S(q) + \lambda T - (1 + \lambda)\theta q$$

s.t.

$$S(q) - T \geq 0$$

or

$$S'(q) = \frac{\theta}{1 + \dfrac{(1 - \alpha)(\beta - 1)}{1 + \lambda}}. \tag{5.24}$$

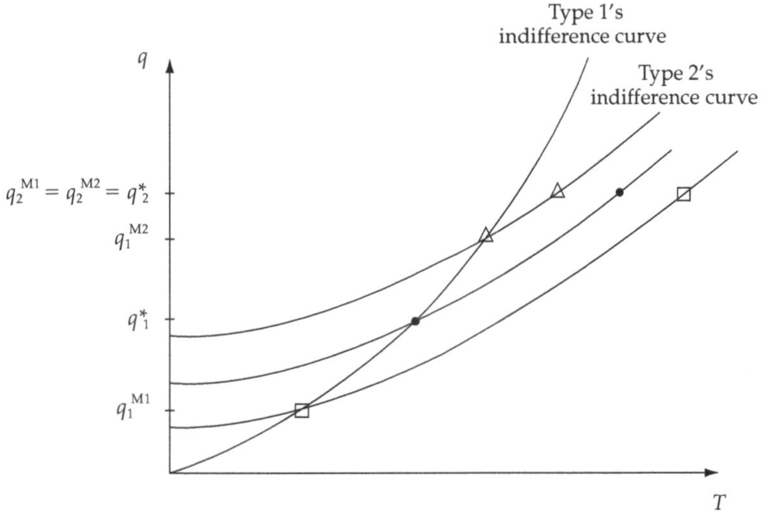

Figure 5.1

We can then show (see Appendix A.5.1) that for β close to 1, optimal pooling is better than political discrimination if λ is small, and majorities are slim (α^* close to 1/2). When α^* is close to 1/2, political discrimination is extreme because the objective functions of majorities differ the most from social welfare. In contrast, political discrimination is better if λ is large enough, because the cost of rents is then high and non-linear tariffs are useful instruments to extract rents.

By continuity we obtain the desired result when α is random:

> PROPOSITION 5.3 Suppose that, when α^* is known, pooling dominates political discrimination (β close to 1, λ small, α^* close to 1/2). Then it remains better if var α^* remains small enough. When var α^* increases, political discrimination eventually becomes better.

5.6 Information Asymmetries, Costly Redistribution and the Cost of Democracy

Let us now discuss the generality of the results obtained in this chapter. In all the cases above, the *ex post* decisions are made by the ruling majority. Even though, in each case, the allocation is *ex post* optimal with the available instruments, from an *ex ante* point of view it corresponds to an inefficient allocation.

As illustrated by Figure 5.2, the democratic alternation between *A* and *B* is detrimental because asymmetric information convexifies the (incentive-compatible) Pareto frontier (see Figure 5.2).[15] It generates an average vector of utilities *C* which is inside the Pareto frontier. An inefficient allocation rule *D* may be *ex ante* superior.

This is reminiscent of Chapter 13 in Buchanan and Tullock (1965), p. 192. Let us reconstruct their argument.

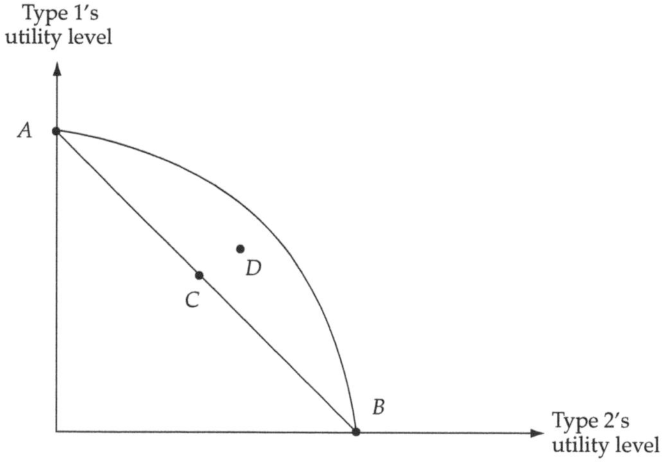

Figure 5.2

[15] See Appendix A.5.2 for another and more explicit example with no restriction on the instruments that can be used by politicians.

First they

> 'assume that the marginal utility of income declines as the individual receives more income in any particular time period', p. 192.

Second, in the face of income uncertainty they recognize that the market fails:

> 'the risk in question would be essentially uninsurable', p. 193.

Actually, it is a moral hazard argument which is behind their idea of non-insurability:

> 'Since the private individual, by modifying his current behavior, is able to affect his claims for compensations, a privately organized insurance plan might be impossible.'

It is the combination of marginal disutility of income and moral hazard which convexifies the Pareto frontier. Then, actors move to public insurance as follows:

> 'Suppose that a constitution is adopted which openly and explicitly states that net-income transfers among individuals and groups will be carried out by simple majority voting ... It seems certain that "redistribution", considered as an activity, will be carried out relatively "too far" under these conditions.' p. 194.

Finally, they conclude that

> 'Side payments will insure that the orthodox Pareto optimality surface will be reached, but the redistribution that will take place through the collective-choice process will not represent the "optimal" shifting among portions on this orthodox optimality surface.' p. 195.

Even in the absence of income effects, we have shown that public ownership and majority rule create socially costly transfers which convexify the Pareto frontier and consequently the 'shifting' among positions on the Pareto frontier due to the democratic alternation is socially detrimental, as in the Buchanan–Tullock analysis.

Only an institutional reform which would share the information rent equally among all citizens could solve the problem. Insurance of the political risk alone would not be enough.

5.7 Conclusion

We have given several examples of normative constitutional analysis. The ingredients of the analysis are informational asymmetries which explain the origin of rents, and political games which choose residual decision makers for *ex ante* non-contractible social decisions. The more instruments politicians have *ex post*, the closer to the (incentive-compatible) Pareto frontier they are and probably the less convex this frontier is, but the more discretion they have in favoring their constituencies. Constitutional choices strike a balance between these two problems. The next two chapters give further examples of this approach.

Appendix 5

A.5.1 Proof of Proposition 5.3

Consider first the pooling equilibrium. Differentiating the first-order condition (5.24), we have

$$\frac{dq^P}{d\beta} = -\frac{(1-\alpha)S'}{(1+\lambda)S''},$$

where S′ and S″ are evaluated at the pooling equilibrium with $\beta = 1$.

For a given α, welfare is

$$W^P(\beta) = [\alpha + \lambda + (1-\alpha)\beta]S(q^P) - (1+\lambda)\theta q.$$

By the envelope theorem

$$\frac{dW^P(\beta)}{d\beta} = (1-\alpha)S(q^P)$$

and

$$\left.\frac{d^2W^P(\beta)}{d\beta^2}\right|_{\beta=1} = (1-\alpha)\,S'\,\frac{dq^P}{d\beta} = \frac{(1-\alpha)^2}{1+\lambda}\frac{S'^2}{(-S'')}.$$

Consider next the equilibrium with majority 2. Then $\alpha = 1 - \alpha^*$. Differentiating the first-order conditions (5.22), (5.23), we have

$$\left.\frac{dq_1^{M2}}{d\beta}\right|_{\beta=1} = \frac{[(1+\lambda)\,a^* - 1]}{(1+\lambda)\,(1-a^*)}\frac{S'}{S''},\quad \left.\frac{dq_2^{M2}}{d\beta}\right|_{\beta=1} = -\frac{S'}{S''}.$$

Welfare is:

$$\begin{aligned} W^{M2}(\beta) &= (1-a^*)(S(q_1)-T_1) + a^*(\beta S(q_2) - T_2) \\ &\quad - (1+\lambda)\,\{\theta[(1-a^*)q_1 + a^*q_2] - (1-a^*)T_1 - a^*T_2\} \\ &= -\,(1-a^*)(\beta-1)S(q_1) \\ &\quad + [(\beta-1)S(q_1) - (1+\lambda)\,\{\theta[(1-a^*)q_1 + a^*q_2] - \\ &\quad S(q_1) - a^*\beta\,(S(q_2) - S(q_1))\}]. \end{aligned}$$

We can apply the envelope theorem to the second term within brackets, which is proportional to the objective function of majority 2.

$$\begin{aligned} \frac{dW^{M2}(\beta)}{d\beta^2} &= -\,(1-a^*)S(q_1) - (1-a^*)(\beta-1)S'(q_1)\frac{dq_1}{d\beta} \\ &\quad + S(q_1) + (1+\lambda)a^*(S(q_2) - S(q_1)). \end{aligned}$$

$$\begin{aligned} \left.\frac{d^2W^{M2}(\beta)}{d\beta^2}\right|_{\beta=1} &= (2a^*-1)S'\left.\frac{dq_1}{d\beta}\right|_{\beta=1} \\ &\quad + (1+\lambda)a^*S'\left[\left.\frac{dq_2}{d\beta}\right|_{\beta=1} - \left.\frac{dq_1}{d\beta}\right|_{\beta=1}\right] \\ &= \frac{S'^2}{(-S'')}\left[(2a^*-1)\frac{1-(1+\lambda)a^*}{(1+\lambda)(1-a^*)} + \frac{\lambda a^*}{1-a^*}\right]. \end{aligned}$$

Consider now the equilibrium with majority 1. Then $a = a^*$. Differentiating the first-order conditions (5.21), (5.22), we have

$$\frac{dq_2^{M1}}{d\beta} = -\frac{S'}{S''},\quad \frac{dq_1^{M1}}{d\beta} = \frac{1-a^*}{a^*}\frac{S'}{S''}.$$

Welfare is

$$\begin{aligned} W^{M1}(\beta) &= a^*(S(q_1)-T_1) + (1-a^*)(\beta S(q_2) - T_2) \\ &\quad - (1+\lambda)\{\theta[a^*q_1 + (1-a^*)q_2] - a^*T_1 - (1-a^*)T_2\} \\ &= (1-a^*)(\beta-1)S(q_1) - (1+\lambda)\{[a^*q_1 + (1-a^*)q_2] \\ &\quad - S(q_1) - (1-a^*)\beta(S(q_2) - S(q_1))\}. \end{aligned}$$

Hence

$$\frac{dW^{M1}(\beta)}{d\beta} = (1 - \alpha^*)S(q_1) + (1 - \alpha^*)(\beta - 1)S' \frac{dq_1}{d\beta}$$
$$+ (1 + \lambda)(1 - \alpha^*)(S(q_2) - S(q_1)).$$

$$\left.\frac{d^2W^{M1}(\beta)}{d\beta^2}\right|_{\beta=1} = 2(1 - \alpha^*)S' \left.\frac{dq_1}{d\beta}\right|_{\beta=1}$$
$$+ (1 + \lambda)(1 - \alpha^*)S' \left[\left.\frac{dq_2}{d\beta}\right|_{\beta=1} - \left.\frac{dq_1}{d\beta}\right|_{\beta=1}\right]$$
$$= [2(1 - \alpha^*) - (1 + \lambda)(1 - \alpha^*)] \frac{1 - \alpha^*}{\alpha^*} \frac{(S')^2}{S''}$$
$$- (1 + \lambda)(1 - \alpha^*) \frac{(S')^2}{S''}$$
$$= \frac{1 - \alpha^*}{\alpha^*}(2\alpha^* - 1 + \lambda) \frac{S'^2}{(-S'')}.$$

Since welfare is the same in all cases for $\beta = 1$, welfare with pooling is better in a neighborhood of $\beta = 1$ if

$$\frac{(1 - \alpha^*)^2}{1 + \lambda} + \frac{\alpha^{*2}}{1 + \lambda} > (2\alpha^* - 1) \frac{[1 - (1 + \lambda)\alpha^*]}{(1 + \lambda)(1 - \alpha^*)}$$
$$+ \lambda \frac{\alpha^*}{1 - \alpha^*} + (2\alpha^* - 1 + \lambda)(\frac{1 - \alpha^*}{\alpha^*}).$$

Consequently, we see that political discrimination is better if λ is large and α^* close to 1. Alternatively, if α^* is close to 1/2 and λ is small, then pooling dominates.

A.5.2 An Example

We consider an economy with only two agents, who have different tastes about a public good decision. Each agent can be viewed as representing a large number of similar voters. In each period the level of a public good must be decided. Agent 1 has preferences represented by the utility function

$$\theta_1 q - \frac{q^2}{2} + t_1,$$

where q is the quantity of public good (whose cost is embedded in the utility function for simplicity or assumed to be zero), t_1 is a quantity of private good (money) and $\theta_1 \in [\underline{\theta}, \bar{\theta}]$ is a taste parameter which represents private knowledge of the agent.[16]

Each period, θ_1 is drawn from a probability distribution with a cumulative distribution function $F(\cdot)$ on $[\underline{\theta}, \bar{\theta}]$ with the regularity condition $\frac{1 - F(\theta)}{f(\theta)}$ non-increasing.

Similarly, agent 2 has preferences represented by

$$\theta_2 q - \frac{q^2}{2} + t_2,$$

where θ_2 is also drawn (independently of θ_1) from the distribution $F(\cdot)$.

The efficient public decision rule is defined by

$$q^*(\theta_1, \theta_2) = \frac{\theta_1 + \theta_2}{2}.$$

The democratic rules of this admittedly quite simple economy are summarized by the fact that in each period agent 1 (or agent 2) controls the government, and therefore the decision over the public good, with probability 1/2.[17]

There is no discount factor, and the 'majority' controlling the government must respect constitutional rules which we take here to be that the individual rationality (IR) constraints of the 'opposition' must be preserved.

Let us see first what would happen under complete information.

If type 1 has control (has the majority), it maximizes its utility under the constraint that type 2 has a non-zero utility level,[18] namely the IR constraint, or

[16] Exceptionally, we consider a case of continuous types in this Appendix. The reader unfamiliar with the relevant technicalities (see Guesnerie and Laffont (1984)) can take as given the characterization of the incentive constraints.

[17] The democratic alternation may reflect very small random changes in the sizes of the two populations, changes which can be neglected in the welfare analysis.

[18] We assume that the public project can be realized only if both agents participate.

$$\text{(I)}\quad \max_q \quad \theta_1 q - \frac{q^2}{2} + t$$

$$\theta_2 q - \frac{q^2}{2} - t \geq 0 \tag{5.25}$$

(5.25) is the IR constraint. We have written transfers in a form which expresses the fact that agent 1 has power and can impose a transfer in private good to agent 2 as long as, with the choice of public good, agent 2's IR constraint is satisfied.

The solution of program (I) is immediately

$$q^{\text{CI}}(\theta_1, \theta_2) = \frac{\theta_1 + \theta_2}{2} \tag{5.26}$$

$$t^{\text{CI}}(\theta_1, \theta_2) = \theta_2 q^{\text{CI}}(\theta_1, \theta_2) - \frac{[q^{\text{CI}}(\theta_1, \theta_2)]^2}{2}. \tag{5.27}$$

When agent 1 is in power, the expected utility of agent 2 is

$$U_2^{\text{M1}} = 0$$

and the expected utility of agent 1 is

$$U_1^{\text{M1}} = E_{\theta_1, \theta_2}\{\theta_1 q^{\text{CI}}(\theta_1, \theta_2) - \frac{[q^{\text{CI}}(\theta_1, \theta_2)]^2}{2} + t^{\text{CI}}(\theta_1, \theta_2)\}. \tag{5.28}$$

Substituting (5.26) and (5.27) in (5.28) we obtain

$$U_1^{\text{M1}} = (E\theta)^2 + \frac{1}{2}\text{Var }\theta, \tag{5.29}$$

where

$$E\theta = \int_{\underline{\theta}}^{\bar{\theta}} \theta \text{d}F(\theta), \quad \text{Var }\theta = \int_{\underline{\theta}}^{\bar{\theta}} (\theta - E\theta)^2 \text{d}F(\theta).$$

By symmetry, we have

$$U_1^{\text{M2}} = 0, \quad U_2^{\text{M2}} = (E\theta)^2 + \frac{1}{2}\text{Var }\theta$$

and, finally, for each agent an expected utility of

$$\frac{1}{2}(E\theta)^2 + \frac{1}{4}\text{Var }\theta.$$

Figure 5.3 summarizes the analysis.

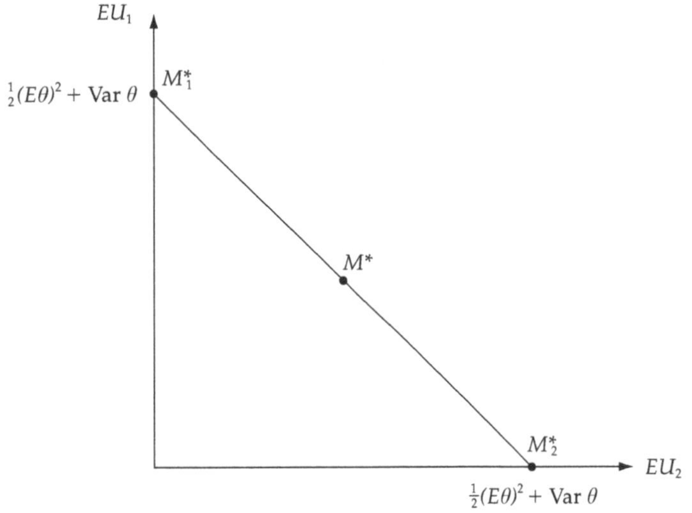

Figure 5.3

M_1^* (resp. M_2^*) represents the expected utilities conditionally on 1 (resp. 2) having control. M^* represents the vector of global expected utilities. Note the essential point that M^* belongs to the *ex ante* Pareto optimal frontier under complete information. It corresponds to the efficient public decision with a symmetric treatment of the agents. In such a world the fluctuation in the allocation of resources due to the democratic rule (restricted here to the fluctuation in transfers) has no social cost.

We assume now that, when agent 1 has control, he does not know agent 2's taste characteristic. The revelation principle tells us that there is no loss of generality in restricting the policies of agent 1 to choosing in the family of revelation mechanisms, i.e. public good decision functions $q(\theta_1, \theta_2)$ and transfer functions $t(\theta_1, \theta_2)$ which induce truthful revelation of agent 2's taste in a Bayesian equilibrium.

Then, agent 1's best policy is to maximize his expected (with respect to θ_2) welfare under the incentive and IR constraint of agent 2. Let us first derive these constraints:

$$\hat{U}_2(\theta_2, \tilde{\theta}_2) = E_{\theta_1}\left[\theta_2 q(\theta_1, \tilde{\theta}_2) - \frac{[q(\theta_1, \tilde{\theta}_2)]^2}{2} - t(\theta_1, \tilde{\theta}_2)\right]$$

is agent 2's expected utility when he is of type θ_2 and envisions to claim he is a $\tilde{\theta}_2$-type in a revelation mechanism $q(\tilde{\theta}_1, \tilde{\theta}_2)$, $t(\tilde{\theta}_1, \tilde{\theta}_2)$.

Let $U_2(\theta_2) = \hat{U}_2(\theta_2, \theta_2)$, i.e., his utility when he tells the truth.

The first-order condition of incentive compatibility tells us that the rate of increase of agent 2's utility level, $\dot{U}_2(\theta_2)$, equals the expectation of the level of public good decision:

$$\dot{U}_2(\theta_2) = E_{\theta_1} q(\theta_1, \theta_2).$$

A necessary link exists between the use which is made of agent 2's information (namely, the public good decision) and the rent that must be given up to him to induce truth telling.

The second-order condition of incentive compatibility puts a sign constraint on the public good decision function, which does not matter if the objectives of the two agents are not too conflicting:

$$E_{\theta_1} q(\theta_1, \theta_2)$$

non-decreasing.

The IR constraint[19] is

$$U_2(\theta_2) \geq 0 \quad \text{for any } \theta_2 \in [\underline{\theta}, \bar{\theta}].$$

Agent 1's optimization program can then be written[20] as (by noting that $t = E_{\theta_1}(\theta_2 q - \frac{1}{2} q^2 + U_2)$)

$$\max_{q(\cdot,\cdot)} E_{\theta_1, \theta_2} ((\theta_1 + \theta_2) q(\theta_1, \theta_2) - [q(\theta_1, \theta_2)]^2 - U(\theta_2))$$

s.t.

$$\dot{U}_2(\theta_2) = E_{\theta_1} q(\theta_1, \theta_2)$$

$$U_2(\theta_2) \geq 0 \text{ for any } \theta_2 \in [\underline{\theta}, \bar{\theta}]$$

$$E_{\theta_2} q(\theta_1, \theta_2) \quad \text{non-decreasing.}$$

The solution of this problem[21] is

[19] This IR constraint is an interim constraint, i.e. it is written after agent 2 has discovered his private information but before knowing agent 1's information.

[20] We assume here that majority 1 chooses the mechanism before knowing its private information parameter. However, the mechanism is played after agents learn their information.

[21] We make assumptions on $F(\cdot)$ and $[\underline{\theta}, \bar{\theta}]$ such that q^{M1} is always non-negative. Note that we can also add constants to the utility functions when the public good is realized, in order to make sure that the IR constraints are satisfied for the chosen probabilistic specifications.

$$q^{\mathrm{M1}}(\theta_1, \theta_2) = \frac{1}{2}\left[\theta_1 + \theta_2 - \frac{(1 - F(\theta_2))}{f(\theta_2)}\right].$$

Hence,

$$\dot{U}_2(\theta_2) = \frac{1}{2} E_{\theta_1}\left[\theta_1 + \theta_2 - \frac{(1 - F(\theta_2))}{f(\theta_2)}\right].$$

$$U_2^{\mathrm{M1}} = E_{\theta_2}U_2(\theta_2) = \frac{1}{2}\int_{\underline{\theta}}^{\bar{\theta}}\int_{\underline{\theta}}^{\bar{\theta}}\left[\int_{\underline{\theta}}^{\theta_2}\left(\theta_1 + \tilde{\theta}_2 - \frac{(1 - F(\tilde{\theta}_2))}{f(\tilde{\theta}_2)}\right)\mathrm{d}\tilde{\theta}_2\right]\mathrm{d}F(\theta_2)\mathrm{d}F(\theta_1)$$

$$U_1^{\mathrm{M1}} = E_{\theta_1\theta_2}[(\theta_1 + \theta_2)q^{\mathrm{M1}}(\theta_1, \theta_2) - [q^{\mathrm{M1}}(\theta_1, \theta_2)]^2] - \mathrm{U}_2^{\mathrm{M1}}.$$

In particular

$$U_1^{\mathrm{M1}} + U_2^{\mathrm{M2}} = (E\theta)^2 + \frac{1}{2}\,\mathrm{Var}\,\theta - \mathrm{E}\,\{\frac{1}{4}(\frac{(1 - F(\theta))}{f(\theta)})^2\}.$$

Note that by symmetry

$$U_1^{\mathrm{M2}} = U_2^{\mathrm{M1}}, \qquad U_2^{\mathrm{M2}} = U_1^{\mathrm{M1}}.$$

Since $U_1^{\mathrm{M1}} + U_2^{\mathrm{M1}} < (E\theta)^2 + \frac{1}{2}\,\mathrm{Var}\,\theta$, the allocation M_1 which corresponds to expected utilities under majority 1 is now below the complete information Pareto frontier.

The global expected utility of agent 1 is

$$\frac{1}{2}U_1^{\mathrm{M1}} + \frac{1}{2}U_1^{\mathrm{M2}} = \frac{1}{2}(U_1^{\mathrm{M1}} + U_2^{\mathrm{M1}}).$$

Figure 5.4 summarizes the analysis. M_1 and M_2 represent the expected utility allocations under majority 1 and 2 respectively and M the average of these. The incomplete information generates a loss with respect to the full information Pareto frontier:

$$A(\theta) = (E\theta)^2 + \frac{1}{2}\,\mathrm{Var}\,\theta$$

$$B(\theta) = A(\theta) - \frac{1}{4}E\left(\frac{1 - F(\theta)}{f(\theta)}\right)^2.$$

Define now the bureaucratic rule

$$q = E\,\frac{\theta_1 + \theta_2}{2}$$

with no transfer which maximizes *ex ante* social welfare and leaves no discretion to politicians. Then

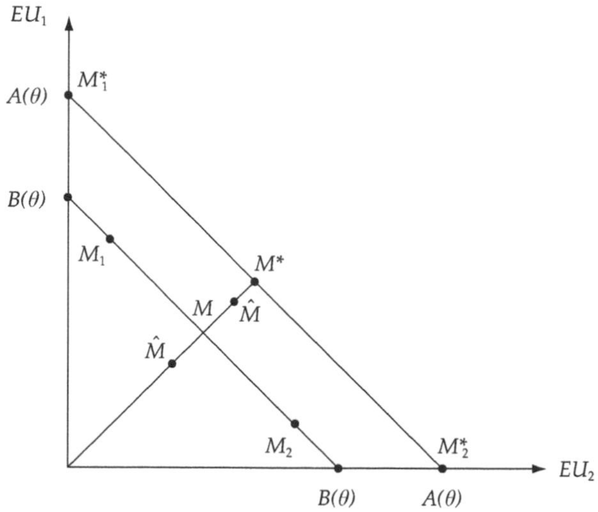

Figure 5.4

$$EU_1 + EU_2 = (E\theta)^2.$$

$\hat{M}$ represents in Figure 5.4 the associated expected utility allocation. $\hat{M}$ can Pareto dominate or be Pareto dominated by M according to the following proposition.

PROPOSITION 5.4 The bureaucratic rule dominates democratic political discrimination if

$$\text{Var } \theta < E\,\frac{1}{2}\left(\frac{(1 - F(\theta))}{f(\theta)}\right)^2.$$

If the importance of asymmetric information measured by Var θ is not too great, the bureaucratic rule which is not responsive to private information but avoids the excessive fluctuations of majority decision making dominates the more informed democratic decision rule.

Under incomplete information the allocations obtained by either the democratic rule or the bureaucratic rule should not be compared with the Pareto frontier under complete information. The relevant normative benchmark is the Pareto frontier under incentive constraints, called the incentive Pareto frontier, which we derive below. It is the convexity of this frontier which creates the possible trade-off between inflexibility (or insensitivity to information) of rules and political discretion inducing a socially costly risk.

The *ex ante* Pareto frontier under incentive constraints that we call the incentive Pareto frontier is determined by varying δ in [0,1] in the following program:

$$\max_{q(\cdot,\cdot)} E_{\theta_1,\theta_2}\left[\delta\left(\theta_1 q - \frac{q^2}{2} + t\right) + (1-\delta)\left(\theta_2 q - \frac{q^2}{2} - t\right)\right]$$

s.t.

$$\begin{aligned} \dot{U}_1(\theta_1) &= E_{\theta_2} q(\theta_1, \theta_2) \\ \dot{U}_2(\theta_2) &= E_{\theta_1} q(\theta_1, \theta_2) \\ U_1(\underline{\theta}) &\geq 0 \\ U_2(\underline{\theta}) &\geq 0 \end{aligned}$$

with

$$U_1(\theta_1) = E_{\theta_2}\left\{\theta_1 q(\theta_1, \theta_2) - \frac{[q(\theta_1, \theta_2)]^2}{2} + t(\theta_1, \theta_2)\right\}$$

$$U_2(\theta_2) = E_{\theta_1}\left\{\theta_1 q(\theta_1, \theta_2) - \frac{[q(\theta_1, \theta_2)]^2}{2} + t(\theta_1, \theta_2)\right\}.$$

If $\delta > \frac{1}{2}$, the coefficient of t in the social welfare function is negative. Consequently, the IR constraint of agent 2 is binding while that of agent 1 is not. The optimization program can be rewritten

$$\max E_{\theta_1,\theta_2}[(\theta_1 + \theta_2)q - q^2 - \frac{2\delta - 1}{2\delta} U_2(\theta_2)]$$

s.t.

$$\begin{aligned} \dot{U}_2(\theta_2) &= E_{\theta_1} q(\theta_1, \theta_2) \\ U_2(\underline{\theta}) &= 0, \end{aligned}$$

with an optimal public decision rule

$$q(\theta_1, \theta_2) = \frac{1}{2}\left[\theta_1 + \theta_2 - \frac{(2\delta - 1)}{2\delta}\frac{1 - F(\theta_2)}{f(\theta_2)}\right]$$

and a symmetric solution when $\delta > \frac{1}{2}$. When $\delta = \frac{1}{2}$, none of the IR contraints is binding and the efficient public decision is implemented.

The incentive Pareto frontier is represented by the dotted non-linear curve $M_1 M_2$ in Figure 5.5.

So, we see that asymmetric information convexifies the incentive Pareto frontier. The social cost of fluctuations in decision making follows from this convexity, as well as the potential superiority of a bureaucratic rule which is not even incentive Pareto efficient.

So far, we have assumed that each majority was selecting its mechanism before knowing its private information. Suppose on the contrary that such a selection is made at the interim stage. We now have an informed principal problem and we must take into account the information transmitted by the ruling majority's offer of mechanism. From Maskin and Tirole (1990), we know that it is as if the agent was informed about the majority's characteristics. When majority 1 occurs, this changes the IR constraint of agent 2 from an interim constraint to an *ex post* constraint

$$U_2(\theta_1, \theta_2) \geq 0 \quad \text{for any } \theta_1, \theta_2.$$

However, it is easy to see that it does not change the decision rule and that, because of the linearity of agent 2's utility in θ_1, it does not change expected utilities either. So the information transmission is harmless.

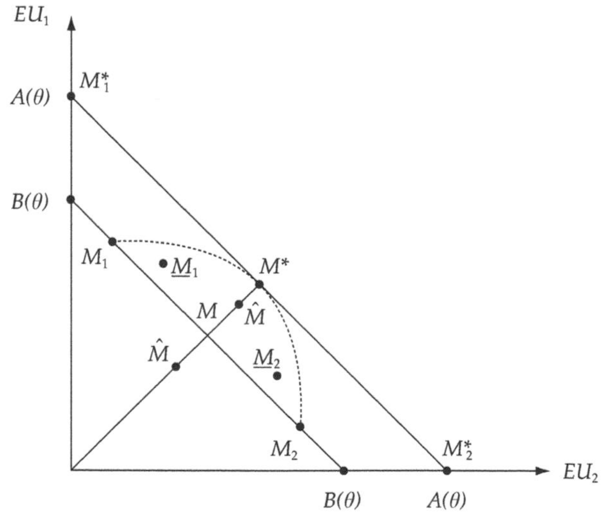

Figure 5.5

6

Political Economy and the Marginal Cost Pricing Controversy

> 'Le meilleur de tous les tarifs serait celui qui ferait payer à ceux qui passent sur une voie de communication un péage proportionnel à l'utilité qu'ils retirent du passage . . . '
>
> 'Il est évident que l'effet d'un tel tarif serait: d'abord de laisser passer autant de monde que si le passage était gratuit; ainsi point d'utilité perdue pour la société; ensuite de donner une recette toujours suffisante pour qu'un travail utile pût se faire.'
>
> 'Je n'ai pas besoin de dire que je ne crois pas à la possibilité d'application de ce tarif volontaire; il rencontrerait un obstacle insurmontable dans l'improbité universelle des passants, mais c'est là le type dont il faut chercher à s'approcher par un tarif obligatoire.'
>
> Jules Dupuit (1849), p. 223

6.1 Introduction

In a very elegant *Econometrica* paper, Hotelling (1938) provided the appropriate formulas assessing the social costs of marginal departures from marginal cost pricing when the interrelations between commodities are taken into account. In so doing he generalized the work of Dupuit (1844) and Marshall (1890). He went further. He advocated marginal cost pricing for industries with large fixed costs and more generally increasing returns:

> 'This proposition has revolutionary implications, for example in electric power and railway economics, in showing that society would do well to cut rates drastically and replace the revenue thus lost by subsidies derived largely from income and inheritance taxes and the site value of land.' Hotelling (1939), p. 151.

In his introduction he suggested that Dupuit also advocated marginal cost pricing. A whole generation of economists took it for granted and did not question the historical origin of the policy consisting of pricing commodities at marginal cost and financing the deficit with the general budget. Ekelund (1968) convincingly demonstrated[1] that Dupuit never proposed marginal cost pricing. Actually, from Adam Smith (1776) to Edgeworth (1913) most major figures of economics warned against the dangers of deficits financed by the general budget. Adam Smith (1776) was particularly clear on this point:

> 'It does not seem necessary that the expense of those public works should be from (that) public revenue ... The greater part of such public works may easily be so managed, as to afford a particular revenue sufficient for defraying their own expense ... ' p. 682 (1937 edition).

Smith seems to suggest prices proportional to marginal cost so as to cover costs, what in France we call the Allais rule:

> 'When the carriages ... pay toll in proportion to their weight or their tunnage, they pay ... in proportion to the wear and tear ... ' p. 683.

What is most interesting are the reasons given by Smith to motivate his proposal. A major argument is an informational one:

> 'When high roads, bridges, canals ... are in this manner made and supported by the commerce which is carried on by means

[1] According to Ekelund, Dupuit was emphatically opposed to the caprice of political influence in the granting of subsidies. His opposition was based on the belief that the political selection of projects to be subsidized would not be grounded in economic criteria. Dupuit clearly saw that the usefulness of a road is maximized when its toll is zero:

> 'L'utilité d'une voie de communication est la plus grande possible lorsque le péage est nul.' p. 247.

However, he understood the deadweight loss of the financing:

> 'On comprend que pour traiter ainsi la seule question de savoir si on doit ou on ne doit pas établir des péages, il y aurait à examiner par quel impôt ou par quelle aggravation d'impôt ils devraient être remplacés et quels seraient les effets de ces impôts.' p. 247.

Dupuit's viewpoint was to be formalized by Edgeworth (1913).

of them, they can be made only where that commerce requires them and consequently where it is proper to make them.' p. 683.

Of course it is not quite right[2] but the next argument, a political economy one, is compelling:

> 'A magnificent high road cannot be made through a desert country where there is little or no commerce, or merely because it happens to lead to the country villa of the intendant of the province, or that of some great lord to whom the intendant finds it convenient to make his court. A great bridge cannot be thrown over a river at a place where nobody passes, or merely to embellish the view from the windows of a neighbouring palace.' p. 683.

Smith understands that the decision process for public works must be delegated and he worries about the incentives created by the delegation of pricing rules to policy makers. Note that he does not question the benevolence of the executive power itself since he relies upon it to conduct an appropriate redistribution policy through third-degree price discrimination:

> 'When the toll upon carriages of luxury, upon coaches, post-chaises, etc. is made somewhat higher in proportion to their weight, than upon carriages of necessary use, such as carts, waggons, etc., the indolence and vanity of the rich is made to contribute in a very easy manner to the relief of the poor ... ' p. 683.

Walras (1897) essentially follows Smith's point of view:

> 'L'Etat interviendra soit pour exercer lui-même le monopole soit pour l'organiser de façon à ce qu'il soit exercé sans bénéfice ni perte.'

without being clear on the allocation of fixed costs in the multi-product case:

> 'Le monopole des chemins de fer devrait être exercé purement et simplement, soit par l'Etat soit pour son compte, au prix de revient.'

[2] It is a sufficient but not a necessary test.

However, he mentions the point of view of J.B. Say (1840), who wants to treat the communication means—roads, canals, etc.—as public goods and who therefore proposes marginal cost pricing (zero price) in a special case.[3] Walras also considers that communication means produce some public goods (if only for the armed forces) which justify subsidies.

Hotelling was aware of a number of criticisms of marginal cost pricing but he dismissed them all on the following grounds.

First, the financing of the deficits induces debatable effects on the distribution of wealth. He argues mainly that the marginal cost pricing rule will be applied for many different projects and

> 'A rough randomness in distribution should be ample to ensure such a distribution of benefits that most persons in every part of the country would be better off by reason of the program as a whole.' Hotelling (1939), p. 259.

Second, in his answer to R. Frisch (1939), Hotelling (1939) recognizes, following A. Lerner (1937), that the income tax he plans to use to finance deficits

> 'is a sort of excise tax on effort and on waiting ... [and] is to some extent objectionable because it affects the choice between effort and leisure ... '

If this turns out to be a real problem, Hotelling finds an easy escape by appealing to land taxes and externality taxes:

> 'Public revenue should be derived primarily from rents of land and other scarce goods, inheritance and windfall taxes, and taxes designed to reduce socially harmful consumption.'

Hotelling's argument rests on the assumption that lump-sum taxes somehow exist. In practice it is recognized that the social cost of public funds is not negligible, ranging from 0.3 in devel-

[3] One motivation of Say is that price equal to average cost may not be sufficient to balance the budget of some projects despite their social usefulness:

> 'Les frais de confection d'un canal, même les frais indispensables, peuvent être tels que les droits de navigation ne soient pas suffisants pour payer les intérêts de l'avance; quoique les avantages qu'en retirerait la nation fussent très supérieurs au montant de ces intérêts. Il faut bien alors que la nation supporte gratuitement les frais de son établissement, si elle veut jouir du bien qui peut en résulter.'

oped countries to more than 1 in developing countries. A first line of criticism that was to be followed eventually even by great defenders of marginal cost pricing such as W. Vickrey is that, even after using land taxes and externality taxes, the financial needs of the government are such that distortive taxes need to be used at the margin. Second-best optimality then requires some form of Ramsey pricing, with the well-known informational difficulties about price elasticities, cream skimming and bypass.

The third main criticism Hotelling considers is the fact that it is necessary to find out whether the creation of a project is a wise social policy, and sometimes to select a limited number of proposed investments, corresponding to the available capital, from among a large number of possibilities. He then provides an answer which ignores both incentive and political questions:

> 'When the question arises of building new railroads, or new major industries of any kind, or of scrapping the old, we shall face not a historical, but a mathematical and economic problem ... This will call for a study of demand and cost functions by economists, statisticians, and engineers, and perhaps for a certain amount of large scale experimentation for the sake of gaining information about these functions.' p. 269.

The intellectual framework of Hotelling is clearly the paradigm of the benevolent social maximizer who can become informed by social experimentation. The two main lines of criticism that Hotelling considered but dismissed are related to this point of view. Incomplete information makes lump-sum taxation ineffective and pushes us toward a second-best world leading to Ramsey pricing. However, the potential lack of benevolence for decision makers may question this conclusion.

This introduction leaves us with many questions, which we will consider in turn. First, what is then the exact intellectual origin of the policy of pricing at marginal cost with public funding of deficits? Second, what was the content of the marginal cost controversy? Third, how can we discuss today the incentives and political economy issues, concerning pricing rules of increasing returns industries, for simplicity restricting the discussion to natural monopolies?

6.2 The Marginal Cost Pricing Rule

Schumpeter attributes to a German economist, W. Launhardt (1885), the paternity of the marginal cost pricing rule:

> '[T]he work of W. Launhardt ... contained the theorem—his argument for government ownership is based upon it—that the social advantage from railroads will be maximized if charges be not higher than—as we should say—marginal cost. It follows from this that the whole overhead would have to be financed from the government's general revenue—the theorem that has been much discussed in our own day after having been independently discovered by Professor Hotelling.' Schumpeter (1954), p. 948.

The idea also came up in the debates following the discussions of Marshall's idea that decreasing returns to scale industries should be taxed and increasing returns to scale industries should be subsidized.

Pigou (1952) qualified Marshall's suggestion:

> 'provided that the funds for the bounty can be raised by a mere transfer that does not inflict any indirect injury on production', p. 224.

> 'Those results ... are results in pure theory.' p. 226.

Pigou then raised the practical difficulty of determining the type of returns to scale (the empty boxes controversy) but hoped that economists would be able to fill those boxes with statistical techniques in the future. J. Robinson (1934) also clarified fairly confused discussions:

> 'The obvious example is a railway system which is working at falling average cost and which is limited to just cover its costs ... The whole problem really boils down to the familiar difficulty that when any concern is running at falling average cost it is impossible to fix a price which both enables it to cover its cost and enables consumers to buy the output whose marginal cost to the firm is equal to the marginal utility to them. The difficulty can be removed by subsidizing the firm ... Whether, on general grounds, such subsidies are desirable, or feasible, is another story.'

The idea of pricing at marginal cost and financing the deficit with public money became familiar during the controversy of socialism (Lange and Taylor (1938), Lerner (1937)). It was even an alledged advantage of public ownership over private ownership for which subsidies were not even considered. Finally, we can also note the political economy defense of marginal cost pricing by Vickrey (1948):

> 'Whether the operation is in private or in public hands, if rates are set above marginal cost in an attempt to cover the entire costs of the operation, the solution of the problem of how to fix rates so as to achieve this end with the least possible misallocation of resources calls, at best, for the exercise of very refined judgment, even in a milieu free from contending interests. In practice, moreover, contention by interested parties makes the achievement of a close approach to the best solution even more difficult ...
>
> 'This uncertainty often produces a situation in which it becomes very easy for the decisions to be made primarily on the grounds of political expediency ... Such considerations can be excluded from rate-fixing problems only by setting rates at marginal costs.'

He also voices a very modern argument in our world of deregulation:

> 'Subsidized operation at marginal cost will usually eliminate the need that is often felt for surrounding such de facto public monopolies with legal prohibitions against competition. As long as it is necessary to cover costs from revenues, it is often deemed necessary to prohibit private competitors from operating in the same field, in order to prevent "skimming the cream" and impairment of revenues or uneconomical duplication of services ...
>
> 'With rates at marginal cost, however, no such prohibitions would be necessary and, indeed, they would be undesirable.'

6.3 Frisch's Comment

It is interesting to see the type of criticisms Frisch made of Hotelling's paper. We argued above that Hotelling was thinking in terms of an informed benevolent social maximizer. Frisch's comment goes even further with all the virtue of logic within a well-defined model. Quite rightly within the model Frisch (1939, p. 145) considers, and in the same spirit as Kahn (1935), he points out:

> 'The only relevant question is whether the excise taxes are proportional or non proportional to the prices that existed before the imposition of the excise taxes. It is the non proportionality of the excise taxes, and only this, that produces a reduction in satisfaction.'

He then claims that Hotelling is considering a case of measure zero, that there is a continuum of other systems leading to the same result:

> 'One consists in telling the individual that under any circumstances his income tax will be so adjusted to the other facts of the situation that his total tax will equal *t*' (i.e. will be constant).

And later:

> 'There exists an infinity of others that are equally good, namely all those whose excise taxes are proportional to the original prices ...'

Frisch is saying that all decompositions of taxes between excise taxes and income taxes which keep consumer prices proportional and which raise the same total revenue are equivalent. Hotelling's answer is also quite interesting. He recognizes Frisch's logical point, but criticizes the other systems proposed by Frisch on informational grounds which are outside the model: tax evasion of excise taxes, difficulty in taxing all commodities, non-linear taxation possibilities with income taxes.

In his 1987 paper in *The New Palgrave*, Vickrey, who wrote 40 papers on marginal cost pricing, recognizes the second-best nature of the problem and the need for taking into account the marginal cost of public funds. Marginal cost pricing cum funding of the deficit with public funds must acknowledge this cost. The second criticism anticipated by Hotelling was the need for testing the validity of the project. Two questions are raised here: first, assuming costs are imperfectly known, what is the best pricing method—the main point raised by Coase (1946)? Second, if subsidies exist, one must take into account their rent-seeking implications. As Vickrey (1987) puts it:

> 'One reason for wanting to avoid such a subsidy is that if an agency is considered eligible for a subsidy much of the pressure on management to operate efficiently will be lost and management effort will be diverted from controlling costs to pleading for an enhancement of the subsidy.'

Hence the tendency to revert to self-financing projects:

> 'This effect can be minimized by establishing the base for the subsidy in a manner as little susceptible as possible to untoward pressure from management. But it is unlikely that this can be as effective in preserving incentives for cost containment as a requirement that the operation be financially self-sustaining.'

These historical debates show that there are two major criticisms against marginal cost pricing. The first is due to the social cost of public funds, which is non-negligible and leads to some form of Ramsey pricing. However, such pricing methods raise informational issues.[4] More importantly, Ramsey pricing opens up the possibility of political manipulations of price elasticities as well as the need to control entry (with possibilities of capture) to avoid cream skimming. The second criticism of marginal cost pricing concerns the political manipulations of fixed costs, which may lead to inefficient decisions.

Therefore, it appears that two attitudes are possible. One is to stick to pure theory and conclude that asymmetric information requires Ramsey pricing or some generalized version developed in Laffont and Tirole (1993). A more policy-oriented attitude must take into account political constraints, i.e. the fact that the regulatory pricing rules will be mandated by politicians who have

[4] Laffont and Tirole (1996) argue that these informational issues are best dealt with by delegating pricing to the firm through a price cap combined with a profit-sharing scheme.

some discretion because the Constitutions, being quite incomplete contracts, cannot control them perfectly.

Such a political economy of pricing is required. Clearly, the various pricing rules are sensitive to different types of political influence and a complete theory should consider, in each policy case, the most relevant dimensions of discretion. The policy conclusions will certainly be country- and industry-specific, since they should, broadly speaking, trade off the inefficiencies of the pricing rules which derive from marginal cost pricing or Ramsey pricing and the political distortions they are associated with.

Some, as Frisch (1970), might think that it is not politically correct to develop such a theory. Frisch's attitude is based on a quite idealistic view of politicians and of the relations between economists and politicians. In his Nobel lecture he calls for cooperation between them:

> 'This will be of basic importance for clarifying what the political authorities really are aiming at'

and, later, describing the dialogue between authorities and experts:

> 'the expert will have to end by saying politely: your Excellencies, I am sorry but you cannot have at the same time all these things on which you insist. The excellencies, being intelligent persons, will understand the philosophy of the preference questions ...'

Taking into account interest groups and the private agendas of politicians is necessary to move from the world of pure theory to public policy, as Frisch clearly wished to. The next two sections are a first step toward such a political economy of pricing rules.[5] They imply a view of the relations between economists and politicians which is quite different from Frisch's view.

6.4 Smith, Edgeworth, Hotelling

The economics of incentives has provided the tools needed for modeling the rents captured by interest groups as a function of

[5] See also Section 5.5 in Chapter 5.

the underlying economic parameters. Therefore, it is an essential input into political economy which is often described as a game of redistribution of rents. We will now give some simplified examples of political games in which the 'constitutional' choice of the pricing rules for natural monopolies can be discussed.

We have already mentioned that Adam Smith proposed inflating marginal costs proportionally to cover costs. Edgeworth (1913) proposed price discrimination to help cover costs[6] with less efficiency distortions. These two rules have different implications for the efficiency distortions under majority voting and also for the realization of the project.

We consider a natural monopoly producing q units of a private good with a cost function

$$C = \theta q + K. \tag{6.1}$$

As in Chapter 5, the population of consumers is composed of two types, type 1 in proportion α with the utility function $S(q)$ for the good produced by the monopoly and type 2 in proportion $1 - \alpha$ with the utility function $\beta S(q)$, with $\beta > 1$. Variable α takes the value $\alpha^* > \frac{1}{2}$ with probability π and the value $1 - \alpha^*$ with probability $1 - \pi$. The policy decisions of this simple model are the production level and the financing of the natural monopoly. If $\alpha = \alpha^*$, type 1 has the majority and takes the policy decisions within the constitutional constraints which maximize the welfare of type 1 consumers. And similarly with type 2 when $\alpha = 1 - \alpha^*$.

The constitutional constraints are represented by various rules. Consider first the Smith rule. Let q_i be the consumption of type i, $i = 1, 2$. Budget balance is achieved by prices which inflate the marginal cost θ by a factor δ such that revenues cover costs:

$$(\delta - 1)\theta(\alpha q_1 + (1 - \alpha)q_2) = K. \tag{6.2}$$

Consumers' optimization leads to

$$S'(q_1) = \delta\theta \tag{6.3}$$

$$\beta S'(q_2) = \delta\theta. \tag{6.4}$$

[6] 'If a railway cannot be made to pay with rates and fares assigned on the principle of cost of service, it is better that it should practise discrimination than that it should not exist.' p. 223. As we saw above, Dupuit was led to a similar idea as an approximation of his ideal pricing.

The solutions q_1, q_2, δ are different according to the value of a and therefore according to the type of majority. We index the solutions by an upper index i, $i = 1, 2$, depending on the majority.

Then expected welfare is

$$W^S = \pi \{\alpha^*[S(q_1^1) - \delta^1\theta q_1^1] + (1 - \alpha^*)[\beta S(q_2^1) - \delta^1\theta q_2^1]\} \\ + (1 - \pi)\{(1 - \alpha^*)[S(q_1^2) - \delta^2\theta q_1^2] + \alpha^*[\beta S(q_2^2) - \delta^2\theta q_2^2]\}. \quad (6.5)$$

Let $q_1^1(\beta)$, $q_2^1(\beta)$, $\delta^1(\beta)$ and $q_1^2(\beta)$, $q_2^2(\beta)$, $\delta^2(\beta)$ be the solutions of (6.2)–(6.4) in the case of majorities 1 and 2 respectively. Substituting these expressions into W^S, we obtain $W^S(\beta)$. To compare the Smith rule with other rules in the neighborhood of $\beta = 1$, we will need the derivative of expected social welfare with respect to β, at $\beta = 1$.

$$\frac{dW^S}{d\beta}(\beta) = \pi\left[-\alpha^*\theta q_1^1 - (1 - \alpha^*)\theta q_2^1\right]\frac{d\delta^1}{d\beta} + \pi(1 - \alpha^*)S(q_2^1) \\ + (1 - \pi)\left[-(1 - \alpha^*)\theta q_1^2 - \alpha^*\theta q_2^2\right]\frac{d\delta^2}{d\beta} + (1 - \pi)\,\alpha^*S(q_2^2). \quad (6.6)$$

For $\beta = 1$, $q_1^1 = q_2^1 = q_1^2 = q_2^2 = \bar{q}$ and

$$\left.\frac{d\delta^1}{d\beta}\right|_{\beta=1} = \frac{(\delta - 1)(1 - \alpha^*)S'}{(\delta - 1)\theta + \bar{q}S''} \quad (6.7)$$

$$\left.\frac{d\delta^2}{d\beta}\right|_{\beta=1} = \frac{(\delta - 1)\alpha^*S'}{(\delta - 1)\theta + \bar{q}S''}, \quad (6.8)$$

where S', S'' (and later S) are evaluated at $\bar{q}$. Hence

$$\left.\frac{dW^S}{d\beta}\right|_{\beta=1} = \left[\pi(1 - \alpha^*) + (1 - \pi)\alpha^*\right]S \\ - \left[\pi(1 - \alpha^*) + (1 - \pi)\alpha^*\right]\frac{\theta\bar{q}(\delta - 1)S'}{(\delta - 1)\theta + \bar{q}S''}. \quad (6.9)$$

Consider now the Edgeworth rule, which we interpret here as second-degree price discrimination. Let (T_1, q_1), (T_2, q_2) be a nonlinear schedule. Incentive compatibility and budget balance[7] require

[7] We assume that we are in a domain of parameter values such that individual rationality constraints are not binding. This will be the case if the valuations of the commodity considered are high enough.

$$S(q_2) - S(q_1) \leqslant T_2 - T_1 \leqslant \beta[S(q_2) - S(q_1)] \qquad (6.10)$$

$$\alpha T_1 + (1 - \alpha)T_2 = \theta[\alpha q_1 + (1 - \alpha)q_2] + K. \qquad (6.11)$$

Under majority 1, the type-2 incentive constraint is binding and the optimal non-linear price is the solution of

$$\max \alpha^*[S(q_1^1) - T_1^1] \qquad (6.12)$$

s.t. (6.10), (6.11), yielding

$$S'(q_1^1) = \frac{\alpha^*}{1 - \beta(1 - \alpha^*)}\theta \qquad (6.13)$$

$$\beta S'(q_2^1) = \theta \qquad (6.14)$$

$$T_1^1 = \theta[\alpha^* q_1^1 + (1 - \alpha^*)q_2^1] + K - (1 - \alpha^*)\beta[S(q_2^1) - S(q_1^1)] \quad (6.15)$$

$$T_2^1 = T_1^1 + \beta[S(q_2^1) - S(q_1^1)]. \qquad (6.16)$$

Under majority 2, the type 1 incentive constraint is binding and the optimal non-linear price is the solution of

$$\max \alpha^*[\beta S(q_2^2) - T_2^2] \qquad (6.17)$$

s.t. (6.10), (6.11), yielding

$$S'(q_1^2) = \theta \qquad (6.18)$$

$$\beta S'(q_2^2) = \frac{\alpha^*\beta}{\beta - (1 - \alpha^*)}\theta \qquad (6.19)$$

$$T_1^2 = \theta[(1 - \alpha^*)q_1^2 + \alpha^* q_2^2] + K - \alpha^*[S(q_2^2) - S(q_1^2)] \quad (6.20)$$

$$T_2^2 = T_1^2 + S(q_2^2) - S(q_1^2). \qquad (6.21)$$

Then expected welfare is[8]

$$\begin{aligned} W^E = \pi\{&\alpha^*[S(q_1^1) + (1 - \alpha^*)\beta[S(q_2^1) - S(q_1^1)] - \theta[\alpha^* q_1^1 + (1 - \alpha^*)q_2^1] \\ &- K] + (1 - \alpha^*)[\beta S(q_2^1) - \alpha^*\beta[S(q_2^1) - S(q_1^1)\,] - \theta[\alpha^* q_1^1 \\ &+ (1 - \alpha^*)q_2^1] - K]\} + (1 - \pi)\{(1 - \alpha^*)[S(q_1^2) + \alpha^*[S(q_2^2) \\ &- S(q_1^2)] - \theta[(1 - \alpha^*)q_1^2 + \alpha^* q_2^2] - K] + \alpha^*[\beta S(q_2^2) - \\ &(1 - \alpha^*)[S(q_2^2) - S(q_1^2)] - \theta[(1 - \alpha^*)q_1^2 + \alpha q_2^2] - K]\} \end{aligned} \qquad (6.22)$$

[8] The index E refers to the Edgeworth rule, as the previous index, S, refers to the Smith rule.

and

$$\frac{dW^E}{d\beta}\bigg|_{\beta=1} = \left[\pi(1-\alpha^*) + (1-\pi)\alpha^*\right]S. \qquad (6.23)$$

We illustrate in Figures 6.1 and 6.2 the distortions implied by political discrimination. If we continue to assume that, when social welfare is maximized, individual rationality constraints are not binding, we obtain the first-best optimal allocation such that $S'(q_1^*) = \beta S'(q_2^*) = \theta$. From (6.13) and (6.14), $q_1^1 < q_1^*$ and $q_2^1 = q_2^*$. From (6.18) and (6.19), $q_1^2 = q_1^*$ and $q_2^2 > q_2^*$.

So political discrimination is excessive in two ways: first, it leads to marginal prices which are different from marginal costs and induces larger differences in quantities consumed than at the optimum; second, it leads to higher differences in utility levels. Majority 1 tries to use majority 2 to fund the project through the budget balance equation. To increase this funding still respecting incentive constraints leads majority 1 to inflate $\beta[S(q_2) - S(q_1)]$ by decreasing $S(q_1)$ (given that type 2's incentive constraint is binding). Majority 2 must satisfy type 1 incentive constraint $T_2 - T_1 \geqslant S(q_2) - S(q_1)$ and chooses, so as to increase T_1, to increase both T_2 and q_2. Again, this mechanism is less effective when the size of the majority increases and the distortion is then decreased.

The allocation marked by * in Figure 6.1 is the first-best allocation most favorable to type 1 given the incentive constraints, i.e.

$$T_2 = T_1 + \beta[S(q_2^*) - S(q_1^*)].$$

The allocation marked by □, which obtains under majority 1, leads to a higher welfare of type 1, a lower welfare of type 2, and more (marginal) price discrimination.

The allocation marked by ∗ in Figure 6.2 is now the first-best allocation most favorable to type 2 given the incentive constraints, i.e.

$$T_2 = T_1 + [S(q_2^*) - S(q_1^*)].$$

The allocation marked by △ in Figure 6.2, which obtains under majority 2, leads to a lower welfare of type 1 and a higher welfare of type 2 and to more (marginal) price discrimination.

From the above, we can note that the distortions of the Smith rule concern both types and increase with the size of the fixed cost

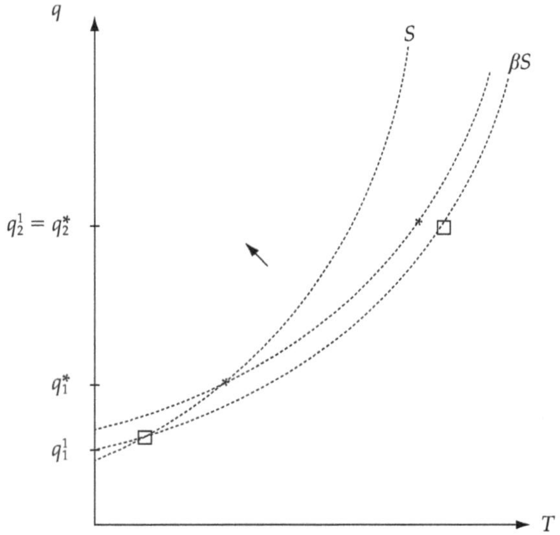

Figure 6.1

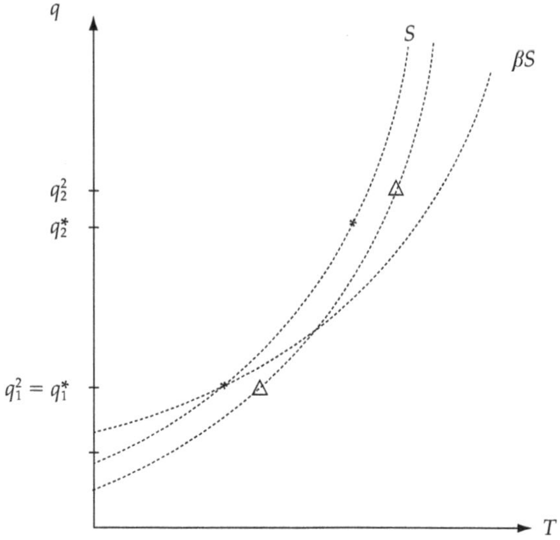

Figure 6.2

and decrease or increase for both types with the heterogeneity parameter β according to the way δ changes with β (see (6.7), (6.8)). The Edgeworth rule introduces a price distortion only for the type which has the majority (see (6.13), (6.19)). Furthermore, these distortions are higher for both types when heterogeneity is high. They are also higher when the majorities are thin (α^* close to 1/2).[9]

Intuitively we can expect the Smith rule to be bad when fixed costs are high and the Edgeworth rule to be bad when heterogeneity is high and majorities thin. Let us compare these rules more formally. We denote by η the price elasticity for the Smith rule at $\beta = 1$. From (6.9), (6.23) we immediately obtain:

PROPOSITION 6.1 For $K > 0$ and $\beta = 1$, the Edgeworth rule is first-best optimal and the Smith rule is not. For β close to 1, if

$$\eta > \frac{\delta}{\delta - 1} \tag{6.24}$$

the Edgeworth rule's advantage increases with β; if

$$\eta < \frac{\delta}{\delta - 1} \tag{6.25}$$

the Edgeworth rule's advantage decreases with β, suggesting that political second-degree discrimination may become dominated by proportional marginal cost pricing with budget balance.

When fixed costs decrease, $\frac{\delta}{\delta - 1}$ increases and for a given price elasticity of demand (6.25) may be satisfied—similarly when the price elasticity decreases. Therefore, under (6.25) when heterogeneity increases, the Smith rule improves relative to the Edgeworth rule. Example 1 of Appendix A.6.2 shows that for a high enough heterogeneity the Smith rule dominates.

PROPOSITION 6.2 For $\beta > 1$ and $K = 0$, the Smith rule is first-best optimal and the Edgeworth rule is not.

[9] The independence of the Edgeworth rule with respect to the fixed cost is due to the fact that we consider only the case where individual rationality constraints are not binding. This is also the reason why the Edgeworth rule, which finances the project from direct payments from consumers, is first-best optimal if $\beta = 1$.

Then,

$$\frac{\mathrm{d}W^{\mathrm{E}}}{\mathrm{d}K} = -1 \tag{6.26}$$

$$\frac{\mathrm{d}W^{\mathrm{S}}}{\mathrm{d}K} = -\pi\left\{1 - \frac{(\delta - 1)\theta\left[\dfrac{a^*}{-S''(q_1^1)} + \dfrac{(1-a^*)}{\beta(-S''(q_2^1))}\right]}{a^* q_1^1 + (1 - a^*)q_2^1}\right\}^{-1}$$

$$- (1 - \pi)\left\{1 - \frac{(\delta - 1)\theta\left[\dfrac{(1-a^*)}{-S''(q_1^2)} + \dfrac{a^*}{\beta(-S''(q_2^2))}\right]}{a^* q_2^1 + (1 - a^*)q_2^2}\right\}^{-1} < -1. \tag{6.27}$$

As K increases, the Edgeworth rule improves relative to the Smith rule and eventually becomes better. The larger K is, the more useful is price discrimination for covering costs without creating too large distortions between marginal prices and marginal costs. So, despite the fact that second-degree price discrimination opens up the possibility of discretionary political discrimination, when fixed costs are large enough discrimination is better (see Example 2 in Appendix A.6.2). The distortions due to the discretion embedded in the Edgeworth rule become less damaging than the distortions due to proportional marginal cost pricing when the fixed cost is large enough. This is simply because they are independent of the fixed cost, as noted above.

A way to decrease the discretion embedded in second-degree price discrimination may be to impose a pooling contract (q, T) selected by each majority. To first order around $\beta = 1$, this pooling contract is equivalent to the Edgeworth rule. To second order it is dominated by the Edgeworth rule (see Appendix A.6.1).

A further way to fight discretion is to impose a single quantity transfer and cover costs with a uniform transfer. We then refer to the egalitarian rule and index it by Eg. Then $T = \theta q + K$ and expected welfare is

$$W^{\mathrm{Eg}} = \{\pi a^* + (1 - \pi)(1 - a^*) + [\pi(1 - a^*) + (1 - \pi)a^*]\beta\}S(q) - \theta q - K,$$

yielding

$$S'(q) = \frac{\theta}{\pi a^* + (1 - \pi)(1 - a^*) + \beta[\pi(1 - a^*) + (1 - \pi)a^*]}$$

and

$$\left.\frac{dW^{Eg}}{d\beta}\right|_{\beta=1} = \left[\pi(1-a^*) + (1-\pi)a^*\right]S$$

$$\left.\frac{d^2W^{Eg}}{d\beta^2}\right|_{\beta=1} = \left[\pi(1-a^*) + (1-\pi)a^*\right]^2 \frac{S'^2}{(-S'')}.$$

For $\beta = 1$, the Edgeworth and egalitarian rules coincide and we immediately obtain:

PROPOSITION 6.3 In a neighborhood of $\beta = 1$, the egalitarian rule dominates the Edgeworth rule if:

$$\left[\pi(1-a^*) + (1-\pi)a^*\right]^2 > \frac{2a^*-1}{a^*}.\left[\pi(1-a^*) + (1-\pi)\right].$$

This condition holds in particular for a^* close enough to 1/2. If the size of the majorities is not large enough, the political distortions of the Edgeworth rule are greater than the efficiency distortions of the egalitarian rule. Since for β close to 1 the Smith rule is dominated, the egalitarian rule is then the best rule so far.

Consider now the Hotelling rule (index H), when we take into account the cost of financing the deficit with distortionary taxes. Let $1 + \lambda$ be the cost of public funds. The Hotelling rule is then characterized by

$$S'(q_1) = \theta \tag{6.28}$$

$$\beta S'(q_2) = \theta, \tag{6.29}$$

a cost of public deficit $(1 + \lambda)\, K$, and a welfare

$$W^H = E_a\{a[S(q_1) - \theta q_1] + (1-a)[\beta S(q_2) - \theta q_2]\} - (1+\lambda)K \tag{6.30}$$

$$\frac{dW^H}{dK} = -(1+\lambda) \tag{6.31}$$

$$\left.\frac{dW^H}{d\beta}\right|_{\beta=1} = [\pi(1-a^*) + (1-\pi)a^*]S. \tag{6.32}$$

PROPOSITION 6.4 Suppose that λ is such that the Smith rule and the Hotelling rule coincide for $\beta = 1$. As β increases, if

$$\eta > \frac{\delta}{\delta - 1},$$

the Hotelling rule dominates; if

$$\eta < \frac{\delta}{\delta - 1},$$

the Smith rule dominates.

As fixed costs increase, the social costs of the Hotelling rule (due to the distortionary funding) are linear in those costs, while those of the Smith rule (due to distortionary pricing) increase non-linearly. For fixed costs low enough, the Smith rule dominates. Also, for β large enough, the Hotelling rule dominates the Edgeworth rule, which then suffers from high political discrimination (see Example 1 in Appendix A.6.2).

6.5 Project Selection and Pricing Rules

In Section 6.4 we examined the limits of marginal cost pricing when public funds are costly. In this case, the cost of funding through indirect taxation must be compared with the distortions of political discrimination. Actually, the main criticism voiced against marginal cost pricing is the political discretion it creates when fixed costs can be manipulated to finance with public funds projects which are not socially valuable.

Suppose, for example, that the fixed cost can take two values $\underline{K}$, $\bar{K}$, with probabilities ν and $1 - \nu$, and $\bar{K} > \underline{K}$. Suppose that, when $K = \bar{K}$, the project should not be realized with the Hotelling rule, i.e., for $\alpha = \alpha^*$ or $\alpha = 1 - \alpha^*$:

$$\alpha[S(q_1(\theta)) - \theta q_1(\theta)] + (1 - \alpha)[\beta S(q_2(\theta)) - \theta q_2(\theta)] < (1+\lambda)\bar{K} \quad (6.33)$$

with

$$q_1(\theta) = \arg\max_q [S(q) - \theta q]$$
$$q_2(\theta) = \arg\max_q [\beta S(q) - \theta q],$$

but that it *is* realized if funding of the fixed cost is uniform and if type 2 has the majority because

$$\beta S(q_2(\theta)) - \theta q_2(\theta) - (1+\lambda)\bar{K} > 0, \quad (6.34)$$

while it is *not* realized if type 1 has the majority such that

$$S(q_1(\theta)) - \theta q_1(\theta) - (1+\lambda)\bar{K} < 0. \tag{6.35}$$

When $K = \underline{K}$, it is done in both cases. The expected loss due to the political manipulation of the Hotelling rule is then

$$(1-\pi)(1-\nu)\{(1+\lambda)\bar{K} - (1-\alpha^*)[S(q_1(\theta)) - \theta q_1(\theta)] \\ - \alpha^*[\beta S(q_2(\theta)) - \theta q_2(\theta)]\}, \tag{6.36}$$

where $1-\pi$ is the probability of majority 2 occurring.

Under the Smith rule, the project is (here) always realized[10] when it should be:

$$S(q_1(\delta^1\theta)) - \delta^1\theta q_1(\delta^1\theta) > 0 \quad (<0) \tag{6.37}$$

if

$$(\delta^1 - 1)\theta(\alpha^* q_1(\delta^1\theta) + (1-\alpha^*)q_2(\delta^1\theta)) = \underline{K} \quad (\bar{K}) \tag{6.38}$$

$$\beta S(q_2(\delta^2\theta)) - \delta^2\theta q_2(\delta^2\theta) > 0 \quad (<0) \tag{6.39}$$

if

$$(\delta^2 - 1)\theta[(1-\alpha^*)q_1(\delta^2\theta) + \alpha^* q_2(\delta^2\theta)] = \underline{K} \quad (\bar{K}). \tag{6.40}$$

However, consumption distortions occur with an expected loss of

$$\nu\Big\{\pi\int_{\theta}^{\delta^1\theta}\big[\alpha^* q_1(b) + (1-\alpha^*)q_2(b)\big]db \\ + (1-\pi)\int_{\theta}^{\delta^2\theta}\big[(1-\alpha^*)q_1(b) + \alpha^* q_2(b)\big]db\Big\}. \tag{6.41}$$

Clearly, depending on the value of π, ν, $\underline{K}$, $\bar{K}$, either of the two regimes can dominate. Suppose we have parameter values so that they are equivalent. Let us consider the marginal effect of an increase of both fixed costs.

For the Hotelling rule the marginal loss of welfare is

$$(1-\pi)(1-\nu)(1+\lambda) + (1+\lambda)\nu. \tag{6.42}$$

For the Smith rule, it is

$$\nu\Bigg[\pi\Big(\alpha^* q_1(\delta^1\theta) + (1-\alpha^*)q_2(\delta^1\theta)\Big)\theta\frac{d\delta^1}{d\underline{K}} \\ + (1-\pi)\Big((1-\alpha^*)q_1(\delta^2\theta) + \alpha^* q_2(\delta^2\theta)\Big)\theta\frac{d\delta^2}{d\underline{K}}\Bigg]. \tag{6.43}$$

[10] Of course, as already mentioned, this is not always the case. A general theory would take into account the lost opportunities induced by such a rule.

Differentiating (6.38) and (6.40) and denoting η^1 (resp. η^2) as the price elasticity of global demand when majority 1 (resp. 2) happens, we have

$$\left[\alpha^* q_1(\delta^1\theta) + (1-\alpha^*)q_2(\delta^1\theta)\right]\theta\frac{d\delta^1}{d\underline{K}} = 1/\left(1 - \frac{\delta^1 - 1}{\delta^1}\eta^1\right)$$
$$\left[(1-\alpha^*)q_1(\delta^2\theta) + \alpha^* q_2(\delta^2\theta)\right]\theta\frac{d\delta^2}{d\underline{K}} = 1/\left(1 - \frac{\delta^2 - 1}{\delta^2}\eta^2\right) \quad (6.44)$$

We obtain:

PROPOSITION 6.5 The Smith rule dominates the Hotelling rule when fixed cost increases if

$$(1+\lambda)[(1-\pi)(1-\nu)+\nu] > \nu\left[\frac{\pi}{1 - \frac{\delta^1 - 1}{\delta^1}\eta^1} + \frac{1-\pi}{1 - \frac{\delta^2 - 1}{\delta^2}\eta^2}\right]. \quad (6.45)$$

In the symmetric case, $\pi = 1/2$, for δ^1, δ^2 close to 1, and for a constant elasticity of demand, (6.45) simplifies to

$$2\lambda\nu + (1-\nu)(1+\lambda) > \eta\left[2 - \frac{1}{\delta^1} - \frac{1}{\delta^2}\right]\nu. \quad (6.46)$$

The Hotelling rule is dominated by the Smith rule if the cost of public funds is large, the probability of a bad project is large, and the elasticity of demand is low. Clearly, Smith did not take into account the elasticity of demand, i.e., he assumed implicitly a zero elasticity in which case the superiority of his rule is obvious. Also, we see from (6.41) and (6.42) that, for δ^1 and δ^2 close to 1, the efficiency losses of the Smith pricing rule are second-order, while the efficiency loss of bad projects being realized remains first-order,[11] and, indeed, (6.46) is satisfied.

6.6 *Conclusion*

In a world of complete information where transfers between social groups do not carry large deadweight losses, even if the democratic game leads to politicians who favor their electorate, economists should help politicians optimize their objectives if

[11] I thank J. Hausman for this remark.

they are interested in global social welfare. As majorities change, economic agents will see their relative positions change, but the average utility levels will not be too far from optimal.[12]

In a world of asymmetric information and incentive constraints, transfers between social groups may become very costly, leading to poor average performances. The discretion allowed by the Constitution enables a majority to capture some rent but this is very costly for the other group. In this world two striking results emerge about the economist–politician relationships. First, by working for politicians (e.g. by providing information) economists may help the politicians' agenda of favoring a majority at the expense of the other groups, leading to a worse outcome on average. Second, the economists have an alternative way for being socially useful. By suggesting constitutional rules which decrease the discretion of politicians even at the cost of some efficiency losses, economists can enhance expected social welfare.[13]

As an example we have shown that despite the inefficiencies of the allocation of resources it embodies, the constitutional constraint of the Smith rule can improve expected welfare because it dominates alternative rules which open up too large opportunities for political discrimination. Indeed, this is particularly interesting from a political economy perspective since it prevents both the political manipulations of fixed costs which Adam Smith (1776) was worried about, and the cross-subsidies manipulations which William Vickrey (1948) emphasized.

Appendix 6

A.6.1 The Edgeworth Rule versus a Pooling Contract Selected by Each Majority.

Under the Edgeworth rule and majority 1, we have, by differentiating (6.13) and (6.14),

[12] The argument here requires that the Pareto frontier be fairly flat and that risk aversion not be large.

[13] The budget balance rule being discussed today in the USA is an example of such a rule. See the pioneering work of the Virginia school (e.g. Brennan and Buchanan (1977)).

$$\left.\frac{\mathrm{d}q_1}{\mathrm{d}\beta}\right|_{\beta=1} = \frac{(1-\alpha^*)}{\alpha^*}\frac{S'}{S''}, \qquad \left.\frac{\mathrm{d}q_2}{\mathrm{d}\beta}\right|_{\beta=1} = -\frac{S'}{S''};$$

and the second derivative of welfare with respect to β at $\beta = 1$, with majority 1, is

$$\frac{(1-\alpha^*)(2\alpha^*-1)}{\alpha^*}\left(\frac{S'^2}{-S''}\right).$$

Similarly, differentiating (6.18), (6.19) we obtain

$$\left.\frac{\mathrm{d}q_1}{\mathrm{d}\beta}\right|_{\beta=1} = 0, \quad \left.\frac{\mathrm{d}q_2}{\mathrm{d}\beta}\right|_{\beta=1} = \frac{1}{\alpha^*}\left(\frac{S'}{-S''}\right),$$

a second derivative of welfare

$$\frac{(2\alpha^*-1)}{\alpha^*}\left(\frac{S'^2}{-S''}\right),$$

and an expected second derivative

$$\left.\frac{\mathrm{d}^2W^E}{\mathrm{d}\beta^2}\right|_{\beta=1} = \frac{(2\alpha^*-1)}{\alpha^*}\left(\frac{S'^2}{-S''}\right)\left[\pi(1-\alpha^*)+(1-\pi)\right].$$

Under pooling, majority 1 (i.e. $\alpha > 1/2$) solves

$$\max \alpha^* [S(q) - T]$$
$$T = \theta q + K$$

or $S'(q^1) = \theta$ and $T^1 = \theta q^1 + K$.

Majority 2 solves

$$\max \alpha^* [\beta S(q) - T]$$
$$T = \theta q + K$$

or $\beta S'(q^2) = \theta$ and $T^2 = \theta q^2 + K$.

Expected welfare is

$$\pi\left\{\alpha^*\left[S(q^1) - \theta q^1 - K\right] + (1-\alpha^*)\left[\beta S(q^1) - \theta q^1 - K\right]\right\}$$
$$+ (1-\pi)\left\{(1-\alpha^*)\left[S(q^2) - \theta q^2 - K\right] + \alpha^*\left[\beta S(q^2) - \theta q^2 - K\right]\right\}$$

$$\left.\frac{\mathrm{d}W^P}{\mathrm{d}\beta}\right|_{\beta=1} = \left[\pi(1-\alpha^*) + (1-\pi)\alpha^*\right]S.$$

From the above

$$\left.\frac{dq_1}{d\beta}\right|_{\beta=1} = 0, \qquad \left.\frac{dq_2}{d\beta}\right|_{\beta=1} = -\frac{S'}{S''}$$

and

$$\left.\frac{d^2W^P}{d\beta^2}\right|_{\beta=1} = (1-\pi)(2\alpha^*-1)\frac{S'^2}{(-S'')}.$$

Then

$$\left.\frac{d^2W^E}{d\beta^2}\right|_{\beta=1} - \left.\frac{d^2W^P}{d\beta^2}\right|_{\beta=1} = (2\alpha^*-1)\left[\frac{\pi(1-\alpha^*)+(1-\pi)}{\alpha^*} - (1-\pi)\right]$$

$$\frac{S'^2}{(-S'')} \geqslant (2\alpha^*-1)\pi\frac{(1-\alpha^*)}{\alpha^*}\frac{S'^2}{(-S'')} \geqslant 0.$$

A.6.2 Examples

Example 1:

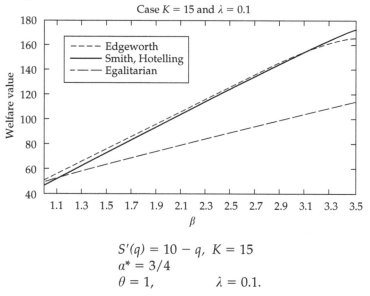

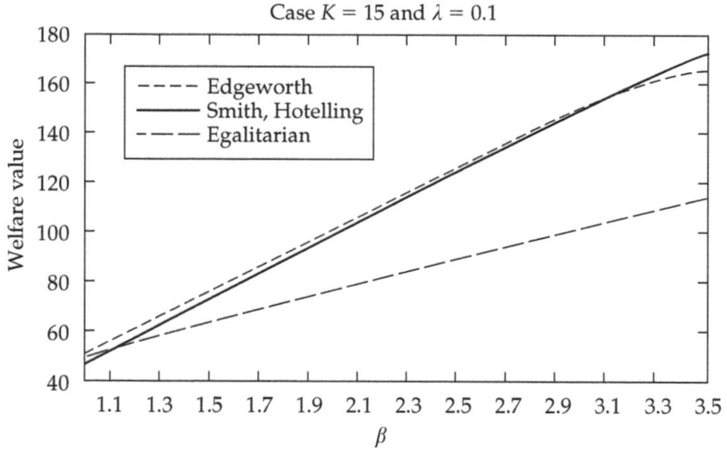

$$S'(q) = 10 - q, \; K = 15$$
$$\alpha^* = 3/4$$
$$\theta = 1, \qquad \lambda = 0.1.$$

- For β large enough, the Smith rule dominates the Edgeworth rule.
- For β large enough, the Hotelling rule dominates the egalitarian rule and the Edgeworth rule. (Note that the Smith

rule and the Hotelling rule are essentially indistinguishable in this figure.)

Example 2:

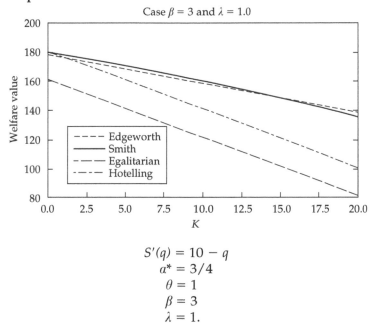

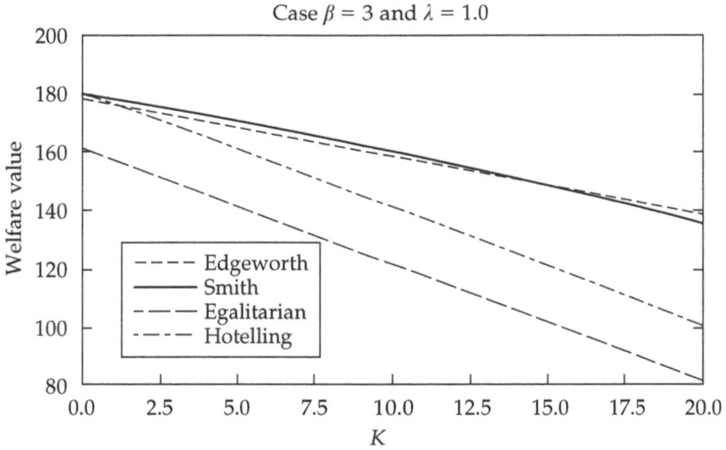

$$S'(q) = 10 - q$$
$$\alpha^* = 3/4$$
$$\theta = 1$$
$$\beta = 3$$
$$\lambda = 1.$$

- For K large enough, the Edgeworth rule dominates the Hotelling rule and, for K even larger, the Smith rule.

7

Toward a Political Theory of the Emergence of Environmental Incentive Regulation

> 'There is no satisfactory theory about the emergence of incentive based mechanisms.'
>
> Hahn (1990).

7.1 Introduction

A large number of instruments have been considered to regulate polluting activities—Pigouvian taxes, quotas, subsidies for pollution reduction, marketable emission permits,[1] deposit refund systems,[2] assignments of legal liabilities,[3] etc. As a result, the choice of policy instruments has become one of the major questions debated in environmental economics.[4] Most of the discussion has taken place within the benevolent social maximizer paradigm. But, starting with Buchanan and Tullock (1975), the necessity of looking for political economy explanations of the choice of instruments has been recognized.[5] However, dissatisfaction remains. Lewis (1997) concludes his survey as follows: 'I see the next progression in [environmental regulation] as being a positive analysis asking which kind of environmental policies will be

[1] Crocker (1966) and Dales (1968a, 1968b) first proposed marketing emission permits.

[2] See Bohm (1981).

[3] There is a large volume of literature on this topic; see in particular Segerson (1995), Boyer and Laffont (1996, 1997) and references therein. See also Gupta, Van Houtven and Cropper (1996) for an empirical analysis of the EPA's decisions regarding the cleanup of Superfund sites.

[4] Cropper and Oates (1992) devote a large part of their survey to this question. See also Segerson (1996) and Lewis (1997).

[5] Beyond the debate about the Buchanan–Tullock paper (Yohe (1976), Dewees (1983), Coelho (1976)), see also Boyer (1979), Noll (1983), Hahn (1990) and Hahn and McGartland (1989).

implemented under information and distribution constraints when special interests try to intervene to affect policy.'

The purpose of this chapter is to use the methodology of this part of the book to construct a formal political economy theory of environmental regulation. Economists' general preferences for sophisticated incentive mechanisms are reconsidered in a political economy approach resting on two main features: private information of economic agents, which explains the rents accruing to them as functions of policy choices, and the incomplete contract nature of Constitutions, which explains the need for politicians as residual decision makers.

Incomplete information is by now well understood as being a major obstacle to first-best efficient regulation. It is only recently that the mechanism-design approach has been developed for environmental economics.[6] A revelation mechanism can be viewed as a command-and-control instrument and it is clearly optimal here: once an optimal revelation mechanism has been obtained, the question of its implementation by various economic instruments or institutions, such as regulatory proceedings, taxes and markets, arises; but, by definition, those institutions then implement the same allocation as the command-and-control approach.[7]

In such a framework the question of instrument choice is empty. Such a question often arose in the literature because authors were not careful enough in defining their instruments. For example, Yohe (1976) correctly shows that the alleged difference between quotas and price controls in Buchanan and Tullock (1975) disappears when instruments are appropriately defined. He writes: 'When the equivalent quantity control is properly specified, both the economist's general preference for taxation and the regulatee's general preference for quotas will disappear.'

Two types of meaningful comparisons of instruments are then possible. In the first type, one considers constraints on instruments (the analysis should explain the origin of these constraints) and various constrained instruments can be compared. This is the

[6] See Baron (1985a), Laffont (1994) and Lewis (1997). Early applications were essentially reinterpreting Groves' mechanisms by treating environmental externalities like public goods (see e.g. Dasgupta, Hammond and Maskin (1980)).

[7] See Laffont (1994) for an example.

essence of Weitzman's (1974) comparison of prices and quantities in a situation where asymmetric information calls for non-linear prices as optimal instruments, as Roberts and Spence (1976) pointed out. Another example is the case of non-convexities due to negative externalities.[8] There, quotas are equivalent to non-linear taxes. Pigouvian (linear) taxes are then dominated by quotas. Similarly, taxes and subsidies which are equivalent when they are accompanied with appropriate lump-sum transfers differ in their absence with respect to the long-run, entry and exit decisions of firms.[9]

In the second type, one considers instruments which could be equivalent in the complete contracting framework and one introduces imperfections elsewhere in the economy that cannot be corrected by the regulator (then a good explanation of this inability of the regulator must be given). This is the case in Buchanan's (1969) example of a polluting monopolist when the subsidies required to correct monopolistic behavior are not available. Then, the Pigouvian tax is clearly dominated by a quota which implements the second-best tax, as devised for example by Lee (1975) and Barnett (1980), and which depends on the firm's market power.

A systematic analysis of instrument choice should then be conducted in well-defined second-best frameworks, which are all methodological shortcuts of an incomplete contract analysis. Constraints such as limited commitment, renegotiation-proof commitment, collusion, favoritism and multiprincipal structures[10] should be considered. Political economy constraints can be viewed also as a special case of this methodology. The lack of finely tuned constitutional control of the politicians (the incomplete contract feature) who have private agendas introduces inefficiencies in the regulatory decision process. It may then become desirable to impose constraints on politicians which

[8] See Starrett (1972) and Baumol and Bradford (1970).

[9] See Kamien, Schwartz and Dolbear (1966), Bramhall and Mills (1966), Kneese and Bower (1968), and Dewees and Sims (1976).

[10] See Baron (1985b) for an early study of the distortions due to the uncoordinated activities of two regulators in the context of environmental problems.

favor particular instruments or to force the use of apparently crude instruments.

Section 7.2 presents the model which introduces pollution in our basic setup. Section 7.3 develops this model, taking as given the delegation of environmental policy to political majorities. More specifically, we compare the policy consisting in the choice of a single pollution level—a typical command-and-control regulation—with the policy consisting in the choice of a menu of pollution–transfer pairs, a typical incentive regulation. We determine the conditions under which the higher discretion associated with the second policy is compensated for by its greater efficiency potential. Section 7.4 explores the foundation of the delegation of environmental policy to politicians. Section 7.5 extends the model to a situation where two types of interest groups, stakeholders in the firm and environmentalists, may benefit from the capture of the government through the size of information rents that the regulation mechanisms leave them. The distortions due to the political process are studied in this more general model, as well as the impact of a dynamics of reelection based on campaign contributions, and the comparison of instruments is extended to this case. Concluding comments are gathered in Section 7.6.

7.2 The Basic Model

We consider a natural monopoly which has delegated to it the realization of a public project which has social value S and costs $C(\theta, d) = \theta(K - d)$ where K is a constant, d is the level of pollution accompanying the completion of the project, and θ is a cost characteristic which is private information of the firm. For a given pollution level, θ measures the efficiency of the firm in realizing the project, a higher θ meaning a higher cost.

Two alternative assumptions are then possible regarding the cost of reducing pollution. The more efficient the firm is, either the more efficient it is also in reducing pollution or the less efficient it is in that regard. In terms of a general cost function $C(\theta, d)$, if we assume $C_\theta > 0$, we have the choice between $C_{\theta d} < 0$ and

$C_{\theta d} > 0$. In order to obtain explicit solutions and carry out numerical simulations, we choose a specific cost function which corresponds to $C_{\theta d} < 0$. This assumption seems to be the most interesting because, with a one-dimensional asymmetry of information, the positive correlation between ability to produce and to reduce pollution seems more compelling than the alternative assumption and leads to more striking results. However, we will point out how our results change with the alternative assumption $C_{\theta d} > 0$. We assume that θ can take two values $\{\underline{\theta}, \bar{\theta}\}$ with $\Delta\theta = \bar{\theta} - \underline{\theta}$, and ν is the probability that $\theta = \underline{\theta}$.

Let t be the compensatory monetary transfer from the regulator to the firm, which then has a rent equal to

$$U = t - \theta(K - d).$$

The social disutility of pollution is $V(d)$ (with $V' > 0$, $V'' > 0$). Consumers' welfare is

$$S - V(d) - (1 + \lambda)t.$$

The utilitarian social welfare is then

$$W = S - V(d) - (1 + \lambda)\theta(K - d) - \lambda U. \tag{7.1}$$

We assume that S is large enough to make the realization of the project always desirable. Under complete information, a benevolent social welfare maximizer would set $V'(d) = (1 + \lambda)\,\theta$ and $t = \theta(K - d)$ to nullify the rent of the firm which is socially costly because $\lambda > 0$. The chosen pollution levels would depend on λ and θ.

Under incomplete information about θ, the firm's individual rationality and incentive compatibility constraints must be taken into account. Only the type-$\underline{\theta}$ firm receives a rent, which is equal to

$$\underline{U} = \Delta\theta\,(K - \bar{d}),$$

where $\bar{d}$ is the pollution level requested from the less efficient type of firm by the separating regulation mechanism $((\underline{t}, \underline{d}), (\bar{t}, \bar{d}))$. The firm of type $\underline{\theta}$ can always pretend to be of type $\bar{\theta}$ and realize the project with a pollution level of $\bar{d}$ at a cost of $\underline{\theta}(K - \bar{d})$; since it is entitled to a transfer $\bar{t} \geq \bar{\theta}(K - \bar{d})$, it realizes a profit (rent) of at least $(\bar{\theta} - \underline{\theta})(K - \bar{d})$, a decreasing function of $\bar{d}$, which must then be a lower bound on its welfare or profit when it acts according to its real type. Note that this rent decreases with the pollution level of the inefficient firm.[11]

The optimal pollution levels obtained from the maximization of the expected value of social welfare (7.1) under the informational constraints can be characterized by the following program:

$$\max_{(\underline{d},\bar{d})} W(\underline{d},\bar{d}) = [\nu(S - V(\underline{d}) - (1+\lambda)\underline{\theta}(K-\underline{d}) - \lambda\Delta\theta(K-\bar{d})) + (1-\nu)(S - V(\bar{d}) - (1+\lambda)\bar{\theta}(K-\bar{d}))], \quad (7.2)$$

yielding

$$\begin{aligned} V'(\underline{d}^*) &= (1+\lambda)\underline{\theta} \\ V'(\bar{d}^*) &= (1+\lambda)\bar{\theta} + \lambda\left(\frac{\nu}{1-\nu}\right)\Delta\theta. \end{aligned} \quad (7.3)$$

7.3 Controlling the Discriminatory Power of Politicians through Constraints on the Choice of Instruments

We have a continuum [0, 1] of agents in the economy. As in Chapter 5, let a represent in each period the measure of consumers who do not share the firm's rent, the non-stakeholders, and $1 - a$ be the measure of those who share the rent, i.e. the stakeholders. Let a be drawn independently in each period, taking the value $a^* \in (\frac{1}{2}, 1)$ with probability $\frac{1}{2}$ and $1 - a^*$ with probability $\frac{1}{2}$. When $a = a^*$, the non-stakeholders' majority, of measure a^*, is in power; when $a = 1 - a^*$, the stakeholders' majority is in power and the measure of this majority is also a^*.

We will assume that politicians have the discretion of using their private information about the economy as exemplified here by λ, the social cost of public funds, whose distribution is common knowledge but whose value is either observed by the government (the majority in power) only or is commonly observed *ex post* but cannot be made verifiable by a court. We consider the value of λ either to be a proxy for specific economic conditions

[11] This feature, which follows from our assumptions on the cost function ($C_\theta > 0$, $C_{\theta d} < 0$), will imply that to reduce the costly rent of the efficient firm, one should let pollution increase. However, this striking result would be reversed with the alternative assumptions ($C_\theta > 0$, $C_{\theta d} > 0$) as in $C(\theta, d) = K - d/\theta$, or ($C_\theta < 0$, $C_{\theta d} < 0$) as in $C(\theta, d) = K - \theta d$.

that the government in power is better equipped to observe (from confidential reports of the public service bureaucracy, for example) or to refer to complex economic conditions which cannot be written in a constitutional contract.

The constitutional contract may on the other hand impose constraints on the choice of instruments for pollution abatement. We want to compare two instruments. The first, corresponding to a rather sophisticated incentive regulation of the firm, is a menu of abatement levels and associated transfers in which firms $\underline{\theta}$ and $\bar{\theta}$ will self-select themselves, and the second, corresponding to a single abatement level based on $E\theta$, the expected value of θ, is imposed on both types of firms. In the first case, we let the political majorities decide on the menu of abatement levels, while in the second case they are constrained by a unique level. In each case, they can use their private information on λ.

Let us consider first the sophisticated separation mechanism. If $a = a^*$, we have majority 1, which maximizes the welfare of nonstakeholders who benefit from the project, suffer from the pollution externality and must pay taxes to finance the project (the cost of the project plus the rent of the firm), namely[12]

$$a^* [S - V(d) - (1 + \lambda)t] = a^* [S - V(d) - (1 + \lambda)\theta(K - d) - (1 + \lambda)U]. \tag{7.4}$$

This objective function overestimates the social cost of the firm's rent relative to (7.1) since $1 + \lambda > \lambda$. Similarly, if $a = 1 - a^*$, majority 2 maximizes the welfare of stakeholders who are similar to type-1 agents except that they share the firm's rent, namely

$$a^* [S - V(d) - (1 + \lambda)t] + U = a^* \left[S - V(d) - (1 + \lambda)\theta(K - d) - \left(1 + \lambda - \frac{1}{a^*}\right)U\right]. \tag{7.5}$$

This objective function underestimates the social cost of the firm's rent since $1 + \lambda - 1/a^* < \lambda$.[13]

Majority 1 maximizes over the pollution levels the expected

[12] This formulation presumes that the majorities cannot change the funding of firms through indirect taxation, which is uniformly spread across all agents.

[13] We assume that $1 + \lambda - 1/a^* > 0$. Otherwise, we would have to take into account the agents' individual rationality constraints since majority 2 would like to make U as large as possible.

value of the welfare of non-stakeholders given by (7.4); that is, it solves

$$\max_{(\underline{d},\bar{d})} W^1(\underline{d}, \bar{d}) = \alpha^*[\nu\,(S - V(\underline{d}) - (1+\lambda)\underline{\theta}(K - \underline{d}) - (1+\lambda)\Delta\theta(K - \bar{d})) + (1 - \nu)(S - V(\bar{d}) - (1+\lambda)\bar{\theta}(K - \bar{d}))]. \tag{7.6}$$

Hence

$$\begin{aligned} V'(\underline{d}_1) &= (1+\lambda)\underline{\theta} \\ V'(\bar{d}_1) &= (1+\lambda)\bar{\theta} + (1+\lambda)\left(\frac{\nu}{1-\nu}\right)\Delta\theta, \end{aligned} \tag{7.7}$$

with associated transfers given by $\bar{t} = \bar{\theta}(K - \bar{d}_1)$ and $\underline{t} = \underline{\theta}(K - \underline{d}_1) + \Delta\theta(K - \bar{d}_1)$. Majority 2 similarly maximizes $W^2(\underline{d}, \bar{d})$, the expected value of stakeholders given by (7.5). This leads to

$$\begin{aligned} V'(\underline{d}_2) &= (1+\lambda)\underline{\theta} \\ V'(\bar{d}_2) &= (1+\lambda)\bar{\theta} + (1+\lambda - 1/\alpha^*)\left(\frac{\nu}{1-\nu}\right)\Delta\theta. \end{aligned} \tag{7.8}$$

We obtain (assuming that each majority is in power half the time) the expected social welfare

$$E_{\lambda\alpha}W(\underline{d}, \bar{d}) = \frac{1}{2}E_\lambda W(\underline{d}_1, \bar{d}_1) + \frac{1}{2}E_\lambda W(\underline{d}_2, \bar{d}_2), \tag{7.9}$$

where $W(\underline{d}_m, \bar{d}_m)$ is the expected level, with respect to the firm's type, of social welfare (7.1) evaluated at pollution levels chosen by majority m as a function of λ.

Comparing (7.3), (7.7) and (7.8), we observe that the pollution level of the more efficient firm is optimal whatever the majority in power since $\underline{d}_1 = \underline{d}_2 = \underline{d}^*$. But the pollution level of the less efficient firm is either too large (under a non-stakeholder's majority government) or too low (under a stakeholder's majority government): $\bar{d}_1 > \bar{d}^* > \bar{d}_2$. These apparently surprising distortions need some explanation. Since both majorities take fully into account the social cost of pollution $V(d)$, they differ only in their treatment of the information rents accruing to the stakeholders of the more efficient firm. Majority 1 (non-stakeholders) overvalues the social cost of the firm's information rent (it uses a weight of $(1 + \lambda)$ instead of λ)

because it does not share these rents. For that majority, the cost of inducing abatement from the less efficient firm, which is the source of the rent of the more efficient firm, is therefore larger than its social cost net of the rent. Majority 1's regulation therefore leads to too much pollution from the less efficient firm because it does not value the positive effect of a more stringent abatement level $\bar{d}$ on the efficient firm's rent. In contrast, majority 2 (stakeholders) undervalues the social cost of the firm's information rent (it uses a weight of $(1 + \lambda - 1/\alpha^*) < \lambda$) because it captures the totality of that rent. For that majority, the net cost of inducing abatement is less than its social cost. Majority 2's regulation leads therefore to too little pollution from the less efficient firm.

We now consider the case of a non-discriminating pollution abatement mechanism which the constitutional contract may impose on the politicians. The latter then have a more limited discretion for promoting the interest of their constituency. Each majority can now select only a single abatement level, rather than a menu of pollution abatement and transfer levels.

If the non-stakeholders' majority is in power, it now solves

$$\max_{d} W^1(d) = \alpha^*[S - V(d) - (1 + \lambda)E\theta\,(K - d) - \nu(1 + \lambda)\Delta\theta(K - d)] \tag{7.10}$$

yielding

$$V'(d_1) = (1 + \lambda)E\theta + (1 + \lambda)\nu\Delta\theta = (1 + \lambda)\bar{\theta}. \tag{7.11}$$

Similarly, the stakeholders' majority chooses a pollution level d_2 characterized by

$$V'(d_2) = (1 + \lambda)E\theta + (1 + \lambda - 1/\alpha^*)\nu\Delta\theta = (1 + \lambda)\bar{\theta} - \frac{1}{\alpha^*}\nu\Delta\theta. \tag{7.12}$$

We obtain an expected social welfare level given by (assuming that each majority is in power half the time)[14]

$$E_{\lambda\alpha}W(d) = \frac{1}{2}E_{\lambda}W(d_1) + \frac{1}{2}E_{\lambda}W(d_2), \tag{7.13}$$

[14] Again, $d_2 < d^* < d_1$, where d^* is the optimal non-discriminating pollution abatement level under the same informational constraints.

where $W(d_m)$ is the social welfare (7.1) evaluated at the single pollution level chosen by majority m as characterized by (7.11) and (7.12).

The emergence of the delegated (separating) incentive mechanism (DIM) hinges on its *ex ante* comparison with the delegated pooling mechanism (DPM) obtained above. We carry out this comparison for small asymmetries of information represented by $\Delta\theta$.

> PROPOSITION 7.1 For $\bar{\theta}$ close enough to $\underline{\theta}$, we have $E_{\lambda a}W(\underline{d}, \bar{d}) > E_{\lambda a}W(d)$; that is, the delegated (separating) incentive mechanism (DIM) chosen by the political majorities dominates the delegated pooling mechanism (DPM) selected by political majorities if and only if

$$\text{var}(\lambda) > H(v, a^*, E\lambda) \equiv -v^2\left(\frac{a^* - \frac{1}{2}}{a^{*2}}\right) - 1 + 2v - 2(1-v)E\lambda - (E\lambda)^2. \tag{7.14}$$

The proof of this proposition uses the same techniques as in Chapter 6 and is given in Appendix A.7.1.

In this context of political delegation, the emergence of the sophisticated separating incentive mechanisms discriminating between the pollution abatement levels requested from the different firms will be associated with increases in $E\lambda$, var(λ) and a^* and with decreases in v. For $E\lambda$ or var(λ) is large, the larger sensitivity of the separating incentive mechanism dominates. Increases in v have two effects. A larger v implies a strong concern for rents accruing to the firm with probability v, but also larger distortions from social welfare maximization in the objective function of the majorities since

$$W(\underline{d}_1, \bar{d}_1) = \frac{W^1(\underline{d}_1, \bar{d}_1)}{a^*} + v\Delta\theta(K - \bar{d}_1) \tag{7.15}$$

$$W(\underline{d}_2, \bar{d}_2) = \frac{W^2(\underline{d}_2, \bar{d}_2)}{a^*} + \left(1 - \frac{1}{a^*}\right)v\Delta\theta(K - \bar{d}_2). \tag{7.16}$$

It turns out that the second distortions are larger and therefore a large v favors a non-discriminating policy (DPM).

Similarly, increases in the asymmetry of information $\Delta\theta$ have *a priori* an ambiguous effect. However, we can show both in the case of a quadratic $V(d)$ function and with simulations for the other cases that (a) if separation (DIM) dominates for small $\Delta\theta$, it dominates always; (b) if pooling (DPM) dominates for small $\Delta\theta$, there exists a $\Delta\theta^0$ beyond which separation becomes better. For large $\Delta\theta$, the greater ability of discriminating mechanisms to extract rents dominates the negative effects of political discretion. A small α^*, i.e. close to $\frac{1}{2}$, corresponds to the case where political agendas differ the most from social welfare; then pooling is favored to decrease the discretionary pursuit of private agendas.

For a quadratic $V(\cdot)$ function, social welfare is quadratic in $\bar{\theta}$. We can then derive the global superiority of the pooling mechanism or the sophisticated separating mechanism from Proposition 7.1 and the fact that all welfare levels coincide at $\bar{\theta} = \underline{\theta}$.[15] However, for more general $V(\cdot)$ functions, the increase in $\bar{\theta}$, which is favorable to letting the majorities choose separating mechanisms, may lead to the superiority of this mechanism over the pooling mechanism even when $\text{var}(\lambda) < H(\cdot)$; that is, even when the pooling mechanism dominates for values of $\bar{\theta}$ close to $\underline{\theta}$. Figure 7.1 provides an example where $\text{var}(\lambda) = 0 < H(\cdot) = 0.08$, but nevertheless the separating incentive mechanism chosen by the political majorities dominates the delegated pooling mechanism selected by political majorities when $\bar{\theta}$ is large enough.

Majorities can favor their respective constituency by choosing menus of pollution levels and transfers which maximize their respective welfare functions, yielding the delegated separating incentive regulation regime. Proposition 7.1 compared this delegation of powers with a constitutional requirement that the majorities select a unique pollution abatement level to be imposed on all firms. One can take a more positive approach to constitutional reform and wonder if moving toward the use of an incentive mechanism with delegated discretion may emerge from unanimous *ex ante* consent and not simply by appealing to social welfare maximization under the veil of ignorance. For this purpose we can compare *ex ante* the per capita welfare of the two types of agents in a DIM and a DPM. We obtain (see Appendix A.7.2):

[15] The first derivatives of the expected welfare functions with respect to $\bar{\theta}$, evaluated at $\bar{\theta} = \underline{\theta}$, are negative and equal. If $V(d)$ is quadratic, then the second derivatives are independent of $\bar{\theta}$.

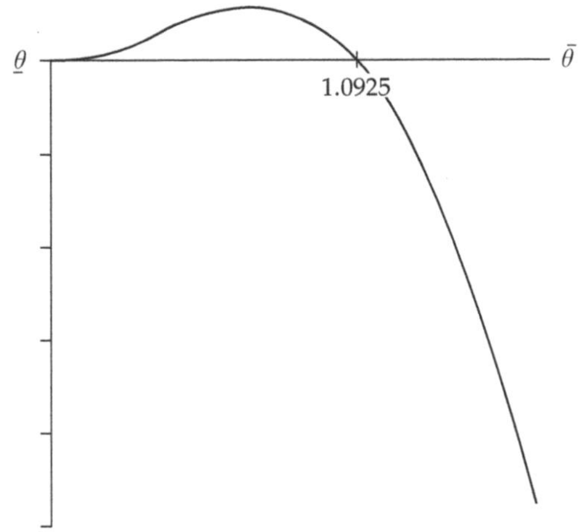

Figure 7.1: The differential expected welfare $E_{\lambda a}W(d) - E_{\lambda a}W(\underline{d}, \bar{d})$ as given by (7.13) and (7.9) as a function of $\bar{\theta}$ for $V(d) = \frac{1}{4}d^4$, $E\lambda = 0.4$, $\mathrm{var}(\lambda) = 0$, $\alpha^* = 0.8$, $K = 5$, $\underline{\theta} = 1$, $\nu = 0.85$

PROPOSITION 7.2 For $\bar{\theta}$ close to $\underline{\theta}$, majority 1 prefers the optimal DIM over the optimal DPM if

$$\mathrm{var}(\lambda) > H^1(\nu, \alpha^*, E\lambda) \equiv \frac{1}{2}\frac{\nu^2}{\alpha^{*2}} - 1 - 2E\lambda - (E\lambda)^2, \qquad (7.17)$$

while majority 2 does if

$$\mathrm{var}(\lambda) > H^2(\nu, \alpha^*, E\lambda) \equiv 2\frac{\nu}{\alpha^*} - \frac{1}{2}\frac{\nu^2}{\alpha^{*2}} - 1 - 2\left(1 - \frac{\nu}{\alpha^*}\right)E\lambda - (E\lambda)^2. \qquad (7.18)$$

Comparing $H^1(\cdot)$, $H^2(\cdot)$ and $H(\cdot)$, we obtain directly the following corollary:

COROLLARY 7.1 We have

$$H^1(\nu, \alpha^*, E\lambda) < H(\nu, \alpha^*, E\lambda) < H^2(\nu, \alpha^*, E\lambda). \qquad (7.19)$$

The non-stakeholders (majority 1) are more active proponents of delegating discretionary power to politicians over environmental policy, i.e. of a DIM scheme, than the stakeholders in environmentally risky businesses (majority 2). Majority 1 prefers a DIM scheme as soon as the variance of λ reaches the threshold $H^1(\cdot)$, while majority 2 still prefers to stick to the DPM scheme until the variance of λ has reached the higher threshold $H^2(\cdot)$. Indeed, the net cost of pollution abatement is higher for majority 1 and therefore raises the value of the more efficient incentive pollution abatement mechanism DIM above that of the cruder DPM as soon as $H^1(\cdot)$ is reached. If unanimous approval is needed for constitutional reform in favor of a sophisticated separating incentive mechanism with delegated discretion, it will happen less often than socially desirable because $H^2(\cdot) > H(\cdot)$; that is, because of the resistance of the stakeholders in environmentally risky businesses.

7.4 Delegating Discriminatory Power to the Politicians

The gain from delegating discretionary power to politicians comes from the use they can make of their information, which in the present context is their knowledge of the social cost of public funds λ. The cost of such delegation is the excessive fluctuation of their decisions $(\underline{d}, \bar{d})$ as a function of λ, as private agendas are taken into account by successive majorities. Alternatively, the constitutional convention may decide not to delegate such discretionary power but instead impose an incentive mechanism $((\underline{t}^P, \underline{d}^P), (\bar{t}^P, \bar{d}^P))$ determined at the constitutional level to maximize expected social welfare. This incentive mechanism can be characterized as the solution to the social maximization program

$$\max_{(\underline{d},\bar{d})} W(\underline{d}, \bar{d}) = \nu(S - V(\underline{d}) - (1 + E\lambda)\underline{\theta}(K - \underline{d}) - (E\lambda)\Delta\theta(K - \bar{d})) + (1 - \nu)(S - V(\bar{d}) - (1 + E\lambda)\bar{\theta}(K - \bar{d})), \quad (7.20)$$

yielding

$$V'(\underline{d}^P) = (1 + E\lambda)\underline{\theta}$$

$$V'(\bar{d}^P) = (1 + E\lambda)\bar{\theta} + (E\lambda)\left(\frac{\nu}{1-\nu}\right)\Delta\theta.$$

The pollution levels $\underline{d}^P$ and $\bar{d}^P$ now depend on $E\lambda$.

At the constitutional level, the choice is then between imposing a separating incentive regulation mechanism which maximizes expected social welfare on the basis of the expected value $E\lambda$, a mechanism which we will denote as a constitutional incentive mechanism (CIM), or delegating to the political majorities the choice of a separating incentive regulation mechanism which will then be a function of the value of λ, i.e. the delegated separating mechanism DIM. In the latter case, the choice of pollution regulation mechanisms will reflect private agendas. The emergence of the latter DIM which depends on λ hinges on its *ex ante* comparison with the former CIM.

PROPOSITION 7.3 The difference in expected welfare between the CIM and the DIM converges to 0 as $\Delta\theta \to 0$ and $\text{var}(\lambda) \to 0$. For a given $\Delta\theta$, the CIM dominates if $\text{var}(\lambda)$ is small. For a given $\text{var}(\lambda)$, the DIM dominates if $\Delta\theta$ is small.

Clearly, the CIM dominates the DIM chosen by the majorities when the variance of λ is small for a given level of asymmetric information, as represented by $\Delta\theta$. Indeed, the CIM is optimal when $\text{var}(\lambda) = 0$, while the DIM is not. By continuity, for low levels of the variance in λ, allowing political majorities to use the observed value of λ in choosing *ex post* an incentive mechanism generates little social value but it generates a significant social cost given the pursuit of private agendas. As $\text{var}(\lambda)$ increases, the value of adjusting policies to the realized value of λ increases and therefore it may eventually be better to give political majorities greater latitude in setting policies and choosing the mechanism.

Similarly, for a given variance in λ, the delegation of authority to politicians is socially valuable—and, indeed, optimal—if $\Delta\theta = 0$. By continuity, for small values of $\Delta\theta$, the delegation of authority allows the politicians to fine-tune the choice of the incentive mechanism to the realized value of λ while the pursuit of their private agendas generates little unwarranted distortions in pollution abatement. Since $\Delta\theta$ is small, maximizing any majority welfare function is almost equivalent to maximizing the social welfare function because there are (almost) no rents. Again, as $\Delta\theta$ increases, for the same given variance of λ one expects that the distortions generated by the pursuit of private agendas will eventually exceed the benefit of fine-tuning the incentive abatement mechanism chosen by the majorities and will therefore lead to the dominance of the CIM.

It has been suggested that one of the main concerns of politicians is to remain in power through reelection. One may wonder what effects such reelection concerns have on the relative social welfare value of different regulation regimes from an *ex ante* constitutional point of view. In the next section we will model the interaction between reelection objectives and the pursuit of private agendas by assuming that the probability of reelection is negatively affected by the pursuit of private agendas.

7.5 Multiple Privately Informed Interest Groups

In the previous sections we have seen how the delegation of environmental policy to politicians enables them to distribute information rents to interest groups. In this section we want to explore the extent to which competing interest groups may mitigate the distortions in the allocation of resources that politicians might find profitable. For this purpose, we extend the model by introducing, in addition to reelection concerns of majorities, first the financing of political coalitions or majorities through campaign contributions and, second, an information asymmetry regarding the damages of pollution. In the same way as θ is private information of stakeholders, the disutility of pollution is now assumed to be $\beta V(d)$ with $\beta \in \{\underline{\beta}, \bar{\beta}\}$, $\Delta\beta = \bar{\beta} - \underline{\beta}$ and μ is the probability that $\beta = \underline{\beta}$.[16] The parameter β is private information of the environmentalists, who suffer the pollution damage, have no stake in the polluting firm, and will be compensated for the cost of pollution. This compensation assumption should be interpreted as a reduced-form formulation of a political constraint on the level of hardship that a majority can impose on the minority; this assumption can also be interpreted as a threshold under which civil disobedience would be triggered. Since β is private information of the environmentalists who are compensated for the cost of pollution, they will also be able to capture an information rent. This is one reason why the environmentalists will here favor higher pollution levels which provide them with higher information rents. Their information rent is

[16] As for θ, the value of β is assumed to be drawn anew every period.

$$U_1 = s - \beta V(d),$$

where s is the transfer from the government. The stakeholders who do not suffer the pollution damage have an informational rent of

$$U_2 = t - \theta(K - d).$$

The taxpayers who are now distinct from stakeholders and environmentalists have utility

$$U_3 = S - (1 + \lambda)(t + s).$$

Assuming that each group (environmentalists, stakeholders, taxpayers) represents one-third of the population, utilitarian social welfare is proportional to

$$W = U_1 + U_2 + U_3 = S - (1 + \lambda)(\theta(K - d) + \beta V(d)) - \lambda(U_1 + U_2 + U_3). \tag{7.22}$$

Under complete information, the optimal pollution is now characterized by $\beta V'(d) = \theta$.[17] Under incomplete information, a revelation mechanism is now a triple $\{d(\theta, \beta), t(\theta, \beta), s(\theta, \beta)\}$. The relevant incentive compatibility and individual rationality constraints are

$$\begin{aligned}
E_\beta\{t(\underline{\theta}, \beta) - \underline{\theta}(K - d(\underline{\theta}, \beta))\} &\geq E_\beta\{t(\bar{\theta}, \beta) - \underline{\theta}(K - d(\bar{\theta}, \beta))\} \\
E_\beta\{t(\bar{\theta}, \beta) - \bar{\theta}(K - d(\bar{\theta}, \beta))\} &\geq 0 \\
E_\theta\{s(\theta, \underline{\beta}) - \underline{\beta}V(d(\theta, \underline{\beta}))\} &\geq E_\theta\{s(\theta, \bar{\beta}) - \underline{\beta}V(d(\theta, \bar{\beta}))\} \\
E_\theta\{s(\theta, \bar{\beta}) - \bar{\beta}V(d(\theta, \bar{\beta}))\} &\geq 0.
\end{aligned}$$

Assuming Bayesian Nash behavior of stakeholders and environmentalists, the revelation mechanism which maximizes expected social welfare

$$W(\vec{d}) = E_{\theta,\beta}\{S - (1 + \lambda)[\theta(K - d) + \beta V(d]\} - \lambda\mu\underline{U}_1 - \lambda v\underline{U}_2 \tag{7.23}$$

under the above incentive and individual rationality constraints is characterized by

[17] Having an individual rationality constraint for the environmentalists amounts to, and should be interpreted as, assuming that they are indemnified at a social cost of $(1 + \lambda)$. This is why we now obtain $\beta V'(d) = \theta$ instead of $\beta V'(d) = (1 + \lambda)\theta$.

$$\begin{aligned} \underline{\beta}V'(d(\underline{\theta}, \underline{\beta})) &= \underline{\theta} \\ (\bar{\beta} + \tfrac{\lambda}{1+\lambda}\tfrac{\mu}{1-\mu}\Delta\beta)\, V'(d(\underline{\theta}, \underline{\beta})) &= \underline{\theta} \\ \underline{\beta}V'(d(\bar{\theta}, \underline{\beta})) &= \bar{\theta} + \tfrac{\lambda}{1+\lambda}\tfrac{\nu}{1-\nu}\Delta\theta \\ (\bar{\beta} + \tfrac{\lambda}{1+\lambda}\tfrac{\mu}{1-\mu}\Delta\beta)\, V'(d(\bar{\theta}, \bar{\beta})) &= \bar{\theta} + \tfrac{\lambda}{1+\lambda}\tfrac{\nu}{1-\nu}\Delta\theta. \end{aligned} \tag{7.24}$$

Let us assume that the two interest groups use a share of their information rent as campaign contributions to influence politicians. We now consider a two-period model. In period 2, majority 1 is able to favor the interests of environmentalists by maximizing the sum of taxpayers' utility and environmentalists' utility,

$$W^1(\overrightarrow{d_1}) = W(\overrightarrow{d_1}) - \nu\underline{U}_2; \tag{7.25}$$

that is, by not including in its objective function the information rent of the stakeholders, where $\overrightarrow{d_1} = (d_1(\underline{\theta}, \underline{\beta}), d_1(\underline{\theta}, \bar{\beta}), d_1(\bar{\theta}, \bar{\beta}), d_1(\bar{\theta}, \bar{\beta}))$. Similarly, if elected, majority 2 is able to favor the interests of the stakeholders of the firm by maximizing the sum of taxpayers' utility and stakeholders' utility,

$$W^2(\overrightarrow{d_2}) = W(\overrightarrow{d_2}) - \mu\underline{U}_1; \tag{7.26}$$

that is, by not including the information rent of the environmentalists.

Let us assume that each majority makes campaign contributions C_1 and C_2 as a fixed proportion ζ, assumed equal for both majorities, of their average rents: $C_1 = \zeta\mu\underline{U}_1$ and $C_2 = \zeta\nu\underline{U}_2$, with $\underline{U}_1 = \Delta\beta[\nu V(d(\underline{\theta}, \bar{\beta})) + (1 - \nu)V(d(\bar{\theta}, \bar{\beta}))]$ and $\underline{U}_2 = \Delta\theta[\mu(K - d(\bar{\theta}, \underline{\beta})) + (1 - \mu)(K - d(\bar{\theta}, \bar{\beta}))]$. These campaign contributions affect the probability of winning the election that follows. For majority 1, the probability of winning is assumed to be

$$\Psi = \frac{1}{2} + \frac{1}{2} g\zeta(\mu\underline{U}_1 - \nu\underline{U}_2) \tag{7.27}$$

where g is a parameter representing the importance of campaign contributions in the electoral process. The stake of winning the election for period 2 is now, for majority 1, $E^1(\overrightarrow{d_1}, \overrightarrow{d_2}) = W^1(\overrightarrow{d_1}) - W^1(\overrightarrow{d_2})$ and, for majority 2, $E^2(\overrightarrow{d_1}, \overrightarrow{d_2}) = W^2(\overrightarrow{d_2}) - W^2(\overrightarrow{d_1})$. Hence, majority 1 maximizes (for the discount factor δ)

$$W^1(\vec{d_1}) + \delta \Psi E^1(\vec{d_1}, \vec{d_2}), \tag{7.28}$$

leading to

$$\underline{\beta} V'(\hat{d}_1(\underline{\theta}, \underline{\beta})) = \underline{\theta}$$

$$\left(\bar{\beta} + \frac{\lambda}{1+\lambda}\frac{\mu}{1-\mu}\Delta\beta - \frac{1}{2}\frac{\delta\, E^1 g\zeta\Delta\beta\mu}{(1+\lambda)(1-\mu)}\right) V'(\hat{d}_1(\underline{\theta}, \bar{\beta})) = \underline{\theta}$$

$$\underline{\beta} V'(\hat{d}_1(\bar{\theta}, \underline{\beta})) = \bar{\theta} + \frac{\nu}{1-\nu}\Delta\theta + \frac{1}{2}\frac{\delta E^1 g\zeta\Delta\theta\nu}{(1+\lambda)(1-\nu)} \tag{7.29}$$

$$\left(\bar{\beta} + \frac{\lambda}{1+\lambda}\frac{\mu}{1-\mu}\Delta\beta - \frac{1}{2}\frac{\delta\, E^1 g\zeta\Delta\beta\mu}{(1+\lambda)(1-\mu)}\right) V'(\hat{d}_1(\underline{\theta}, \bar{\beta})) = \bar{\theta} + \frac{\nu}{1-\nu}\Delta\theta + \frac{1}{2}\frac{\delta E^1 g\zeta\Delta\theta\nu}{(1+\lambda)(1-\nu)}.$$

Let $\vec{\hat{d}_1} = (\hat{d}_1(\underline{\theta}, \underline{\beta}), \hat{d}_1(\underline{\theta}, \bar{\beta}), \hat{d}_1(\bar{\theta}, \underline{\beta}), \hat{d}_1(\bar{\theta}, \bar{\beta}))$.[18] In comparison with the static case, the environmentalist majority increases the pollution levels in all cases, except in the case $(\underline{\theta}, \underline{\beta})$. The reason is that it now wishes not only to decrease as in the static case the stakeholders' rent (with respect to the social optimum) because it undervalues this rent in its objective function, but also to increase its own rent in order to increase its probability of winning the election through campaign contributions, and furthermore to decrease even further the stakeholders' rent for the same reason.

We obtain symmetric results for the stakeholders' majority choosing $\vec{\hat{d}_2}$. In comparison with the static case, the stakeholders' majority decreases the pollution levels in all cases, except in the case $(\underline{\theta}, \underline{\beta})$. The reason is similar to that for which the environmentalist majority increased the pollution levels. Recalling the social welfare function $W = U_1 + U_2 + U_3$, let

$$E_{\lambda a}\hat{W}(\vec{\hat{d}}) = \frac{1}{2}E_\lambda W(\vec{\hat{d}_1}) + \frac{1}{2}E_\lambda W(\vec{\hat{d}_2}). \tag{7.30}$$

The above DIM with two specific interest groups (DIM2) is to be compared with a constitutional pooling mechanism which determines a unique welfare-maximizing pollution-abatement level as a function of λ but common to all firms and environmentalists (or specific values of θ and β) and common to all majorities in power, i.e. a CPM2 regulation. The latter can be characterized as follows:

[18] One should note that the second-period pollution levels can be obtained from (7.29) with $\delta = 0$.

$$\max_d W(d) = S - (1 + \lambda)(E\theta(K - d) + E\beta V(d)) - \lambda\mu\Delta\beta V(d) \\ - \lambda\nu\Delta\theta(K - d), \tag{7.31}$$

yielding

$$\left(E\beta + \frac{\lambda}{1+\lambda}\mu\Delta\beta\right) V'(\hat{d}) = \left(E\theta + \frac{\lambda}{1+\lambda}\nu\Delta\theta\right), \tag{7.32}$$

leading to

$$E_\lambda W(\hat{d}). \tag{7.33}$$

The use of sophisticated delegated incentive schemes DIM2 leads to two additional sources of distortions. First, campaign contributions are losses from a welfare point of view; and, second, incentive distortions are reinforced. In a situation where the CPM2 scheme given by (7.32) is dominated in the static case by a DIM2 scheme,[19] we may expect that it will dominate the latter for g, ζ or δ large enough. Figure 7.2 provides such an example. Curve A illustrates the basic case ($\underline{\theta} = 1$, $\bar{\theta} = 1.5$, $\underline{\beta} = 1$, $\bar{\beta} = 1.5$) in which, for large enough values of δ, the CPM2 scheme dominates the sophisticated DIM2 scheme. Curve B illustrates the same basic case except that $\bar{\theta} = 1.7$; it shows that as the informational asymmetry $\Delta\theta$ is increased, the domination of the CPM2 scheme occurs for values of δ larger than 5.35. Curve C illustrates the same basic case except that $\bar{\beta} = 1.7$; it shows again that as the informational asymmetry $\Delta\beta$ is increased, the domination of the CPM2 scheme occurs for values of δ larger than 7.15.

In this context, the emergence of sophisticated delegated incentive mechanisms (DIM2) would therefore be associated with *decreases* in δ, a measure of the desire of politicians to remain in power over time, with *decreases* in g, a measure of the importance of campaign contributions in the electoral process, and *decreases* in ζ, a measure of the willingness of agents to make campaign contributions out of their information rents. Hence, politicians with long-term plans and objectives, together with the private financing of electoral campaigns, favor simple command-and-control schemes over more sophisticated delegated separating

[19] The static regulation values for the CPM2 scheme can be obtained from (7.29) with $\delta = 0$.

incentive mechanisms. This negative effect of reelection concerns with multiple privately informed interest groups should be combined with any positive reputation effect which could come from voters realizing in period 1 that politicians pursue social objectives. The presence of multiple interest groups may transform valuable reforms toward delegated incentive mechanisms into undesirable reforms because these powerful mechanisms raise the stake of political conflicts generating additional distortions.

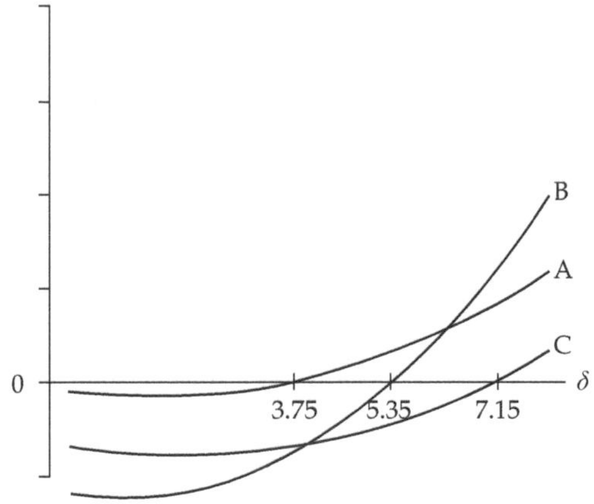

Figure 7.2: The differential expected welfare

$E_{\lambda}W(\hat{d}) - E_{\lambda\alpha}\hat{\hat{W}}(\overrightarrow{\hat{d}})$ as given by (7.33) and (7.30) as a function of δ for $V(d) = \frac{1}{2}d^2$, $E\lambda = 1$, $\text{var}(\lambda) = 0$, $\nu = 0.6$, $\mu = 0.6$, $K = 5$, $g = 1$, $\zeta = 0.75$

7.6 Conclusion

We have interpreted the political economy of environmental policy as an analysis of the economic implications of politicians' discretion in pursuing the private agendas of their constituencies: some voters are more concerned than others by pollution; some voters have stakes in the information rents of the polluting firms.

Sophisticated environmental policy depends on non-verifiable variables that cannot be contracted upon in the Constitution. Consequently, it must be delegated to politicians, thereby creating an incentive problem when politicians' motivations are to stay in power by pleasing to a certain degree a majority of voters rather than to maximize social welfare. We have shown that the larger the social cost of public funds, i.e., the larger is $E\lambda$ and the greater the variability of economic variables (var(λ), $\Delta\theta$, $\Delta\beta$) is, the more valuable is flexibility and therefore the greater the delegation of authority to politicians. However, the thinner majorities are (the lower α^* is) or the larger the information rents are (the larger ν and/or the larger μ are), the more the politicians' objectives are biased away from maximizing social welfare, providing a justification of cruder environmental policies which leave them less discretion.

Reelection considerations lead to conflicting influences on this basic trade-off. If, through reputation effects and a better social control, pursuing excessively private agendas today is costly for the next election, more sophisticated environmental policies may emerge as socially optimal. On the other hand, if the campaign contributions favoring reelection are important (large g) and significantly related (large ζ) to the information rents of the various interest groups, politicians are led to greater distortions to favor even more the interest groups supporting them. When this is added to the waste of campaign contributions themselves, it favors giving up sophisticated policies which become costly political stakes. Depending on the relative importance of these conflicting effects of reelection considerations, a longer-term view in politics (larger δ) may favor (if the reputation effect dominates the combined g-effect and ζ-effect) or not (otherwise) the emergence of sophisticated market-based or incentive mechanisms.

The approach developed in this chapter could be extended to other types of social and economic regulations. It should also be broadened by considering more detailed and realistic electoral processes and by introducing various institutions (bureaucracy, courts, etc.) which mitigate the incentive problems associated with the delegation of public policy responsibilities to political majorities.[20]

[20] See in particular Breyer (1992) and Pollak (1995).

Appendix 7

A.7.1 Proof of Proposition 7.1

To compare the two schemes, DPM and DIM, we first note that the two expected welfare functions evaluated at $\bar{\theta} = \underline{\theta}$ are equal (equations (7.7), (7.8), (7.11) and (7.12) all give the same values) and that their first derivatives with respect to $\bar{\theta}$ evaluated at $\bar{\theta} = \underline{\theta}$ are negative and equal. Hence, we compare the DPM and DIM schemes by computing the second derivatives of the expected social welfare with respect to $\bar{\theta}$ at $\bar{\theta} = \underline{\theta}$. Consider first the case of the DIM scheme, where separating incentive mechanisms are chosen by the political majorities. Social welfare when majority 1 decides, $W(\underline{d}_1, \bar{d}_1)$, can be written from (7.1) and (7.4) as

$$W(\underline{d}_1, \bar{d}_1) = \frac{W^1(\underline{d}_1, \bar{d}_1)}{\alpha^*} + \nu\Delta\theta\,(K - \bar{d}_1),$$

where $W^1(\cdot, \cdot)$ is the objective function of majority 1. Using the envelope theorem for $W^1(\underline{d}_1, \bar{d}_1)$, we have

$$\frac{\mathrm{d}W(\underline{d}_1, \bar{d}_1)}{\mathrm{d}\bar{\theta}} = -\,(1 + \lambda - \nu)(K - \bar{d}_1) - \nu\Delta\theta\,\frac{\mathrm{d}\bar{d}_1}{\mathrm{d}\bar{\theta}},$$

where, from (7.7),

$$\frac{\mathrm{d}\bar{d}_1}{\mathrm{d}\bar{\theta}} = \frac{1 + \lambda}{(1 - \nu)V''(\bar{d}_1)}$$

and therefore

$$\frac{\mathrm{d}^2W(\underline{d}_1, \bar{d}_1)}{\mathrm{d}\bar{\theta}^2} = \frac{(1 + \lambda - 2\nu)(1 + \lambda)}{(1 - \nu)V''(\bar{d}_1)}.$$

Similarly, when majority 2 decides, we have

$$W(\underline{d}_2, \bar{d}_2) = \frac{W^2(\underline{d}_2, \bar{d}_2)}{\alpha^*} + \left(1 - \frac{1}{\alpha^*}\right)\nu\Delta\theta(K - \bar{d}_2),$$

yielding

$$\frac{\mathrm{d}W(\underline{d}_2, \bar{d}_2)}{\mathrm{d}\bar{\theta}} = -\,(1 + \lambda - \nu)(K - \bar{d}_2) - \left(1 - \frac{1}{\alpha^*}\right)\nu\Delta\theta\,\frac{\mathrm{d}\bar{d}_2}{\mathrm{d}\bar{\theta}},$$

where, from (7.8),

$$\frac{\mathrm{d}\bar{d}_2}{\mathrm{d}\bar{\theta}} = \frac{1 + \lambda - \nu/\alpha^*}{(1 - \nu)V''(\bar{d}_2)}$$

and therefore

$$\frac{\mathrm{d}^2 W(\underline{d}_2, \bar{d}_2)}{\mathrm{d}\bar{\theta}^2} = \frac{(1 + \lambda - \nu/\alpha^*)}{(1 - \nu)V''(\bar{d}_2)}\left(1 + \lambda + \frac{\nu}{\alpha^*} - 2\nu\right).$$

Hence the expected second derivative at $\bar{\theta} = \underline{\theta}$ (implying that $\bar{d}_1 = \underline{d}_1 = (1 + \lambda)\underline{\theta}$) in the case of the DIM (assuming that each majority is in power half the time) is given by

$$\left.\frac{\mathrm{d}^2 E_{\lambda\alpha} W(\underline{d}, \bar{d})}{\mathrm{d}\bar{\theta}^2}\right|_{\bar{\theta}=\underline{\theta}} = \frac{\nu^2\left(\frac{\alpha^* - \frac{1}{2}}{\alpha^{*2}}\right) + 1 - 2\nu + 2(1 - \nu)E\lambda + (E\lambda)^2 + \operatorname{var}(\lambda)}{(1 - \nu)V''(d^0)}, \tag{7.34}$$

where $V'(d^0) = (1 + \lambda)\underline{\theta}$.

Consider now the DPM scheme where the political majorities are restricted to choosing a single abatement level as a function of λ. We obtain from (7.11) and (7.12)

$$\left.\frac{\mathrm{d}d_1}{\mathrm{d}\bar{\theta}}\right|_{\bar{\theta}=\underline{\theta}} = \frac{1 + \lambda}{V''(d^0)}$$

and

$$\left.\frac{\mathrm{d}d_2}{\mathrm{d}\bar{\theta}}\right|_{\bar{\theta}=\underline{\theta}} = \frac{1 + \lambda - \frac{\nu}{\alpha^*}}{V''(d^0)}$$

The social welfare, when majority 1 is in power, is given by

$$W(d_1) = \frac{W^1(d_1)}{\alpha^*} + \nu\Delta\theta(K - d_1)$$

and, similarly, the social welfare, when majority 2 is in power, is given by

$$W(d_2) = \frac{W^2(d_2)}{a^*} + \left(1 - \frac{1}{a^*}\right)\nu\Delta\theta(K - d_2).$$

Hence,

$$\frac{\mathrm{d}W(d_1)}{\mathrm{d}\bar{\theta}} = -(1 + \lambda - \nu)(K - d_1) - \nu\Delta\theta\frac{\mathrm{d}d_1}{\mathrm{d}\bar{\theta}}$$

and

$$\frac{\mathrm{d}W(d_2)}{\mathrm{d}\bar{\theta}} = -(1 + \lambda - \nu)(K - d_2) - \left(1 - \frac{1}{a^*}\right)\nu\Delta\theta\frac{\mathrm{d}d_2}{\mathrm{d}\bar{\theta}}.$$

We therefore obtain

$$\left.\frac{\mathrm{d}^2W(d_1)}{\mathrm{d}\bar{\theta}^2}\right|_{\bar{\theta}=\underline{\theta}} = (1 + \lambda - 2\nu)\frac{(1 + \lambda)}{V''(d^0)}$$

and

$$\left.\frac{\mathrm{d}^2W(d_2)}{\mathrm{d}\bar{\theta}^2}\right|_{\bar{\theta}=\underline{\theta}} = \left(1 + \lambda + \frac{\nu}{a^*} - 2\nu\right)\frac{\left(1 + \lambda - \frac{\nu}{a^*}\right)}{V''(d^0)}.$$

Hence the expected second derivative at $\bar{\theta} = \underline{\theta}$ in the case of a DPM scheme (assuming again that each majority is in power half the time) is given by

$$\left.\frac{\mathrm{d}^2E_{\lambda a}W(d)}{\mathrm{d}\bar{\theta}^2}\right|_{\bar{\theta}=\underline{\theta}} = \frac{\nu^2\left(\frac{a^* - \frac{1}{2}}{a^{*2}}\right) + 1 - 2\nu + 2(1 - \nu)E\lambda + (E\lambda)^2 + \mathrm{var}(\lambda)}{V''(d^0)}$$

Therefore, the second derivative of the expected social welfare under the DPM scheme is $(1 - \nu)$ times the second derivative of the expected social welfare under the DIM scheme as given by (7.34). These derivatives are of the sign of the numerator, which is positive iff (7.14) holds. If $\mathrm{var}(\lambda) > H(\cdot)$, the DIM dominates the DPM for $\bar{\theta}$ close to $\underline{\theta}$ and vice versa if $\mathrm{var}(\lambda) < H(\cdot)$.

A.7.2 Proof of Proposition 7.2

We want to compare the expected welfare of each majority under a DPM imposed by the Constitution and under a DIM to determine the eagerness of each majority to support the latter constitutional rule. So we want to compare

$$E_{\lambda a} W^1(d) - E_{\lambda a} W^1(\underline{d}, \bar{d})$$

and

$$E_{\lambda a} W^2(d) - E_{\lambda a} W^2(\underline{d}, \bar{d})$$

for $\bar{\theta}$ close to $\underline{\theta}$. First note that both differences and their first derivatives with respect to $\bar{\theta}$ vanish at $\Delta\theta = 0$. So we consider second derivatives. Straightforward computations (the proof follows steps similar to those in the proof of Proposition 7.1) lead to

$$E_{\lambda a} \frac{\partial^2 W^1(d)/a^*}{\partial \bar{\theta}^2} - E_{\lambda a} \frac{\partial^2 W^1(\underline{d}, \bar{d})/a^*}{\partial \bar{\theta}^2} > 0 \text{ if and only if } \mathrm{var}(\lambda) > H^1(v, a^*, E\lambda)$$

and, similarly,

$$E_{\lambda a} \frac{\partial^2 W^2(d)/a^*}{\partial \bar{\theta}^2} - E_{\lambda a} \frac{\partial^2 W^2(\underline{d}, \bar{d})/a^*}{\partial \bar{\theta}^2} > 0 \text{ if and only if } \mathrm{var}(\lambda) > H^2(v, a^*, E\lambda).$$

Part III

Coalition Formation and Constitutional Design

'Recently David Easton has offered a definition that combines all these and, besides, fits politics into the general scheme of social sciences. Politics, he said, is the authoritative allocation of value . . .'

Riker (1962), p. 10.

'the greater part of the study of the authoritative allocation of value is reduced to the study of coalitions'.

Riker (1962), p. 12.

8

Optimal Constitutional Response to Coalition Formation

'It does *not* follow, because all of the individuals in a group would gain if they achieved their group objective, that they would act to achieve that objective, even if they were all rational and self interested.'

M. Olson (1965), p. 2.

8.1 Introduction

Politics is about collective decision making. To understand how interest groups form to influence the political process of collective decision making, one must understand the nature of the transaction costs affecting coalition formation. Olson (1965) has argued that small groups have lower per capita transaction costs for example, and this argument is often used to explain why taxpayers often do not form an interest group while managers of an industry do. To model Olson's intuition we need a theory which makes these transaction costs endogenous, contrary to the modeling of Chapters 2 to 5. We believe that asymmetric information between agents who want to enter collusive agreements is one major force explaining the transaction costs within coalitions.[1] In this chapter we explain a methodology[2] to write group incentive

[1] In his study of political coalitions using cooperative game theory, Riker (1962), p. 77, also insists on the role of uncertainty but in a different direction: 'The uncertainty of the real world and the bargaining situation forces coalition members to aim at a subjectively estimated minimum winning coalition rather than at an actual minimum. In decision-systems large enough so that participants do not know each other or what each is doing, the actual size and weight of a coalition may be in doubt, if only because of lack of communication and because of participants' inability to estimate each others' weights.'

[2] This methodology was first developed in Laffont and Martimort (1997) and (1999).

constraints when colluding partners have private information. It provides an important step toward a systematic analysis of group incentives in organizations such as governments and a framework to model Olson's ideas.[3]

The literature on collusion in collective decision mechanisms started with Green and Laffont (1979), who proved that Groves' mechanisms (which are individually incentive compatible) are not robust to the formation of coalitions when agents freely share their private information. Also, with dominant strategy mechanisms for which agents communicate only their own private information, Laffont and Maskin (1980) have shown that, with a continuum of types, only pooling decision rules can be implemented. Crémer (1996) shows that, even if one takes into account asymmetric information within coalitions, Groves' mechanisms are not collusion-proof.

Maskin (1999) obtained very positive results for Nash implementation (i.e. under complete information of the agents), even with no restriction on agents' characteristics, by showing that any monotonic social-choice rule satisfying no veto power was implementable in Nash equilibria. In the same environments and with at least three alternatives, Maskin (1979) showed that any social-choice rule satisfying no veto power is not robust to collusion (i.e. is not implementable in strong Nash equilibria).

In this chapter we will study, in a Bayesian setting,[4] horizontal collusion between two interest groups which try to manipulate collective decision making defined by constitutional rules.

In Section 8.2 we present the model which allows for correlation of the private pieces of information for the two interest groups. When the interest groups do not collude, their Bayesian-Nash-maximizing behavior in mechanisms proposed by the constitutional level does not put any restriction on the set of interim individually rational allocations that can be achieved by the Constitution whatever the (non-zero) degree of correlation ρ. Under Bayesian implementation, the flexibility of available mon-

[3] However, in this book we will not formalize the dependence of transaction costs on the number of members in an interest group.

[4] See Laffont and Maskin (1979) for preliminary work on collusion with Bayesian Nash behavior.

etary transfers enables the Constitution to obtain information revelation at no cost. Efficiency does not conflict with incentives. A discontinuity then holds at a correlation coefficient of zero. We know that in this 'independent' case the principal cannot reach the complete information optimum, whereas he can do it for any degree of non-zero correlation. Section 8.2 explains within our model this result due to Crémer–McLean (1988) in the context of auction mechanisms.

Section 8.3 discusses the various issues raised by the modeling of collusion with soft information and justifies the choices made in our analysis. Section 8.4 deals with the case when interest groups can costlessly share their private information, and provides a precise framework where the characterization of the additional incentive constraints due to collusion follows the tradition of Green and Laffont (1979) and others. It follows that the complete-information optimum can no longer be reached as the collusion-proof constraints prevent the use of Crémer–McLean mechanisms. When the degree of correlation becomes small, this restores the continuity of the optimal mechanism at $\rho = 0$ and calls for distortions even when correlation becomes perfect. A second lesson from this section is that the usual approach implicitly restricts the mechanisms used by the principal to mechanisms for the revelation of only the (original) private information of the agents (before joint disclosure). Section 8.5 considers more general mechanisms which elicit the information obtained by agents after their joint disclosure of private information. Then, the complete information optimum can in general be reached.

In Section 8.6 we model collusion under incomplete information, provide a collusion-proof principle with soft information, characterize the collusion-proof constraints and the optimal constitutional mechanism. Again, this optimal mechanism restores continuity at $\rho = 0$ through the working of collusion-proof constraints. Furthermore, when correlation becomes perfect, the principal approaches the efficient allocation contrary to what is obtained in Section 8.4. It shows the crucial role of the transaction costs inside the coalition due to asymmetric information. As correlation becomes perfect, these transaction costs turn out to be so effective that collusion-proof constraints become slack. Section 8.7 concludes by outlining the numerous directions for further research revealed by the analysis of this chapter.

8.2 The Model

We now consider an extension of Chapter 2 with a benevolent Constitution or *principal* and two politicians, suppliers of essential inputs necessary to perform a two-stage production process. Each politician is fully integrated or captured by the firm he controls. We will refer to the politician–firm pairs as the agents for simplicity. When the Constitution wants to produce a quantity q of a final good, agent 1 produces a quantity q_1 of an intermediate good (good 1) which is used by agent 2 to produce a quantity q_2 of a final good (good 2). The production technologies are Leontieff and one-to-one, and we denote $q = q_1 = q_2$.

Each agent has private information about his constant marginal cost θ_i. These marginal costs (θ_1, θ_2) are drawn from a joint common knowledge distribution with discrete support $\Theta = \{\underline{\theta}, \bar{\theta}\}$, with $\Delta\theta = \bar{\theta} - \underline{\theta} > 0$, and we denote

$$\begin{aligned} p_{11} &= \Pr(\theta_1 = \underline{\theta} \text{ and } \theta_2 = \underline{\theta}) \\ p_{12} &= \Pr(\theta_1 = \underline{\theta} \text{ and } \theta_2 = \bar{\theta}) \\ p_{21} &= \Pr(\theta_1 = \bar{\theta} \text{ and } \theta_2 = \underline{\theta}) \\ p_{22} &= \Pr(\theta_1 = \bar{\theta} \text{ and } \theta_2 = \bar{\theta}). \end{aligned}$$

Let $\rho = p_{11}p_{22} - p_{12}p_{21}$ be the measure of correlation which is assumed to be non-negative. For simplicity, we restrict the analysis to the symmetric case where $p_{12} = p_{21} \neq 0$.

As usual, we denote the utility of agent i by

$$U_i = t_i - \theta_i q, \quad \mathrm{i} = 1, 2,$$

where t_i is the monetary transfer received from the constitutional level.

Social welfare is given by

$$W = S(q) - (1 + \lambda)(t_1 + t_2) + U_1 + U_2 = S(q) - (\theta_1 + \theta_2)\, q - \lambda t_1 - \lambda t_2.$$

We adopt the following notation: the index 1 refers to an efficient type and the index 2 to an inefficient type. Then t_{ij} is the transfer received by a type-i agent when the other agent is of type j; q_{ij} is the production level with a type-i agent and a type-j agent.

The complete-information social optimum is characterized by

$$\begin{aligned} S'(q_{11}^*) &= 2(1 + \lambda)\underline{\theta} \\ S'(q_{12}^*) &= S'(q_{21}^*) = (1 + \lambda)(\underline{\theta} + \bar{\theta}) \end{aligned}$$

$$S'(q_{22}^*) = 2(1 + \lambda)\bar{\theta}$$

$$t_{11}^* = \underline{\theta} q_{11}^*, \quad t_{12}^* = \underline{\theta} q_{12}^*, \quad t_{21}^* = \bar{\theta} q_{21}^*, \quad t_{22}^* = \bar{\theta} q_{22}^*.$$

Note that $t_{12}^* \neq t_{21}^*$ even though $q_{12}^* = q_{21}^*$. The transfer t_{12}^* (resp. t_{21}^*) is received by the efficient (resp. inefficient) agent when there is a pair of efficient and inefficient agents.

Under asymmetric information about the production characteristics (θ_1, θ_2), the Constitution can exploit the correlation of types to design a mechanism with yardstick competition which extracts all the agents' information rents and achieves the complete information optimum. Below, we characterize the transfers which implement this solution.

From the revelation principle, we can restrict the analysis to revelation mechanisms which are truthful and interim individually rational in the Bayesian sense. Using symmetry, a revelation mechanism is defined by

$$t_{11}, q_{11}; \quad t_{12}, t_{21}, q_{12} = q_{21}; \quad t_{22}, q_{22}.$$

First we write the incentive constraints. For a $\underline{\theta}$-agent, it must be the case that he prefers to tell the truth rather than lying when he anticipates that the other agent is telling the truth, i.e.

$$\frac{p_{11}}{p_{11} + p_{12}} (t_{11} - \underline{\theta} q_{11}) + \frac{p_{12}}{p_{11} + p_{12}} (t_{12} - \underline{\theta} q_{12})$$

$$\geq \frac{p_{11}}{p_{11} + p_{12}} (t_{21} - \underline{\theta} q_{21}) + \frac{p_{12}}{p_{11} + p_{12}} (t_{22} - \underline{\theta} q_{22}). \tag{8.1}$$

Indeed, $\frac{p_{11}}{p_{11} + p_{12}}$ (resp. $\frac{p_{12}}{p_{11} + p_{12}}$) is his belief that the other agent is of type $\underline{\theta}$ (resp. of type $\bar{\theta}$) when he is himself of type $\underline{\theta}$. Multiplying by $(p_{11} + p_{12})$ we can rewrite (8.1) as

$$p_{11}(t_{11} - \underline{\theta} q_{11}) + p_{12}(t_{12} - \underline{\theta} q_{12}) \geq p_{11}(t_{21} - \underline{\theta} q_{21}) + p_{12}(t_{22} - \underline{\theta} q_{22}). \tag{8.2}$$

Similarly, we obtain for the incentive constraint of type $\bar{\theta}$ and the individual rationality constraints of type $\underline{\theta}$ and $\bar{\theta}$ respectively

$$p_{21}(t_{21} - \bar{\theta} q_{21}) + p_{22}(t_{22} - \bar{\theta} q_{22}) \geq p_{21}(t_{11} - \bar{\theta} q_{11}) + p_{22}(t_{12} - \bar{\theta} q_{12}) \tag{8.3}$$

$$p_{11}(t_{11} - \underline{\theta} q_{11}) + p_{12}(t_{12} - \underline{\theta} q_{12}) \geq 0 \tag{8.4}$$

$$p_{21}(t_{21} - \bar{\theta}q_{21}) + p_{22}(t_{22} - \bar{\theta}q_{22}) \geq 0. \tag{8.5}$$

The Constitution wishes to maximize expected social welfare under the constraints (8.2) to (8.5):

$$p_{11}[S(q_{11}) - 2\underline{\theta}q_{11} - 2\lambda t_{11}] + 2p_{12}[S(q_{12}) - (\underline{\theta} + \bar{\theta})q_{12} - \lambda(t_{12} + t_{21})] + p_{22}[S(q_{22}) - 2\bar{\theta}q_{22} - 2\lambda t_{22}]. \tag{8.6}$$

We obtain a special case of the Crémer–McLean (1988) theorem:[5]

PROPOSITION 8.1 For $\rho \neq 0$, the Constitution achieves the complete-information optimum.

PROOF: We can find transfers which saturate the four constraints, i.e., which satisfy incentive compatibility without leaving any expected rent at the interim stage to any agent. Indeed, for $\rho \neq 0$ the following system is invertible because the determinant is $-\rho^2$.

$$\begin{bmatrix} 0 & 0 & p_{11} & p_{12} \\ p_{21} & p_{22} & 0 & 0 \\ p_{11} & p_{12} & 0 & 0 \\ 0 & 0 & p_{21} & p_{22} \end{bmatrix} \begin{bmatrix} t_{11} \\ t_{12} \\ t_{21} \\ t_{22} \end{bmatrix} = \begin{bmatrix} \underline{\theta}(p_{11}q_{21} + p_{12}q_{22}) \\ \bar{\theta}(p_{21}q_{11} + p_{22}q_{12}) \\ \underline{\theta}(p_{11}q_{11} + p_{12}q_{12}) \\ \bar{\theta}(p_{21}q_{21} + p_{22}q_{22}) \end{bmatrix} \tag{8.7}$$

The transfers that implement the complete-information solution are obtained by solving (8.7) for $\rho \neq 0$.

$$\hat{t}_{11} = \frac{\underline{\theta}p_{22}(p_{11}q_{11} + p_{12}q_{12}) - \bar{\theta}p_{12}(p_{21}q_{11} + p_{22}q_{12})}{\rho}$$

$$\hat{t}_{12} = \frac{\bar{\theta}p_{11}(p_{21}q_{11} + p_{22}q_{12}) - \underline{\theta}p_{21}(p_{11}q_{11} + p_{12}q_{12})}{\rho}$$

$$\hat{t}_{21} = \frac{\underline{\theta}p_{22}(p_{11}q_{21} + p_{12}q_{22}) - \bar{\theta}p_{12}(p_{21}q_{21} + p_{22}q_{22})}{\rho}$$

$$\hat{t}_{22} = \frac{\bar{\theta}p_{11}(p_{21}q_{21} + p_{22}q_{22}) - \underline{\theta}p_{21}(p_{11}q_{21} + p_{12}q_{22})}{\rho}.$$

We observe that as p_{12} goes to zero, all *ex post* rents $u_{ij} = t_{ij} - \theta_i q_{ij}$ go to zero. With penalties and rewards which converge to zero, one can achieve the optimum.

[5] See also McAfee and Reny (1991) and Riordan and Sappington (1988).

Conversely, if ρ goes to zero, then t_{11} and t_{21} go to $-\infty$ and t_{12} and t_{22} go to $+\infty$.

It may not be surprising that when agents are very similar, it is relatively simple to extract their rents by yardstick competition. The more intriguing result is that the result remains true for any degree of correlation of types, even if it is infinitesimal. The mechanism exploits the risk neutrality of the agents by specifying extreme rewards and penalties. A $\underline{\theta}$-agent faces, when he tells the truth, an extreme reward if the other agent is a $\bar{\theta}$-agent and an extreme penalty if the other agent is a $\underline{\theta}$-agent. And similarly for a $\bar{\theta}$-agent. Those numbers can be arranged in such a way that he always wants to tell the truth.

The result raises two concerns. First, it is not realistic to think that unbounded penalties (or even unbounded rewards) can be implemented because of the limited resources of the agents (or the principal). Second, a striking discontinuity occurs at $\rho = 0$. Indeed, for independent types the Constitution cannot achieve the complete information optimum (while it can for any infinitesimal degree of correlation).

For the independent case, define

$$\nu = \Pr(\theta_1 = \underline{\theta}) = \Pr(\theta_2 = \underline{\theta}).$$

Then

$$p_{11} = \nu^2, \quad p_{12} = p_{21} = \nu(1 - \nu), \quad p_{22} = (1 - \nu)^2.$$

Following the methods of Chapter 2, we obtain the optimal mechanism characterized as follows:

$$S'(q_{11}^I) = 2(1 + \lambda)\underline{\theta}$$

$$S'(q_{12}^I) = (1 + \lambda)(\underline{\theta} + \bar{\theta}) + \lambda \frac{\nu}{1 - \nu} \Delta\theta$$

$$S'(q_{22}^I) = 2(1 + \lambda)\bar{\theta} + \frac{2\lambda\nu}{1 - \nu} \Delta\theta.$$

The Constitution gives up information rents to the $\underline{\theta}$-agents and, to decrease those rents, distorts production downward ($q_{12}^I < q_{12}^*$; $q_{22}^I < q_{22}^*$).

Continuity at $\rho = 0$ can be restored by imposing exogenous limited-liability constraints for the agents, where

$$t_{ij} \geq k \quad \text{for any} \quad i, j,$$

or limited resource constraints for the principal, where

$$t_{ij} \leq k \quad \text{for any} \quad i, j.$$

In this chapter, we will explore a different solution. The ability to extract all the rents from agents through yardstick competition is susceptible of triggering collusive behavior. The principal will have to take into account not only individual incentive constraints but also coalitional incentive constraints. A by-product of the analysis will be to restore the continuity of the optimal mechanism at $\rho = 0$.

8.3 *Modeling Collusion*

Modeling collusion requires a large number of choices. What is the timing of information flows and of contracting: do agents learn their private information before or after contracting with the principal or the ringmaster; do colluding partners contract with the ringmaster before or after contracting with the principal? Does collusion entail sharing information or not and, if it is possible to share information, does it happen also without collusion? Do the colluding parties have access to an uninformed third party, the ringmaster, to organize their collective response to the mechanism proposed by the Constitution, or does the offer of collusion come from an informed partner? Is the colluding contract binding, can it use monetary transfers or should it be self-enforcing because colluding contracts are illegal? Are there transaction costs in these illegal contracts?

In this chapter we will offer two examples of such modeling, bearing in mind that each particular problem requires careful attention to the details of this modeling.

In the two cases the timing will be as follows:

Agents obtain their private information	Constitution offers mechanism G	Agents accept or reject G	Agents share information or do not	An uninformed ringmaster offers a collusion contract S	$G \circ S$ is played

First, each agent i, $i = 1, 2$, learns his type θ_i. Then the Constitution (principal) offers a revelation mechanism[6] G that we write as $q(\tilde{\theta}_1, \tilde{\theta}_2)$, $t_1(\tilde{\theta}_1, \tilde{\theta}_2)$, $t_2(\tilde{\theta}_1, \tilde{\theta}_2)$, where $\tilde{\theta}_1$ and $\tilde{\theta}_2$ are the announcements of agent 1 and agent 2 respectively. If one agent rejects G, the game stops and all players get a payoff of zero. If both agents accept G, we will consider two cases: in the first, we assume that agents have a technology enabling them to share their private information; in the second case this step does not exist. Then, an uninformed third party offers to agents a collusive contract S which entails a manipulation of reports and side transfers maximizing the expected sum of utilities of the agents under incentive constraints and individual rationality constraints ensuring to agents at least as much as what they obtain by non-cooperatively playing G. If one agent rejects S, G is played non-cooperatively. Otherwise $G \circ S$ is played.

The most debatable assumption here is the access to a ringmaster who can enforce a contract. Using an uninformed third party as a ringmaster weakens the power of a coalition when agents share their private information, because the informed parties could commit to an informational alliance which eliminates the individual incentive constraints. On the contrary, when the colluding partners are uninformed about each other, the use of an uninformed party avoids informed-principal inefficiencies and increases the power of the coalition. What is more problematic in all these cases is that a binding contract is postulated, despite the fact that it is illegal. Either one must appeal to a third party like the Mafia or to reputation, in which case it should be viewed as a shortcut to a truly dynamic analysis.

The main virtue of our modeling is to allow for a collusion-proof principle which, as the revelation principle, leads to a characterization of implementable allocations and therefore of the optimal constitutional response to individual and group incentives.

[6] One can show (Laffont and Martimort (1999)) that, in the case of no sharing of information between agents, there is no gain to expect from a more general mechanism (see also Section 8.5). However, we assume that G cannot be conditional on an announcement by the agents of the collusion contract S because agents coordinate their response to G. Implicitly, the ringmaster is assumed to be always able to undo mechanisms designed for inducing agents to reveal their common information S.

8.4 Collusion under Complete Information

For a given mechanism G, $(q(\cdot), t_1(\cdot), t_2(\cdot))$, the ringmaster offers the manipulation of reports $\phi(\theta_1, \theta_2)$ and side transfers $y_1(\theta_1, \theta_2)$, $y_2(\theta_1, \theta_2)$ which maximize the expected sum of the agents' utilities under the incentive, individual rationality and balanced transfers constraints.[7] Since agents share their private information, the constraints are written under complete information, so that the ringmaster's program can be decomposed in a maximization program for each profile (θ_1, θ_2).

$$\text{(I)} \quad \max_{\phi(.), y_1(.), y_2(.)} t_1(\phi(\theta_1, \theta_2)) + t_2(\phi(\theta_1, \theta_2)) - (\theta_1 + \theta_2)\, q(\phi(\theta_1, \theta_2))$$

s.t.

$$y_1(\theta_1, \theta_2) + y_2(\theta_1, \theta_2) = 0 \tag{8.8}$$

$$\begin{aligned} & t_1(\phi(\theta_1, \theta_2)) - \theta_1 q(\phi(\theta_1, \theta_2)) + y_1(\theta_1, \theta_2) \\ & \geq t_1(\phi(\tilde{\theta}_1, \theta_2)) - \theta_1 q(\phi(\tilde{\theta}_1, \theta_2)) + y_1(\tilde{\theta}_1, \theta_2) \text{ for } \tilde{\theta}_1 \neq \theta_1 \end{aligned} \tag{8.9}$$

$$\begin{aligned} & t_2(\phi(\theta_1, \theta_2)) - \theta_2 q(\phi(\theta_1, \theta_2)) + y_2(\theta_1, \theta_2) \\ & \geq t_2(\phi(\theta_1, \tilde{\theta}_2)) - \theta_2\, q(\phi(\theta_1, \tilde{\theta}_2)) + y_2(\theta_1, \tilde{\theta}_2) \text{ for } \tilde{\theta}_2 \neq \theta_2 \end{aligned} \tag{8.10}$$

$$t_1(\phi(\theta_1, \theta_2)) - \theta_1 q(\phi(\theta_1, \theta_2)) + y_1(\theta_1, \theta_2) \geq U_1^G(\theta_1, \theta_2) \tag{8.11}$$

$$t_2(\phi(\theta_1, \theta_2)) - \theta_2 q(\phi(\theta_1, \theta_2)) + y_2(\theta_1, \theta_2) \geq U_2^G(\theta_1, \theta_2) \tag{8.12}$$

where $U_i^G(\theta_1, \theta_2)$ denotes the utility of agent i when G is played non-cooperatively under complete information.

Note that here the restriction to revelation mechanisms for the principal and the third party is a strong restriction, because both know that the agents are informed and could use Maskin games asking each agent to reveal all his information (θ_1, θ_2). We explore these more general mechanisms in Section 8.5.

Under the above restrictions, one immediately obtains a generalization of the revelation principle.

> PROPOSITION 8.2 The collusion-proof principle: any Bayesian perfect equilibrium of the two-stage game of contract offer and collusion contract offer, $G \circ S$, can be achieved by a truth-

[7] Through this assumption we consider the case most favorable to collusive behavior organized by an uninformed third party.

telling revelation mechanism offered by the principal such that the best response of the third party is to offer no manipulation of reports and no side transfers.

PROOF: Consider $\tilde{G} = G \circ S$ for the optimal collusion contract S offered by the third party when the principal offers G. Then, $\tilde{G}$ is a truth-telling revelation mechanism such that the null-collusion contract (no manipulation of reports; no side transfers) is the best response of the third party. Suppose it is not the case. $\tilde{G}$ is truth-telling by construction. Suppose then that the third party can offer a new contract $\tilde{S}$ which is better for the coalition for at least some profile (θ_1, θ_2). But then $\tilde{S} \circ S$ is better than S for the coalition, a contradiction of the optimality of S.

It remains to write the implications that $\phi(\cdot) = i(\cdot)$; $y_1 = y_2 = 0$ is the optimal contract offer in (I) to describe the collusion-proof constraints.

PROPOSITION 8.3 A revelation mechanism G is collusion-proof if and only if

$$\begin{aligned}
2(t_{11} - \underline{\theta} q_{11}) &\geq t_{12} + t_{21} - 2\underline{\theta} q_{12} \\
&\geq 2(t_{22} - \underline{\theta} q_{22}) \\
t_{12} + t_{21} - (\underline{\theta} + \bar{\theta}) q_{12} &\geq 2t_{22} - (\underline{\theta} + \bar{\theta}) q_{22} \\
&\geq 2t_{11} - (\underline{\theta} + \bar{\theta}) q_{11} \\
2(t_{22} - \bar{\theta} q_{22}) &\geq t_{12} + t_{21} - 2\bar{\theta} q_{12} \\
&\geq 2(t_{11} - \bar{\theta} q_{11}).
\end{aligned}$$

PROOF: Call $\zeta, \delta_1, \delta_2, \nu_1, \nu_2$ the multipliers of (8.8), (8.9), (8.10), (8.11), (8.12) respectively in (I).

Maximizing with respect to $y_1(\theta_1, \theta_2)$ and $y_2(\theta_1, \theta_2)$ gives

$$\zeta + \delta_1 + \nu_1 = 0 = \zeta + \delta_2 + \nu_2 \text{ or } \delta_1 + \nu_1 = \delta_2 + \nu_2 \equiv \delta + \nu.$$

Maximizing with respect to $\phi(\theta_1, \theta_2)$ gives

$$\begin{aligned}
\phi(\theta_1, \theta_2) \in \arg\max_{\tilde{\phi}} \{ & t_1(\tilde{\phi}) + t_2(\tilde{\phi}) - (\theta_1 + \theta_2)\, q(\tilde{\phi}) \\
& + \delta_1(t_1(\tilde{\phi}) - \theta_1 q(\tilde{\phi})) + \delta_2(t_2(\tilde{\phi}) - \theta_2 q(\tilde{\phi})) \\
& + \nu_1(t_1(\tilde{\phi}) - \theta_1 q(\tilde{\phi})) + \nu_2(t_2(\tilde{\phi}) - \theta_2 q(\tilde{\phi}))\}
\end{aligned}$$

or

$$\phi(\theta_1, \theta_2) \in \arg\max_{\tilde{\phi}} (1 + \delta + \nu)[t_1(\tilde{\phi}) + t_2(\tilde{\phi}) - (\theta_1 + \theta_2)\, q(\tilde{\phi})].$$

Hence the result.

It is as if the incentive constraints of the agents were not binding for the third party and the collusion-proof constraints are identical to the incentive constraints of a merger of the two agents. However, individual incentive constraints remain in the principal's problem since an agent could reject the null side-contract offered by the third party and deviate if the contract offered by the principal was not truth-telling.[8]

Substituting these transfers into the principal's objective function (8.6), we maximize with respect to quantities and we get:

PROPOSITION 8.4 The optimal collusion-proof Constitution is characterized by

$$S'(q_{11}) = 2(1 + \lambda)\,\underline{\theta}$$

$$S'(q_{12}) = (1 + \lambda)(\underline{\theta} + \bar{\theta}) + \lambda\Delta\theta\,\frac{p_{11}}{p_{12}}$$

$$S'(q_{22}) = 2(1 + \lambda)\,\bar{\theta} + 2\lambda\Delta\theta\,\frac{p_{12}}{p_{22}}.$$

With collusion under complete information, the principal cannot achieve the complete information allocation and gives up an expected rent to the efficient type. He gets less than if he was facing a single agent with three states of nature: $2\underline{\theta}$, $\underline{\theta} + \bar{\theta}$, and $2\bar{\theta}$. In the last case the distortions would be

$$S'(q_{12}) = (1 + \lambda)(\underline{\theta} + \bar{\theta}) \quad + \frac{1}{2}\lambda\Delta\theta\,\frac{p_{11}}{p_{12}}$$

$$S'(q_{22}) = 2(1 + \lambda)\bar{\theta} + \frac{2p_{12} + p_{11}}{p_{22}}\,\lambda\Delta\theta.$$

For the timing we have chosen, we must take into account interim individual rationality constraints (because agents accept G before sharing information) and *ex post* individual and collective incentive constraints. As usual, we can expect the inefficient type's participation constraint and the upward incentive constraints to be binding, i.e.

[8] Writing dominant-strategy individual and collective incentive constraints is the approach followed by Green and Laffont (1979).

$$t_{11} - \underline{\theta}q_{11} = t_{21} - \underline{\theta}q_{12} \tag{8.13}$$

$$t_{12} + t_{21} - (\underline{\theta}+\bar{\theta})q_{12} = 2t_{22} - (\underline{\theta}+\bar{\theta})q_{22} \tag{8.14}$$

$$t_{12} - \underline{\theta}q_{12} = t_{22} - \underline{\theta}q_{22} \tag{8.15}$$

$$p_{21}(t_{21} - \bar{\theta}q_{21}) + p_{22}(t_{22} - \bar{\theta}q_{22}) = 0. \tag{8.16}$$

From (8.13) to (8.16) we obtain

$$t_{11} = \underline{\theta}q_{11} + \Delta\theta q_{12} \tag{8.17}$$

$$t_{21} = \bar{\theta}q_{12} \tag{8.18}$$

$$t_{22} = \bar{\theta}q_{22} \tag{8.19}$$

$$t_{12} = \underline{\theta}q_{12} + \Delta\theta q_{22}. \tag{8.20}$$

When the correlation goes to zero and ρ goes to zero, with the notation of Section 8.2

$$\frac{p_{11}}{p_{12}} \text{ and } \frac{p_{21}}{p_{22}} \text{ go to } \frac{\nu}{1-\nu}$$

and

$$S'(q_{12}) = (1 + \lambda)(\bar{\theta} + \underline{\theta}) + \lambda\Delta\theta\frac{\nu}{1-\nu}$$

$$S'(q_{22}) = 2(1 + \lambda)\bar{\theta} + 2\lambda\Delta\theta\frac{\nu}{1-\nu},$$

i.e. we restore the continuity at $\rho = 0$ of the optimal mechanism without any exogenous assumption of limited liability. It is easy to see why collusion-proof constraints prevent the use of the Crémer–McLean mechanisms when ρ goes to zero. One of the collusion-proof constraints is

$$2(t_{11} - \underline{\theta}q_{11}) \geq 2(t_{22} - \underline{\theta}q_{12}). \tag{8.21}$$

As ρ goes to zero, we saw that, in a Crémer–McLean mechanism, t_{11} goes to $-\infty$ and t_{22} to $+\infty$, clearly violating (8.21).

8.5 Collusion under Complete Information with Extended Mechanisms

Since agents are able to share their private information, the principal and the ringmaster can use more general mechanisms than the ones used in Section 8.4, in which the agents are asked to reveal both their own private information and the private information of the other agent. Actually, the revelation principle applies for these message spaces (see Repullo (1986), Moore (1992)) and we can proceed with revelation mechanisms.

Let $m_1 = (\tilde{\theta}_1^1, \tilde{\theta}_2^1)$ and $m_2 = (\tilde{\theta}_1^2, \tilde{\theta}_2^2)$ be the messages of agents 1 and 2 respectively.

The third party easily avoids conflicting reports m_1 and m_2 with sufficiently large penalties and is left with the incentive constraints of the merger of the two agents. Hence, the same collusion-proof constraints as in Proposition 8.3 should be used.

The major difference with the previous section is that the principal can also avoid conflicting reports in the same way and consequently individual incentive constraints vanish. We are left with the collusion-proof incentive constraints and the interim Bayesian participation contraints since agents accept G before sharing information.

The relevant constraints are the upward collusion-proof constraints and the participation constraints:

$$2(t_{11} - \underline{\theta}q_{11}) \geq t_{12} + t_{21} - 2\underline{\theta}q_{12} \qquad (8.22)$$

$$t_{12} + t_{21} - (\underline{\theta} + \bar{\theta})q_{12} \geq 2t_{22} - (\underline{\theta} + \bar{\theta})q_{22} \qquad (8.23)$$

$$p_{11}(t_{11} - \underline{\theta}q_{11}) + p_{12}(t_{12} - \underline{\theta}q_{12}) \geq 0 \qquad (8.24)$$

$$p_{21}(t_{21} - \bar{\theta}q_{21}) + p_{22}(t_{22} - \bar{\theta}q_{22}) \geq 0. \qquad (8.25)$$

Hence:

PROPOSITION 8.5 If $p_{12} \neq 0$ the optimal collusion-proof extended mechanism achieves the complete-information optimum.

PROOF: If $p_{12} \neq 0$, the system (8.22) to (8.25) is invertible. Transfers which leave no rent to the agents can be found.

Consequently, there is no reason to distort the production decisions.

Note that a discontinuity now exists at $p_{12} = 0$. Indeed, if $p_{12} = 0$, agents are fully informed when they accept the mechanism G. The relevant constraints are then

$$t_{11} - \underline{\theta} q_{11} \geq t_{22} - \underline{\theta} q_{22}$$
$$t_{22} - \bar{\theta} q_{22} \geq 0,$$

and it is as if the principal was facing a single agent. The above mechanism exploits the fact that, at the time they accept G, agents do not know the type of their future colluding partner. The uncertainty remains as long as $p_{12} \neq 0$, but not in the limit for $p_{12} = 0$.

8.6 Collusion under Incomplete Information

The analysis of this section recognizes a major friction in coalition formation, namely that colluding partners often cannot reliably share their private information. This will create a possible transaction cost in the formation of the coalition as the individual incentive constraints may become binding. We continue to assume that the principal cannot offer contracts conditional on the collusive contracts since we assume that the ringmaster can always coordinate agents' responses to undo this type of contract.

The principal now offers a mechanism G which maps messages $m = (m_1, m_2) \in M_1 \times M_2$ into quantities and transfers $q(m)$, $t_1(m)$, $t_2(m)$.

The ringmaster offers agents a revelation mechanism[9] which entails a manipulation of reports $\phi(\theta_1, \theta_2)$ and side transfers $y_1(\theta_1, \theta_2)$, $y_2(\theta_1, \theta_2)$ and which must be interim incentive compatible, interim individually rational and balanced, i.e.

$$y_1(\theta_1, \theta_2) + y_2(\theta_1, \theta_2) = 0 \text{ for any } (\theta_1, \theta_2).$$

[9] This is used here without loss of generality, since we can apply the revelation principle at the last stage of the game.

Let us denote

$$\phi_{11} = \phi(\underline{\theta}, \underline{\theta}); \ \phi_{12} = \phi(\underline{\theta}, \bar{\theta}); \ \phi_{21} = \phi(\bar{\theta}, \underline{\theta}); \ \phi_{22} = \phi(\bar{\theta}, \bar{\theta}).$$

The interim incentive constraints of $\underline{\theta}$-agents[10] are written as

$$\begin{aligned} p_{11}[t_1(\phi_{11}) + y_1(\underline{\theta}, \underline{\theta}) - \underline{\theta}q(\phi_{11})] + p_{12}[t_1(\phi_{12}) + y_1(\underline{\theta}, \bar{\theta}) - \underline{\theta}q(\phi_{12})] \\ \geq p_{11}[t_1(\phi_{21}) + y_1(\bar{\theta}, \underline{\theta}) - \underline{\theta}q(\phi_{21})] \\ + p_{12}[t_1(\phi_{22}) + y_1(\bar{\theta}, \bar{\theta}) - \underline{\theta}q(\phi_{22})] \end{aligned} \quad (8.27)$$

$$\begin{aligned} p_{11}[t_2(\phi_{11}) + y_2(\underline{\theta}, \underline{\theta}) - \underline{\theta}q(\phi_{11})] + p_{12}[t_2(\phi_{21}) + y_2(\bar{\theta}, \underline{\theta}) - \underline{\theta}q(\phi_{21})] \\ \geq p_{11}[t_2(\phi_{12}) + y_2(\underline{\theta}, \bar{\theta}) - \underline{\theta}q(\phi_{12})] \\ + p_{12}[t_2(\phi_{22}) + y_2(\bar{\theta}, \bar{\theta}) - \underline{\theta}q(\phi_{22})]. \end{aligned} \quad (8.28)$$

If agents refuse the collusive contract S, they play G non-cooperatively[11] and obtain an expected utility $U_i^G(\theta_i)$.

The interim individual rationality constraints of $\underline{\theta}$-agents and $\bar{\theta}$-agents are written as

$$p_{11}[t_1(\phi_{11}) + y_1(\underline{\theta}, \underline{\theta}) - \underline{\theta}q(\phi_{11})] + p_{12}[t_1(\phi_{12}) + y_1(\underline{\theta}, \bar{\theta}) - \underline{\theta}q(\phi_{12})] \geq (p_{11} + p_{12})\, U_1^G(\underline{\theta}) \quad (8.29)$$

$$p_{11}[t_2(\phi_{11}) + y_2(\underline{\theta}, \underline{\theta}) - \underline{\theta}q(\phi_{11})] + p_{12}[t_2(\phi_{21}) + y_2(\bar{\theta}, \underline{\theta}) - \underline{\theta}q(\phi_{21})] \geq (p_{11} + p_{12})\, U_2^G(\underline{\theta}) \quad (8.30)$$

$$p_{21}[t_1(\phi_{21}) + y_1(\bar{\theta}, \underline{\theta}) - \bar{\theta}q(\phi_{21})] + p_{22}[t_1(\phi_{22}) + y_1(\bar{\theta}, \bar{\theta}) - \bar{\theta}q(\phi_{22})] \geq (p_{21} + p_{22})\, U_1^G(\bar{\theta}) \quad (8.31)$$

$$p_{12}[t_2(\phi_{12}) + y_2(\underline{\theta}, \bar{\theta}) - \bar{\theta}q(\phi_{12})] + p_{22}[t_2(\phi_{22}) + y_2(\bar{\theta}, \bar{\theta}) - \bar{\theta}q(\phi_{22})] \geq (p_{21} + p_{22})\, U_2^G(\bar{\theta}). \quad (8.32)$$

For any mechanism G: $q(\cdot)$, $t_1(\cdot)$, $t_2(\cdot)$ that the Constitution offers, the (uninformed) ringmaster offers the collusion contract S^* which maximizes the expected welfare of the agents under the above constraints, i.e. which solves

$$\text{(II)} \quad \max_{\substack{\phi_{ij} \\ i,j=1,2}} \sum_{ij} p_{ij}[t_1(\phi_{ij}) + t_2(\phi_{ij}) - (\theta_i + \theta_j)q(\phi_{ij})]$$

[10] The other incentive constraint can be neglected and we check *ex post* that it is satisfied.

[11] We assume here that, following the refusal of contract S, agents do not change their beliefs (see Laffont and Martimort (1999) for a discussion of other out-of-equilibrium beliefs and a more general analysis).

s.t. (8.26) to (8.32).

We can then follow the same reasoning as in Section 8.4. Establish a collusion-proof principle and characterize the collusion-proof constraints by the first-order conditions of the concave problem (II) in which we state that the null-collusion contract is the best contract that the third party can offer (see Appendix A.8.1 for details). We obtain:

PROPOSITION 8.6 A mechanism G is collusion-proof if there exists $\varepsilon \in [0,1)$ such that

$$2t_{11} - 2\theta q_{11} \geq t_1(\theta_1, \theta_2) + t_2(\theta_1, \theta_2) - 2\underline{\theta} q(\theta_1, \theta_2) \quad \text{for any } (\theta_1, \theta_2) \tag{8.33}$$

$$t_{12} + t_{21} - \left(\underline{\theta} + \bar{\theta} + \frac{p_{11}}{p_{12}}\varepsilon\Delta\theta\right)q_{12} \geq t_1(\theta_1, \theta_2) + t_2(\theta_1, \theta_2) - \left(\underline{\theta} + \bar{\theta} + \frac{p_{11}}{p_{12}}\varepsilon\Delta\theta\right)q(\theta_1, \theta_2) \quad \text{for any } (\theta_1, \theta_2) \tag{8.34}$$

$$2t_{22} - 2\left(\bar{\theta} + \Delta\theta\frac{p_{12}\varepsilon}{p_{22} + \frac{\rho\varepsilon}{p_{12}}}\right)q_{22} \geq t_1(\theta_1, \theta_2) + t_2(\theta_1, \theta_2) - 2\left(\bar{\theta} + \Delta\theta\frac{p_{12}\varepsilon}{p_{22} + \frac{\rho\varepsilon}{p_{12}}}\right)q(\theta_1, \theta_2) \quad \text{for any } (\theta_1, \theta_2) \tag{8.35}$$

The optimal mechanism G maximizes expected social welfare under the individual rationality and incentive constraints and under these group incentive constraints. The difficulty, as usual, is to guess which are the relevant constraints.

Note first that (8.33) and (8.34) imply the monotonicity condition

$$q_{11} \geq q_{12}. \tag{8.36}$$

Similarly, (8.34) and (8.35) imply

$$\psi(\varepsilon)(q_{12} - q_{22}) \geq 0, \tag{8.37}$$

with

$$\psi(\varepsilon) = 1 + 2\frac{p_{12}^2\varepsilon}{p_{12}p_{22} + \varepsilon(p_{11}p_{22} - p_{12}^2)} - \frac{p_{11}\varepsilon}{p_{12}}.$$

For ρ small, $\psi(\varepsilon)$ is positive for any ε in [0,1) and we have the usual monotonicity condition $q_{12} \geq q_{22}$. But, for ρ large $\psi(\varepsilon)$ may be negative for ε close to unity. As Proposition 8.5 shows, ε is a free variable in the principal's optimization problem. So (8.37) opens up the possibility of implementing production decisions with $q_{12} < q_{22}$, i.e. enables the principal to violate monotonicity. This new possibility created by Bayesian incentive compatibility, rather than the dominant-strategy incentive compatibility we met in the previous section, turns out to be very valuable for high correlation as we see below.

We distinguish the cases of low and high correlation.

Case 1: Low correlation.

We can expect the upward incentive constraint of the efficient type, the individual rationality constraint of the inefficient type and the upward group incentive constraints to be binding. Then, the optimization program of the principal can be written:

$$\max_{\substack{q_{ij}, t_{ij} \\ i,j=1,2}} p_{11}[S(q_{11}) - 2\underline{\theta} q_{11} - 2\lambda t_{11}] + 2p_{12}[S(q_{12}) - (\underline{\theta} + \bar{\theta})q_{12} - \lambda(t_{12} + t_{21})]$$
$$+ p_{22}[S(q_{22}) - 2\bar{\theta} q_{22} - 2\lambda t_{22}]$$

s.t.

$$p_{11}[t_{11} - \underline{\theta} q_{11}] + p_{12}[t_{12} - \underline{\theta} q_{12}] \geq p_{11}[t_{21} - \underline{\theta} q_{12}] + p_{12}[t_{22} - \underline{\theta} q_{22}] \quad (8.38)$$

$$2t_{11} - 2\underline{\theta} q_{11} \geq t_{12} + t_{21} - 2\underline{\theta} q_{12} \quad (8.39)$$

$$t_{21} + t_{12} - \left(\underline{\theta} + \bar{\theta} + \frac{p_{11}\,\varepsilon}{p_{12}}\Delta\theta\right) q_{12} \geq 2t_{22} - \left(\underline{\theta} + \bar{\theta} + \frac{p_{11}\,\varepsilon}{p_{12}}\Delta\theta\right) q_{22} \quad (8.40)$$

$$p_{12}[t_{21} - \bar{\theta} q_{12}] + p_{22}[t_{22} - \bar{\theta} q_{22}] \geq 0 \quad (8.41)$$

$$q_{11} \geq q_{12} \geq q_{22}. \quad (8.42)$$

Since $q_{22} \leq q_{12}$, $\varepsilon = 0$ is the best choice to weaken constraint (8.40). Solving for transfers, substituting in the objective function and maximizing with respect to quantities yields:

Proposition 8.7 For low correlation, the optimal Constitution is characterized by

$$S'(q_{11}) = 2(1 + \lambda)\underline{\theta}$$

$$S'(q_{12}) = (1 + \lambda)(\underline{\theta} + \bar{\theta}) + \frac{\lambda \Delta\theta p_{11}}{2p_{12}} \left(1 + \frac{p_{12}}{\rho + p_{12}}\right)$$

$$S'(q_{22}) = 2(1 + \lambda)\,\bar{\theta} + \frac{\lambda\Delta\theta}{p_{22}} \left(p_{11} + 2p_{12} - \frac{p_{12}p_{11}}{p_{12} + \rho}\right).$$

Note that, as ρ goes to zero,

$$S'(q_{12}) \text{ goes to } (1 + \lambda)(\underline{\theta} + \bar{\theta}) + \frac{\lambda\Delta\theta p_{11}}{p_{12}}$$

$$S'(q_{22}) \text{ goes to } 2(1 + \lambda)\,\bar{\theta} + \frac{2\lambda\Delta\theta p_{12}}{p_{22}},$$

i.e. we restore the continuity at $\rho = 0$ with the case of independent types since then

$$\frac{p_{11}}{p_{12}} = \frac{p_{12}}{p_{22}} = \frac{\nu}{1 - \nu}.$$

Again the collusion-proof constraints prevent the use of the Crémer–McLean mechanisms.

CASE 2: High correlation.

With high correlation, the principal can achieve a higher payoff than above by exploiting the (possible) non-monotonicity of production. When p_{12} is small, the probability of a pair of $(\underline{\theta}, \bar{\theta})$ agents is low and the principal can afford a low production level in this unlikely event. This enables him, by choosing ε=1, to weaken considerably the collusion-proof constraint (8.40) which becomes

$$t_{12} + t_{21} - \left(\underline{\theta} + \bar{\theta} + \frac{p_{11}\Delta\theta}{p_{12}}\right) q_{12} \geq 2t_{22} - \left(\underline{\theta} + \bar{\theta} + \frac{p_{11}}{p_{12}}\Delta\theta\right) q_{22}. \tag{8.43}$$

Since q_{12} is now very small, the collusion-proof constraint

$$2t_{11} - 2\underline{\theta}q_{11} \geq 2t_{22} - 2\underline{\theta}q_{22} \tag{8.44}$$

replaces (8.39).

Maximizing expected social welfare under the constraints (8.38), (8.44), (8.43), (8.41) and $q_{11} \geq q_{22} \geq q_{12}$, we now obtain:

PROPOSITION 8.8 For high correlation, the optimal Constitution is characterized by

$$S'(q_{11}) = 2(1 + \lambda)\underline{\theta}$$

$$S'(q_{12}) = (1 + \lambda)(\underline{\theta} + \bar{\theta}) + \lambda \frac{p_{11}}{p_{12}}.\Delta\theta$$

$$S'(q_{22}) = 2(1 + \lambda)\bar{\theta} + \frac{2\lambda p_{12}}{p_{22}} \Delta\theta.$$

Note that when p_{12} goes to zero, q_{12} goes to zero,[12] and q_{22} approaches the complete information optimum q_{22}^*.

So, as p_{12} goes to zero we approach in probability the complete-information optimum. We can also check that the expected rent converges to zero. Indeed for p_{12} close enough to zero

$$t_{11} - \underline{\theta}q_{11} \quad \text{goes to} \quad \Delta\theta q_{22}$$

$$t_{12} - \underline{\theta}q_{12} \quad \text{goes to} \quad \Delta\theta q_{22}\left(1 - \frac{p_{11}}{p_{12}}\right)$$

and $p_{11}(t_{11} - \underline{\theta}q_{11}) + p_{12}(t_{12} - \underline{\theta}q_{12})$ goes to $p_{12}\Delta\theta q_{22}$, which goes to zero as p_{12} goes to zero.

The result here is strikingly different from the case of collusion under complete information in Section 8.4. As p_{12} goes to zero, the cost of eliminating production when the messages are $\underline{\theta}$ and $\bar{\theta}$ goes to zero, since the case $(\underline{\theta}, \bar{\theta})$ occurs with a probability going to zero, and the gain is that it eliminates the stake of collusion. The fear of the event $(\underline{\theta}, \bar{\theta})$ remains very large because the *ex post* rent $t_{12} - \underline{\theta}q_{12}$ goes to minus infinity when p_{12} goes to zero, and such a fear is necessary for the third party to be able to induce truth telling.[13] The transaction costs within the coalition become so high that the collusion constraints become ineffective. With complete information within the coalition, this fear is eliminated by a perfect coordination of reports.

The main conclusion here is that the transaction costs within collusion contracts due to asymmetric information can be extremely favorable for the principal. Even if a principal could costlessly provide technologies enabling agents to learn their

[12] $q_{12} \geq 0$ becomes binding if $S'(0)$ is finite.

[13] Note that even a weak limited-liability constraint would prevent such a mechanism and would recreate inefficiencies when p_{12} goes to zero.

types, it is clear that he should not do so for weakening collusion incentive constraints. In general, there will be a trade-off between improving communication within the organization for efficiency purposes and maintaining agents under incomplete information to eliminate more easily incentives for collusion.

8.7 Conclusion

We have modeled the transaction costs existing when colluding partners want to organize an interest group. They are based on asymmetric information within the coalition and we believe that they can provide the foundations of Olson's theory of group behavior. Indeed, Olson (1965) stressed the free rider problem existing within groups. From the recent theory of public goods we know that the real explanation of the free rider problem lies in the combination of asymmetric information and participation constraints. Laffont and Maskin (1979) and Myerson and Satterthwaite (1983) have shown that complete information efficiency cannot then be achieved within a group in general, and Mailath and Postlewaite (1990) proved that the inefficiency grows with the size of the group. Organizing the best response of a group to a mechanism offered by a principal is a public good to be provided under incomplete information and it is not surprising that transaction costs decrease the efficiency of collusion for the benefit of the principal. It remains to extend the analysis to multiagent situations, to model the behavior of subcoalitions, and to prove that small groups may be more powerful interest groups (i.e. groups which affect the collective decision more) than larger groups because of their lower internal transaction costs.

We have stressed in this chapter the methodology enabling us to extend incentive theory to group incentive theory in a model with soft information. In so doing, we have made many assumptions, but we have provided a solid starting point for further analysis.

One major assumption is that we have assumed that colluding partners were always able to coordinate their answers about their collusion contract in such a way that the principal was unable to elicit that information. Following the general approach of Nash implementation, one could attempt to elicit this information with extended mechanisms. One would have to model collusion for such mechanisms and one might be able to design universal mechanisms which again implement the complete information optimum. Even if this were true, it would be quite unrealistic to push the logic of the principal–agent model so far. Either at the cost of some slight departure from the principal–agent model or with a particular assumption of incompleteness for the principal's contract, we are able to offer a modeling of the transaction costs due to the possibility of collusion which is attractive.

This approach is particularly attractive for our purpose of normative political economy because it enables us to extend the revelation principle. We can then characterize implementable allocations and consequently the optimal constitutional response to the activity of interest groups made possible by informational asymmetries.

We can distinguish three lines of further research.

The first one would maintain the basic framework and study the same model with more types, more agents (raising the issue of subcoalitions), inefficiencies in the collusion contract (due to the lack of a third party and particular extensive forms of bargaining), etc.

The second one would model collusion with more general mechanisms used by the principal to elicit information about collusive activities.

The third one would relax the assumption of enforceable collusion contracts and look for a self-enforcement by reputation in dynamic models (see Tirole (1992) and Martimort (1997) for a start).

With this new methodology we have made available a theory of endogenous transaction costs in the formation of coalitions. It offers one line of attack for understanding why some coalitions form and others do not, and therefore a theory of interest groups and some elements for designing institutions able to cope with these interest groups. It is by now well understood that contracts affect the performance of institutions. We can push this insight one step further. The side-contracts that agents can design within an institution, which themselves depend on the information structures, also affect their performance, even if it is only indirectly because of the collusion-proof principle. There are many testable implications of this theory that we hope to investigate.[14]

[14] A related stylized fact is that the occurrence of wars in Africa is known to depend on the distribution of tribes as represented by an index of ethnolinguistic fractionalization (see Collier and Hoeffler (1998)).

Appendix 8

A.8.1 Proof of Proposition 8.6

The game tree of the game induced by the contracts *G* and *S* is as follows:

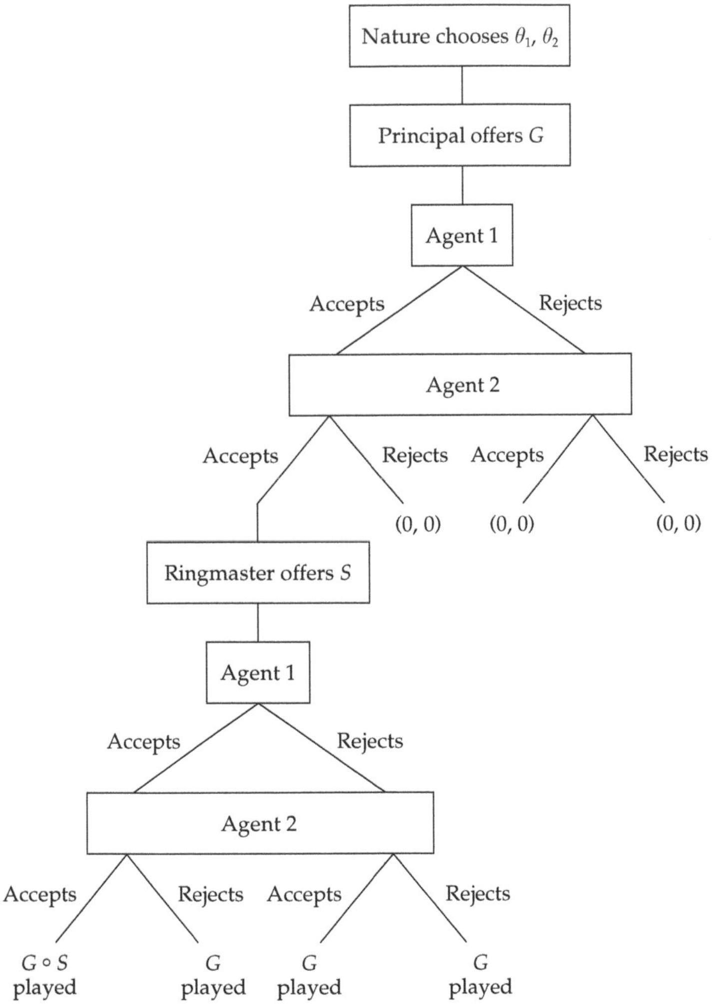

We are interested in characterizing the perfect Bayesian equilibria (PBE) $G^* \circ S^*$ of the whole game described above. G^* maps $M_1 \times M_2$ into the space of allocations (production level and transfers). G^* maximizes the principal's expected welfare taking into account the continuation equilibrium of the game of coalition formation. We assume that the out-of-equilibrium beliefs remain the original beliefs. S^* maps the space of characteristics $\Theta \times \Theta$ (where $\Theta = \{\underline{\theta}, \bar{\theta}\}$) into the space of message spaces and side transfers. S^* maximizes the sum of agents' expected utilities under Bayesian incentive constraints, budget balance and individual rationality constraints which ask for expected utility levels higher than those obtained in the truthful Nash equilibrium play of G^*.

The mechanism $\tilde{G} = G^* \circ S^*$ is a truthful revelation mechanism which implements truthfully the PBE of $G^* \circ S^*$ and for which the optimal strategy of the ringmaster is to offer the null side-contract (with no manipulation of reports and no side transfers). If this was not the case, the ringmaster could offer $\tilde{S}$ achieving higher utility levels than those obtained with $G^* \circ S^*$, which are themselves higher than those obtained playing G^*. This would contradict the optimality of S^*.

Therefore to characterize all the PBE achievable by the principal, it is sufficient to characterize the revelation mechanisms which are interim individually incentive compatible and interim individually rational and for which the best strategy of the third party is to offer the null-collusion contract. This last requirement is achieved by writing the first-order conditions of problem II and inserting that truthful behavior and no side transfers are optimal.

In problem II, call $\rho(\theta_1, \theta_2), \delta_1, \delta_2, \underline{\nu}_1, \underline{\nu}_2, \bar{\nu}_1, \bar{\nu}_2$ the multipliers associated with constraints (8.22) to (8.32) respectively. Maximizing with respect to $y_1(\cdot,\cdot)$ and $y_2(\cdot,\cdot)$ we obtain

$$\rho(\underline{\theta}, \underline{\theta}) + p_{11}(\delta_1 + \underline{\nu}_1) = 0 \tag{8.45}$$

$$\rho(\underline{\theta}, \underline{\theta}) + p_{11}(\delta_2 + \underline{\nu}_2) = 0 \tag{8.46}$$

$$\rho(\underline{\theta}, \bar{\theta}) + p_{12}(\delta_1 + \underline{\nu}_1) = 0 \tag{8.47}$$

$$\rho(\underline{\theta}, \bar{\theta}) - p_{11}\delta_2 + p_{12}\bar{\nu}_2 = 0 \tag{8.48}$$

$$\rho(\bar{\theta}, \underline{\theta}) - p_{11}\delta_1 + p_{12}\bar{\nu}_1 = 0 \tag{8.49}$$

$$\rho(\bar{\theta}, \underline{\theta}) + p_{12}(\delta_2 + \underline{\nu}_2) = 0. \tag{8.50}$$

Note that from (8.41), (8.42)

$$\delta_1 + \underline{v}_1 = \delta_2 + \underline{v}_2, \tag{8.51}$$

from (8.43), (8.44)

$$\delta_1 + \underline{v}_1 = -\frac{p_{11}}{p_{12}}\delta_2 + \bar{v}_2, \tag{8.52}$$

and from (8.45), (8.46)

$$\delta_2 + \underline{v}_2 = -\frac{p_{11}}{p_{12}}\delta_1 + \bar{v}_1. \tag{8.53}$$

Maximizing with respect to ϕ_{11}, ϕ_{12}, ϕ_{21}, ϕ_{22}, we obtain

$$\phi_{11}^* \in \arg\max_{\phi_{11}} \{p_{11}[t_1(\phi_{11}) + t_2(\phi_{11}) - 2\underline{\theta}q(\phi_{11})] + (\delta_1 + \underline{v}_1)p_{11}[t_1(\phi_{11}) - \underline{\theta}q(\phi_{11})] + (\delta_2 + \underline{v}_2)p_{11}[t_2(\phi_{11}) - \underline{\theta}q(\phi_{11})]\}$$

or, using (8.47),

$$\phi_{11}^* \in \arg\max_{\phi_{11}} \{t_1(\phi_{11}) + t_2(\phi_{11}) - \underline{\theta}q(\phi_{11})\}; \tag{8.54}$$

$$\phi_{12}^* \in \arg\max_{\phi_{12}} \{p_{12}[t_1(\phi_{12}) + t_2(\phi_{12}) - (\underline{\theta} + \bar{\theta})q(\phi_{12})] + (\delta_1 + \underline{v}_1)p_{12}[t_1(\phi_{12}) - \underline{\theta}q(\phi_{12})] - p_{11}\delta_2[t_2(\phi_{12}) - \underline{\theta}q(\phi_{12})] + p_{12}\bar{v}_2[t_2(\phi_{12}) - \bar{\theta}q(\phi_{12})]\}$$

or, using (8.48),

$$\phi_{12}^* \in \arg\max_{\phi_{12}} \{t_1(\phi_{12}) + t_2(\phi_{12}) - (\underline{\theta} + \bar{\theta} + \frac{p_{11}}{p_{12}}\varepsilon_1 \Delta\theta)q(\phi_{12})\} \tag{8.55}$$

with

$$\varepsilon_1 = \frac{\delta_2}{1 + \delta_1 + \underline{v}_1}.$$

Symmetrically,

$$\phi_{21}^* \in \arg\max_{\phi_{21}} \left\{t_1(\phi_{21}) + t_2(\phi_{21}) - \left(\underline{\theta} + \bar{\theta} + \frac{p_{11}}{p_{12}}\varepsilon_2 \Delta\theta\right)q(\phi_{21})\right\}$$

with

$$\varepsilon_2 = \frac{\delta_1}{1 + \delta_2 + \underline{v}_2};$$

and

$$\begin{aligned}\phi_{22}^{*} \in \arg\max_{\phi_{22}} \{ & p_{22}[t_1(\phi_{22}) + t_2(\phi_{22}) - 2\bar{\theta}q(\phi_{22})] \\ & - p_{12}\delta_1[t_1(\phi_{22}) - \underline{\theta}q(\phi_{22})] \\ & - p_{12}\delta_2[t_2(\phi_{22}) - \underline{\theta}q(\phi_{22})] \\ & + p_{22}\bar{v}_1[t_1(\phi_{22}) - \bar{\theta}q(\phi_{22})] \\ & + p_{22}\bar{v}_2[t_2(\phi_{22}) - \bar{\theta}q(\phi_{22})]\}.\end{aligned}$$

We rewrite the objective function as

$$\begin{aligned}&(p_{22} - p_{12}\delta_1 + p_{22}\bar{v}_1)[t_1(\phi_{22}) - \bar{\theta}q(\phi_{22}) - \Delta\theta p_{12}\delta_1 q(\phi_{22})] \\ &+ (p_{22} - p_{12}\delta_2 + p_{22}\bar{v}_2)[t_2(\phi_{22}) - \bar{\theta}q(\phi_{22}) - \Delta\theta p_{12}\delta_2 q(\phi_{22})]. \quad (8.56)\end{aligned}$$

Noting that at a symmetric equilibrium $\delta_1 = \delta_2 = \delta$, $\bar{v}_1 = \bar{v}_2 = \bar{v}$ and $\varepsilon_1 = \varepsilon_2 = \varepsilon$. Then from (8.47), (8.48), (8.49):

$$\begin{aligned}p_{22} - p_{12}\delta + p_{22}\bar{v} &= p_{22}\,(1 + \delta + \underline{v}) + p_{22}\left(1 + \frac{p_{11}}{p_{12}}\right)\delta - (p_{22} + p_{21})\delta \\ &= p_{22}\,(1 + \delta + \underline{v}) + \frac{\delta\rho}{p_{12}}.\end{aligned}$$

Dividing (8.53) by $1 + \delta + \underline{v}$ we obtain

$$\left(p_{22} + \frac{\rho\varepsilon}{p_{12}}\right)[t_1(\phi_{22}) + t_2(\phi_{22}) - 2\bar{\theta}] - 2\Delta\theta p_{12}\varepsilon q(\phi_{22});$$

hence

$$\phi_{22}^{*} \in \arg\max_{\phi_{22}} \left\{ t_1(\phi_{22}) + t_2(\phi_{22}) - 2\left(\bar{\theta} + \Delta\theta \frac{p_{12}\varepsilon}{p_{22} + \frac{\rho\varepsilon}{p_{12}}} q(\phi_{22})\right)\right\}. \quad (8.57)$$

Equations (8.54), (8.55), (8.57) summarize the collusion-proof constraints where ε is a free variable in [0,1).

9

Collusion and Decentralization

'Certainly, the benefits derived from delegation come at a price. The principal suffers welfare losses caused by opportunistic behavior on the part of his or her agents. Even under the best of circumstances, agency losses cannot be eliminated.'

Kiewiet and McCubbins (1991), p. 37.

9.1 Introduction

A major debate in the theory of government concerns its proper degree of decentralization.[1] A large part of the information relevant for decision making is dispersed among the members of society. The goal of organizational design is to set up the communication channels and to allocate authority in order to use this information in the least costly way.[2] Under *delegation*, the agents of the periphery have no direct communication with the center. Reports on their information must flow up a hierarchy and then recommendations from the center flow down leaving some decision-making authority at several levels of the hierarchy. In contrast, under *centralization*, the agents of the periphery communicate directly with the center, which centralizes all decision making. What are the costs and benefits of each of these different organizations? How are incentive problems solved under each of those arrangements? What is the exact impact of communication constraints in each case? For a given distribution of asymmetric information, what should be the optimal form of organization?

[1] See CEPR (1993) for a discussion of the related notion of subsidiarity and Kiewiet and McCubbins (1991) for an analysis of delegation in the US Congress.

[2] See Baiman (1982), Baron and Besanko (1992), (1995), Crémer and Riordan (1987) and McAfee and McMillan (1995).

In Section 9.2 we consider the issue of delegation when the Constitution—the principal—faces two privately informed agents who may collude. We show that, for independent private pieces of information and risk-neutral agents, delegation entails no cost for the principal. Section 9.3 even shows that, for a principal with bounded rationality, delegation may even be preferable because of the interaction of collusion constraints and limited communication. Section 9.4 extends the analysis to a particular case of correlated private information between the two agents. This enables us to return to the supervision model of Chapter 2, which is generalized to the case of soft information. Risk-aversion of the agent to whom contracting is delegated (the delegated agent) creates new transaction costs which may become a building block of a general theory of delegation. Section 9.5 concludes.

9.2 The Independent Case

The model is the same as in Chapter 8 but with independent types. We show that delegation entails no cost.

9.2.1 The Optimal Centralized Constitution

The Constitution maximizes expected social welfare under the interim incentive constraint of a $\underline{\theta}$-agent and the interim participation constraint of a $\bar{\theta}$-agent, i.e.

$$\text{(I)} \quad \max_{\substack{(q_{ij},\, t_{ij}) \\ i,j=1,2}} \nu^2[S(q_{11}) - 2\underline{\theta}q_{11} - 2\lambda t_{11}] + 2\nu(1-\nu)[S(q_{12}) - (\underline{\theta}+\bar{\theta})q_{12} - \lambda(t_{12}+t_{21})] + (1-\nu)^2[S(q_{22}) - 2\bar{\theta}q_{22} - 2\lambda t_{22}]$$

s.t.

$$\nu(t_{11} - \underline{\theta}q_{11}) + (1-\nu)(t_{12} - \underline{\theta}q_{12}) \geqslant \nu(t_{21} - \underline{\theta}q_{12}) + (1-\nu)(t_{22} - \underline{\theta}q_{22}) \tag{9.1}$$

$$\nu(t_{21} - \bar{\theta}q_{12}) + (1-\nu)(t_{22} - \bar{\theta}q_{22}) \geqslant 0. \tag{9.2}$$

We note that program (I) can be rewritten with only expected transfers:

$$T_1 = \nu t_{11} + (1-\nu)t_{12}$$
$$T_2 = \nu t_{21} + (1-\nu)t_{22}.$$

$$\text{(II)} \quad \max_{\substack{(q_{ij}, t_{ij})\\ i,j=1,2}} \nu^2[S(q_{11}) - 2\underline{\theta}q_{11}] + 2\nu(1-\nu)[S(q_{12}) - (\underline{\theta}+\bar{\theta})q_{12}]$$
$$+ (1-\nu)^2[S(q_{22}) - 2\bar{\theta}q_{22}] - 2\lambda\nu T_1 - 2\lambda(1-\nu)T_2$$

$$T_1 - \underline{\theta}[\nu q_{11} + (1-\nu)q_{12}] \geq T_2 - \underline{\theta}[\nu q_{12} + (1-\nu)q_{22}] \quad (9.3)$$

$$T_2 - \bar{\theta}[\nu q_{12} + (1-\nu)q_{22}] \geq 0. \quad (9.4)$$

Solving (9.3) and (9.4) for T_1 and T_2 and substituting in (II), we obtain:

$$\text{(III)} \quad \max_{\substack{(q_{ij}, t_{ij})\\ i,j=1,2}} \nu^2[S(q_{11}) - 2\underline{\theta}q_{11}] + 2\nu(1-\nu)[S(q_{12}) - (\underline{\theta}+\bar{\theta})q_{12}]$$
$$+ (1-\nu)^2[S(q_{22}) - 2\bar{\theta}q_{22}] - 2\lambda\nu\underline{\theta}[\nu q_{11} + (1-\nu)q_{12}]$$
$$- 2\lambda(1-\nu)\bar{\theta}[\nu q_{12} + (1-\nu)q_{22}] - 2\lambda\nu\Delta\theta[\nu q_{12} + (1-\nu)q_{22}];$$

hence the solutions (as in Section 8.2):

$$S'(q_{11}) = 2(1+\lambda)\underline{\theta} \quad (9.5)$$

$$S'(q_{12}) = (1+\lambda)(\underline{\theta}+\bar{\theta}) + \frac{\lambda\nu}{1-\nu}\Delta\theta \quad (9.6)$$

$$S'(q_{22}) = 2(1+\lambda)\bar{\theta} + \frac{2\lambda\nu}{1-\nu}\Delta\theta. \quad (9.7)$$

We observe that only the expected transfers T_1 and T_2 are determined. Therefore, we have two degrees of freedom in determining transfers. They can be used to obtain additional properties.

(a) Dominant-strategy implementation and *ex post* individual rationality constraints.[3]

We can choose

$$t_{21} = \bar{\theta}q_{12}, \qquad t_{22} = \bar{\theta}q_{22}.$$

[3] This result is a special case of a theorem in Mookherjee and Reichelstein (1992) which gives general conditions under which Bayesian strategy implementation implies dominant strategy implementation. This theorem is itself a generalization of a result in Laffont and Tirole (1987) where a dominant strategy Vickrey auction is shown to be equivalent to the optimal Bayesian auction.

Then, dominant-strategy implementation requires

$$t_{11} - \underline{\theta}q_{11} \geqslant t_{21} - \underline{\theta}q_{12} = \Delta\theta q_{12}$$
$$t_{12} - \underline{\theta}q_{12} \geqslant t_{22} - \underline{\theta}q_{22} = \Delta\theta q_{22}.$$

We can choose

$$t_{11} = \underline{\theta}\, q_{11} + \Delta\theta q_{12}, \qquad t_{12} = \underline{\theta}q_{12} + \Delta\theta q_{22}.$$

This implies, of course, Bayesian strategy implementation.

(b) Collusion-proof implementation.

Reasoning as in Section 8.5 (for $\rho = 0$), we know that collusion-proofness requires two additional constraints:

$$2t_{11} - 2\underline{\theta}q_{11} \geqslant t_{12} + t_{21} - 2\underline{\theta}q_{12} \tag{9.8}$$

$$t_{21} + t_{12} - (\underline{\theta} + \bar{\theta})q_{12} \geqslant 2t_{22} - (\theta + \bar{\theta})q_{22}. \tag{9.9}$$

Therefore, under Bayesian strategy implementation we can use the two degrees of freedom to ensure collusion-proofness.

> PROPOSITION 9.1 The optimal centralized collusion-proof Constitution is characterized by (9.5), (9.6), (9.7) with associated transfers obtained from (9.1), (9.2), (9.8), (9.9).

We want to evaluate now the cost of the loss of control involved in delegating contracting to one agent.

9.2.2 *Optimal Delegation*

The Constitution has no relationship now with agent 2 and contracts only with agent 1, who himself contracts with agent 2. We assume that agent 1 accepts or rejects the principal's offer before contracting with agent 2. In solving the game backward, there is no loss of generality in assuming in stage 2 that agent 1 uses a revelation mechanism to contract with agent 2.

However, this is an informed principal–agent problem with private values. From Proposition 11 in Maskin and Tirole (1990), the principal neither gains nor loses if his type is revealed to the agent before the game is played. So, we assume that agent 1 maximizes his own expected utility under the participation and incentive constraints of agent 2 aware of agent 1's type.

Let $s(m)$, $q(m)$ be the mechanism offered by the principal to agent 1 where the message m asked from agent 1 maps all the information he has acquired, i.e. $(\theta_1, \theta_2) \in \Theta \times \Theta$, into M.

Let $\phi(\theta_1, \theta_2) \in M$ denote the message which agent 1 commits to transmit to the principal and $y(\theta_1, \theta_2)$ the compensatory payment to agent 2. Agent 1 looks for the optimal internal contract by maximizing his expected utility under the incentive and participation constraints of agent 2, i.e. he solves the program

$$\text{(IV)} \qquad \max_{\phi(\cdot),y(\cdot)} \nu[s(\phi(\theta_1, \underline{\theta})) - y(\theta_1, \underline{\theta}) - \theta_1 q(\phi(\theta_1, \underline{\theta}))] + (1-\nu)[s(\phi(\theta_1, \bar{\theta})) - y(\theta_1, \bar{\theta}) - \theta_1 q(\phi(\theta_1, \bar{\theta}))]$$

s.t.

$$y(\theta_1, \underline{\theta}) - \underline{\theta} q(\phi(\theta_1, \underline{\theta})) \geqslant y(\theta_1, \bar{\theta}) - \underline{\theta} q(\phi(\theta_1, \bar{\theta})) \tag{9.10}$$

$$y(\theta_1, \bar{\theta}) - \bar{\theta} q(\phi(\theta_1, \bar{\theta})) \geqslant 0. \tag{9.11}$$

As usual, we have written only the incentive constraint of the $\underline{\theta}$-agent 2 and the individual rationality constraint of the $\bar{\theta}$-agent 2.

Solving (9.10), (9.11) and inserting in (IV), we get

$$\text{(V)} \quad \max_{\phi(\cdot)} \nu[s(\phi(\theta_1, \underline{\theta})) - (\theta_1 + \underline{\theta}) q(\phi(\theta_1, \underline{\theta})) - \Delta\theta q(\phi(\theta_1, \bar{\theta}))] + (1-\nu)[s(\phi(\theta_1, \bar{\theta})) - (\theta_1 + \bar{\theta}) q(\phi(\theta_1, \bar{\theta}))].$$

Again applying the revelation principle, we know that the Constitution can restrict itself to revelation mechanisms $(s(\cdot), q(\cdot))$ from $\Theta \times \Theta$ into $R \times R_+$ which are truthful. Writing that

$$\phi(\theta_1, \theta_2) = (\theta_1, \theta_2)$$

is optimal in program (V), we immediately have

$$s_{11} - 2\underline{\theta} q_{11} \geqslant s(\theta_1, \theta_2) - 2\underline{\theta} q(\theta_1, \theta_2) \qquad \text{for any } (\theta_1, \theta_2)$$

$$s_{12} - \left(\underline{\theta} + \bar{\theta} + \frac{\nu}{1-\nu}\Delta\theta\right) q_{12} \geqslant s(\theta_1, \theta_2) - \left(\underline{\theta} + \bar{\theta} + \frac{\nu}{1-\nu}\Delta\theta\right) q(\theta_1, \theta_2) \quad \text{for any } (\theta_1, \theta_2)$$

$$s_{21} - (\underline{\theta} + \bar{\theta}) q_{12} \geqslant s(\theta_1, \theta_2) - (\underline{\theta} + \bar{\theta}) q(\theta_1, \theta_2) \qquad \text{for any } (\theta_1, \theta_2)$$

$$s_{22} - \left(2\bar{\theta} + \frac{\nu}{1-\nu}\Delta\theta\right) q_{22} \geqslant s(\theta_1, \theta_2) - \left(2\bar{\theta} + \frac{\nu}{1-\nu}\Delta\theta\right) q(\theta_1, \theta_2) \quad \text{for any } (\theta_1, \theta_2).$$

To these constraints the Constitution must also add the interim participation constraint of agent 1 before he knows agent 2's type. Only the $\bar{\theta}$-agent 1's constraint is expected to bind, as well as the upward incentive constraints obtained above. Taking into account the symmetry of the problem,[4] we obtain the following optimization program for the Constitution:

$$\text{(VI)} \quad \max_{\substack{(q_{ij},\, t_{ij}) \\ i,j=1,2}} v^2[S(q_{11}) - 2\underline{\theta}q_{11} - \lambda s_{11}] + 2v(1-v)[S(q_{12}) - (\underline{\theta} + \bar{\theta})q_{12} - \lambda s_{12}] + (1-v)^2[S(q_{22}) - 2\bar{\theta}q_{22} - \lambda s_{22}]$$

s.t.

$$s_{11} - 2\underline{\theta}q_{11} = s_{12} - 2\underline{\theta}q_{12}$$

$$s_{12} - \left(\underline{\theta} + \bar{\theta} + \frac{v}{1-v}\Delta\theta\right)q_{12} = s_{22} - \left(\underline{\theta} + \bar{\theta} + \frac{v}{1-v}\Delta\theta\right)q_{22}$$

$$v[s_{12} - (\underline{\theta} + \bar{\theta})q_{12} - \Delta\theta q_{22}] + (1-v)(s_{22} - 2\bar{\theta}q_{22}) = 0.$$

Solving (VI), we get (9.5), (9.6), (9.7) again.

PROPOSITION 9.2 The optimal Constitution with delegation is equivalent to the optimal centralized collusion-proof Constitution.

This proposition generalizes (trivially) the result proved in Melumad, Mookherjee and Reichelstein (1995), according to which centralization (without considering the possibility of collusion) is equivalent to delegation.[5] The loss of control is costless for the principal. In delegation, the choice of a contract by agent 1 becomes a moral hazard variable. However, it is fully anticipated by the principal, and because agent 1 is risk-neutral and uninformed about agent 2's type, the principal achieves the same allocation as if he was controlling this variable.[6]

[4] One can easily show that the symmetry $q_{12} = q_{21}$ and $s_{12} = s_{21}$ is not a restriction of generality.

[5] See Itoh (1993) and Balliga and Sjostrom (1996) for studies of delegation and collusion with moral hazard.

[6] It is well known that, for utility functions separable in effort and risk-neutral, moral hazard is innocuous.

9.3 The Independent Case with Limits on Communication

Limits on communication are a fundamental structuring feature of organizations, which was the main center of attention of the theory of organizations until the emergence of incentive theory. Very little research has been done to integrate those two lines of research. Green and Laffont (1982) put constraints on the dimensionality of the messages which can be transmitted, while Green and Laffont (1986) use Shannon's information theory to model these constraints and to study the interaction of these constraints with incentive constraints. One can model the processing of each signal reported as involving a fixed cost (Dye (1985)). Melumad, Mookherjee and Reichelstein (1995) model the incompleteness of communication as the possibility for the agents to report only a finite number of messages on their types even if these types are continuously distributed. All these approaches are debatable, as they are imperfect shortcuts for a missing theory of bounded rationality.

We will assume (the limited communication assumption) that because of bounded rationality of the principal, the whole vector of types cannot be transmitted to the principal. Only the sum of the reports can be received by the principal, who does not obtain the identity of the reports.

> Proposition 9.3 The optimal Constitution with delegation is unaffected by limited communication.

We observed that the symmetry constraints (footnote 4) do not restrict the delegation contract. The asymmetry of transfers is reconstructed within the agents' relationship since the incentive contract offered by agent 1 to agent 2 yields outcomes which vary with agent 2's type.

> Proposition 9.4 The optimal Constitution with centralization (without collusion) is not affected by limited communication.

> Proof: The optimal contract entails, from the symmetry of the problem, $q_{12} = q_{21}$ and, furthermore, we have two degrees of freedom in the choice of contracts. We can use one such degree of freedom to impose $t_{12} = t_{21}$.

Limited communication alone or collusion-proofness alone does not invalidate the equivalence of centralization and delegation. However, when both constraints are imposed, delegation dominates centralization.

PROPOSITION 9.5 The optimal collusion-proof Constitution with centralization is affected by the constraint of limited communication. It entails:

$$S'(q_{11}) = 2(1+\lambda)\underline{\theta}$$

$$S'(q_{12}) = (1+\lambda)(\underline{\theta} + \bar{\theta}) + \frac{\lambda(1+\nu)}{2(1-\nu)}\Delta\theta$$

$$S'(q_{22}) = 2(1+\lambda)\bar{\theta} + \frac{\lambda\nu\Delta\theta}{(1-\nu)}.$$

PROOF: Collusion-proofness requires two degrees of freedom and then the transfers obtained with (9.1), (9.2), (9.8), (9.9) conflict with the limited communication constraint which imposes $t_{12} = t_{21}$.

Imposing anonymity, the relevant constraints become

$$2(t_{11} - \underline{\theta}q_{11}) \geqslant 2(t_{12} - \underline{\theta}q_{12}) \tag{9.12}$$

$$2t_{12} - (\underline{\theta} + \bar{\theta})q_{12} \geqslant 2t_{22} - (\underline{\theta} + \bar{\theta})q_{22} \tag{9.13}$$

$$\nu(t_{12} - \bar{\theta}q_{12}) + (1-\nu)(t_{22} - \bar{\theta}q_{22}) \geqslant 0, \tag{9.14}$$

i.e. the two collusion-proof constraints and the interim $\bar{\theta}$-agent individual rationality constraint.

Note that (9.12) is now identical to a (dominant-strategy) incentive constraint in the $(\underline{\theta}, \underline{\theta})$-state and that (9.13), which is equivalent to

$$2(t_{12} - \underline{\theta}q_{12}) \geqslant 2(t_{22} - \underline{\theta}q_{22}) + \Delta\theta(q_{12} - q_{22}),$$

implies, since $q_{12} > q_{22}$, the other (dominant-strategy) incentive constraint in the $(\underline{\theta}, \bar{\theta})$ state

$$t_{12} - \underline{\theta}q_{12} \geqslant t_{22} - \underline{\theta}q_{22}.$$

These two (dominant-strategy) incentive constraints imply the Bayesian incentive constraint (9.1).

Solving (9.12), (9.13), (9.14) for the transfers, inserting in the expected social welfare and maximizing with respect to quantities together yield Proposition 9.5.

The limited communication assumption creates some scope for collusive behavior. Consider the optimal symmetric mechanism with no collusion obtained in Section 9.2.1 with $t_{12} = t_{21}$ and dominant strategy implementation. The transfers satisfy

$$t_{11} - \underline{\theta} q_{11} = t_{12} - \underline{\theta} q_{12}$$

$$t_{12} - \underline{\theta} q_{12} = t_{22} - \underline{\theta} q_{22}$$

$$\nu(t_{12} - \bar{\theta} q_{12}) + (1 - \nu)(t_{22} - \bar{\theta} q_{22}) = 0.$$

Then $t_{22} - \bar{\theta} q_{22} > t_{22} - \bar{\theta} q_{12} = t_{12} - \bar{\theta} q_{12}$ since $q_{22} < q_{12}$.

We see that the truthful revelation of his type by an efficient agent exerts a negative externality on the inefficient agent (as long as $q_{22} < q_{12}$; setting $q_{22} = q_{12}$ destroys the externality). In this case the inefficient type is willing to bribe the efficient agent so that he misreports his type to the principal. The stake of collusion for the inefficient agent that can be shared by the colluding partners is

$$(t_{22} - \bar{\theta} q_{22}) - (t_{12} - \bar{\theta} q_{12}) = \Delta\theta(q_{12} - q_{22}).$$

The principal can destroy collusion by a pooling contract ($q_{12} = q_{22}$) or by increasing t_{12} to satisfy the collusion constraint

$$2t_{12} - (\underline{\theta} + \bar{\theta}) q_{12} \geqslant 2t_{22} - (\underline{\theta} + \bar{\theta}) q_{22}.$$

So we conclude from Propositions 9.4 and 9.5 that delegation dominates collusion-proof centralization since delegation still achieves the second-best while collusion-proof centralization does not. Delegation is a type of collusion in which all the bargaining power belongs to agent 1, while in centralization the bargaining power is split between the two agents. If the principal can manage to create the asymmetric distribution of bargaining powers that delegation entails, he benefits. The limited communication constraint between the principal and the agents imposes an equal treatment under the centralization regime between a $\underline{\theta}$-agent and a $\bar{\theta}$-agent when there is a pair of $\underline{\theta}$ and $\bar{\theta}$ agents. The asymmetry of delegation eliminates this equal treatment constraint to the benefit of the principal.[7]

[7] See Laffont and Martimort (1998) for further developments.

Because of the revelation principle, delegation can only be valuable for a principal in a second-best framework. We have given here an example of such a framework by postulating constraints on communication. A more general theory of the benefits of delegation will explore additional second-best constraints. The most traditional constraint considered is a limit of commitment for the principal.[8] The literature relies then on the availability of third parties with given preferences to present delegation as a partial solution to the commitment problem (see Rogoff (1985), Spulber and Besanko (1992), Fershtmann, Judd and Kalai (1991)). The question remains about the origin of these preferences.

An alternative is to recognize the non-benevolence of the principal as we have done in Part II. Delegation can then play the same role as above (Seabright (1996)). Within the same framework Faure-Grimaud and Martimort (1999) compare two timings of delegation (before and after elections), which they interpret as (politically) independent or dependent bureaucracies.

9.4 Risk Aversion

Delegation of the choice of a contract creates a moral hazard problem, as we saw in the previous section. To deal with asymmetric information, agent 1 offers agent 2 a contract which is incentive-compatible. Agent 1 is obliged to give up a rent to agent 2 and this rent depends on the type of agent 2: it is risky from the point of view of agent 1, who accepts the contract with the principal before knowing agent 2's type. If agent 1 is risk-averse, a risk premium must be provided to agent 1 for him to bear this risk. This risk premium is a new transaction cost of delegation for the principal.

We could develop this idea in the model of the previous sections. Instead, we go back to the supervision model of Chapter 2 with two major changes in the hypotheses: the signal obtained by the supervisor is soft, as is private information in this chapter. Furthermore, we consider a noisy signal to remain close to the

[8] This constraint itself is often imposed by the Constitution. It is another example of contractual limitation of the Constitution, which settles for a limit on the length of delegation rather than using a more complete contract.

notation of previous sections. We will obtain a new theory of supervision with soft information.[9]

9.4.1 The Benchmark Model

Agent 2 is now the firm producing the public good with a marginal cost $\theta \in \{\underline{\theta}, \bar{\theta}\}$ where we also denote $\theta_1 = \underline{\theta}, \theta_2 = \bar{\theta}$. The information technology of the politician–supervisor consists of two signals τ_1 and τ_2 with the following stochastic structure:

$$p_{ij} = \Pr(\theta = \theta_i, \tau = \tau_j) \quad \text{and} \quad \rho = p_{11}p_{22} - p_{12}p_{21} > 0.$$

Then

$$\Pr(\theta = \theta_i/\tau = \tau_j) = \frac{p_{ij}}{p_{1j} + p_{2j}} \quad \text{for any } i, j$$

and we note that, from $\rho > 0$,

$$\Pr(\theta = \theta_1/\tau = \tau_1) = \frac{p_{11}}{p_{11} + p_{21}} > \frac{p_{12}}{p_{12} + p_{22}} = \Pr(\theta = \theta_1/\tau = \tau_2).$$

So τ_1 (resp. τ_2) is a signal favorable to θ_1 (resp. θ_2). For simplicity, we assume that the signal is also observed by the agent.

We assume that the politician–supervisor (agent 1) has a utility function with constant absolute risk aversion

$$V(s) = 1 - e^{-rs}.$$

The timing is as in Chapter 2. In the absence of collusion between the politician and the firm, the principal learns $\tau \in \{\tau_1, \tau_2\}$ with zero payments to the politician, who is indifferent between all reports.

For each value of τ, the principal maximizes expected social welfare under the incentive and individual rationality constraints of the firm, i.e.

$$\max_{\substack{(q_{ij}, t_{ij}) \\ i,j = 1,2}} \Pr(\theta = \theta_1/\tau = \tau_j)(S(q_{1j}) - \theta_1 q_{1j} - \lambda t_{1j}) + \Pr(\theta = \theta_2/\tau = \tau_j)(S(q_{2j}) - \theta_2 q_{2j} - \lambda t_{2j})$$

[9] See Faure-Grimaud, Laffont and Martimort (1998) for a more detailed exposition.

s.t., for $j = 1, 2$,

$$t_{1j} - \theta_1 q_{1j} \geqslant t_{2j} - \theta_1 q_{2j}$$
$$t_{2j} - \theta_2 q_{2j} \geqslant t_{1j} - \theta_2 q_{1j}$$
$$t_{1j} - \theta_1 q_{1j} \geqslant 0$$
$$t_{2j} - \theta_2 q_{2j} \geqslant 0.$$

As usual, the incentive constraint of the $\underline{\theta}$-agent and the participation constraint of the $\bar{\theta}$-agent are binding, leading to

$$\max_{\substack{(q_{ij}) \\ i,j = 1,2}} \Pr(\theta = \theta_1/\tau = \tau_j)[S(q_{1j}) - (1+\lambda)q_{1j} - \lambda\Delta\theta q_{2j}]$$
$$+\Pr(\theta = \theta_2/\tau = \tau_j)\,[S(q_{2j}) - (1+\lambda)q_{2j}];$$

hence

$$S'(q^*_{1j}) = (1+\lambda)\,\underline{\theta}$$
$$S'(q^*_{2j}) = (1+\lambda)\bar{\theta} + \frac{p_{1j}}{p_{2j}}\Delta\theta \quad j = 1, 2.$$

Because of the positive correlation, $\frac{p_{11}}{p_{21}} > \frac{p_{12}}{p_{22}}$ and $q^*_{22} > q^*_{12}$. The production level when the signal τ_1 is transmitted is smaller than for τ_2 because the posterior probability that the principal is facing an efficient type (to whom a costly information rent will have to be given up) is higher.

9.4.2 *Collusion with Complete Information*

If the politician and the firm can share their private information, and if we continue to consider revelation mechanisms $s(\theta_i, \tau_j)$, $t(\theta_i, \tau_j)$, $q(\theta_i, \tau_j) = q_{ij}$, the individual and collective incentive constraints can be written as

$$t(\theta_1, \tau_1) - \theta_1 q_{11} \geq t(\theta_2, \tau_1) - \theta_1 q_{21}$$
$$t(\theta_1, \tau_2) - \theta_1 q_{12} \geq t(\theta_2, \tau_2) - \theta_1 q_{22}$$
$$s(\theta_1, \tau_1) \geq s(\theta_1, \tau_2)$$
$$s(\theta_1, \tau_2) \geq s(\theta_1, \tau_1)$$
$$s(\theta_2, \tau_1) \geq s(\theta_2, \tau_2)$$
$$s(\theta_2, \tau_2) \geq s(\theta_2, \tau_1)$$

for all θ_i, τ_j, and

$$V(s(\theta_i, \tau_j)) + t(\theta_i, \tau_j) - \theta_i q_{ij} \geq V(s(\theta_{i'}, \tau_{j'})) + t(\theta_{i'}, \tau_{j'}) - \theta_i q_{i'j'}$$

for all $\theta_{i'}$, $\tau_{j'}$.

The fact that the supervisor has a flat utility function (i.e. not depending on the production level) implies a constant payment for him and therefore, from the collusion constraints,

$$t(\theta_1, \tau_1) = t(\theta_1, \tau_2)$$
$$t(\theta_2, \tau_1) = t(\theta_2, \tau_2).$$

The principal is therefore restricted to the unconditional optimum which does not use the message about τ. It is characterized by

$$S'(q_{11}^u) = S'(q_{12}^u) = (1 + \lambda)\underline{\theta}$$

$$S'(q_{21}^u) = S'(q_{22}^u) = (1 + \lambda)\bar{\theta} + \lambda \frac{p_{11} + p_{12}}{p_{21} + p_{22}} \Delta\theta.$$

In this informational context, if the contract is delegated to the politician, since no rent is given up to the firm, the politician's utility function is

$$V[s(\theta, \tau) - \theta q(\theta, \tau)]$$

and the function $V(\cdot)$ is irrelevant for writing incentive and participation constraints. We again obtain the non-conditional optimum, and similarly, of course, if we delegate the contract to the firm (which simply ignores the signal τ).

9.4.3 *Collusion under Incomplete Information*

The characterization of the optimal centralization contract with collusion under incomplete information would follow the methodology of Chapter 8. One conjecture is that, as soon as the third party puts some weight on the politician's welfare, the optimal contract is equivalent to delegation to the politician. Here, we simply compare the two types of delegation.

Delegation to the Agent

Clearly, as above, there is no way to elicit the signal from the agent if he observes it, and no way for the agent to elicit the politician's signal if he does not observe it. We still obtain the unconditional optimum.

Delegation to the Politician

Following Section 9.2, the politician commits to a manipulation of reports $\phi(\theta_i, \tau_j)$ and transfers to the agent $y(\theta_i, \tau_j)$, which maximize his expected utility (conditional to his information τ_j) under the incentive and participation constraints of the agent (who is assumed to have observed τ_j).

The politician's optimization program can be reduced to:

$$\max_{(\phi(\cdot))} \Pr(\theta_1 | \tau_j) V[s(\phi(\theta_1, \tau_j)) - \theta_1 q(\phi(\theta_1, \tau_j)) - \Delta\theta q(\phi(\theta_2, \tau_j))]$$
$$+ \Pr(\theta_2 | \tau_j) V[s(\phi(\theta_2, \tau_j)) - \theta_2 q(\phi(\theta_2, \tau_j))].$$

Applying the revelation principle, we know that the principal can restrict himself to revelation mechanisms $s(\cdot)$, $q(\cdot)$ which induce truthful revelation by the politician of his information (θ_i, τ_j). Expressing the fact that the optimal $\phi(\cdot)$ is the identity function (and using the fact that V is exponential), we obtain the incentive constraints faced by the principal:

$$s_{11} - \theta_1 q_{11} \geq s_{21} - \theta_2 q_{21} + \Delta\theta q_{21} \tag{9.15}$$

$$s_{12} - \theta_1 q_{12} \geq s_{22} - \theta_2 q_{22} + \Delta\theta q_{22}. \tag{9.16}$$

$$s_{11} - \theta_1 q_{11} - \Delta\theta q_{21} - \frac{1}{r}\log\left\{\frac{p_{11}}{p_{11}+p_{21}} + \frac{p_{21}}{p_{11}+p_{21}} e^{-r[s_{21} - \theta_2 q_{21} - s_{11} + \theta_1 q_{11} + \Delta\theta q_{21}]}\right\}$$
$$\geq s_{11} - \theta_1 q_{11} - \Delta\theta q_{22} - \frac{1}{r}\log\left\{\frac{p_{11}}{p_{11}+p_{21}} + \frac{p_{21}}{p_{11}+p_{21}} e^{-r[s_{22} - \theta_2 q_{22} - s_{11} + \theta_1 q_{11} + \Delta\theta q_{22}]}\right\} \tag{9.17}$$

The participation constraints of the politician are:

$$s_{11} - \theta_1 q_{11} - \Delta\theta q_{21} - \frac{1}{r}\log\left\{\frac{p_{11}}{p_{11}+p_{21}} + \frac{p_{21}}{p_{11}+p_{21}} e^{-r[s_{21} - \theta_2 q_{21} - s_{11} + \theta_1 q_{11} + \Delta\theta q_{21}]}\right\} \geq 0 \tag{9.18}$$

$$s_{12} - \theta_1 q_{12} - \Delta\theta q_{22} - \frac{1}{r}\log\left\{\frac{p_{12}}{p_{12}+p_{22}} + \frac{p_{22}}{p_{12}+p_{22}} e^{-r[s_{22} - \theta_2 q_{22} - s_{12} + \theta_1 q_{12} + \Delta\theta q_{22}]}\right\} \geq 0 \tag{9.19}$$

The principal maximizes, under (9.16) to (9.20), his expected utility

$$\sum_{ij} p_{ij} \left(S(q_{ij}) - \theta_i q_{ij} - \lambda s_{ij}\right).$$

Expressing the solution as a function of the index of risk aversion r we obtain

$$S'(q_{11}(r)) = S'(q_{12}(r)) = (1 + \lambda)\underline{\theta} \tag{9.20}$$

$$S'(q_{21}(r)) = (1 + \lambda)\bar{\theta} + \lambda\Delta\theta \frac{p_{11} e^{-r\Delta\theta(q_{22}(r) - q_{21}(r))}}{p_{21} + p_{11}(1 - e^{-r\Delta\theta(q_{22}(r) - q_{21}(r))})} \tag{9.21}$$

$$S'(q_{22}(r)) = (1 + \lambda)\bar{\theta} + \frac{\lambda\Delta\theta}{p_{22}}\left(p_{11} + p_{12} - \frac{p_{21}p_{11} e^{-r\Delta\theta(q_{22}(r) - q_{21}(r))}}{p_{21} + p_{11}(1 - e^{-r\Delta\theta(q_{22}(r) - q_{21}(r))})}\right) \tag{9.22}$$

We summarize the above discussion in:

PROPOSITION 9.6

(a) The optimal Constitution with delegation to the politician entails (9.20), (9.21), (9.22).
(b) $q_{21}(r)$(resp. $q_{22}(r)$) is an increasing (resp. decreasing) function of r. Moreover, for all r, $q_{21}(r) < q_{22}(r)$.
(c) $\lim_{r\to\infty} q_{21}(r) = \lim_{r\to\infty} q_{22}(r) = q_2^u$.

Figure 9.1 describes the behavior of the solution.

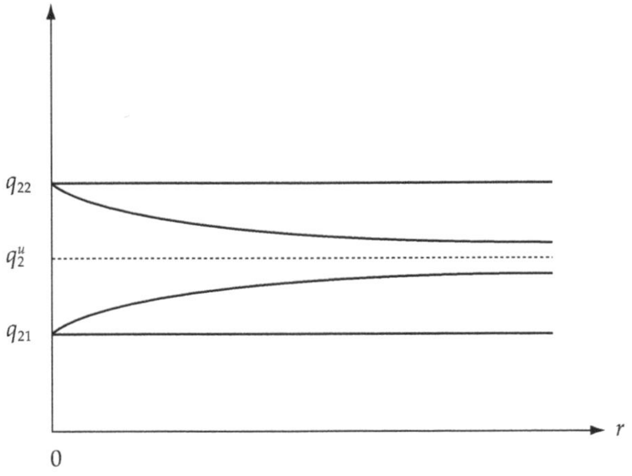

Figure 9.1

When risk aversion goes to zero, we obtain the conditional optimum. Indeed, since the politician is risk-neutral there is no need to give him a risk premium for bearing the risk associated with the contract to the agent. The principal obtains the signal τ at no cost. As risk aversion increases, a costly risk premium must be given to the politician. To mitigate this cost, the principal decreases the riskiness of the incentive payments to be made to the firm by decreasing the spread between q_{22} and q_{21}, i.e., by making the production level less responsive to the politician's information. In the limit as risk aversion goes to infinity, we get the unconditional optimum. The politician observing soft signals becomes useless.

To see the sensitivity of the solution with respect to the informativeness of the signals, consider the special case where

$$\Pr(\tau = \tau_1 \mid \theta = \theta_1) = \Pr(\tau = \tau_2 \mid \theta = \theta_2) = \varepsilon \quad \varepsilon \geq 1/2.$$

When ε goes to 1/2 (uninformative signal), the solution converges to the unconditional optimum. There is continuity at $\varepsilon = 1/2$ with the independent case.

When ε goes to 1 (complete information), we again converge to the unconditional optimum (as in Section 9.4). It is as if collusion is perfect.

This suggests that, if the principal can control the information structure of the politician, he will provide an information structure with an intermediary level of correlation. This reminds us of Proposition 4.1.b.

Furthermore, we can observe that incomplete information between the politician and the agent is a way to endogenize the transaction cost of collusion which was taken exogenously in Chapter 2. Indeed, one can identify[10] the two models with a transaction cost

$$k \approx \frac{r}{2}\left(1 + \frac{\nu\varepsilon}{(1-\nu)(1-\varepsilon)}\right)\Delta\theta\Delta q$$

for $\Delta\theta$, Δq small. This provides a building block for a theory of organizational design which takes these transaction costs into account. For example, when it comes to select who should be the

[10] See Faure-Grimaud, Laffont and Martimort (1998).

supervisor from two agents, this theory favors the choice of the less risk-averse agent to minimize the risk premium required.

Finally, we note that delegation to the politician is better than delegation to the agent in this model. More generally, governmental design will have to solve for the optimal allocation of delegation.

9.5 Conclusion

Delegation does two things. By cutting communication between the principal and one of the two agents, it makes impossible the use of Maskin games through which the principal extracts common information by relying on the possibility of conflicting reports. It basically restricts the principal to the use of revelation mechanisms designed to elicit all the information of the delegated agent, both his own private information and the information he acquires on the other agent.

Second, delegation introduces a moral hazard problem since the choice of the contract between the delegated agent and the agent becomes non-observable, and therefore non-directly controllable. With risk-neutral agents, this loss of control is irrelevant.

The combination of risk neutrality and our way of modeling collusion under centralization then leads to the absence of any efficiency loss in delegation. Decentralization appears costless.

When the principal has bounded rationality and can absorb only a limited amount of information, it is clear that decentralization which uses all the information may dominate centralization which will use a limited amount of information despite the conflicting objectives of the principal and the agents. Section 9.3 gives a more subtle result to the extent that it is the combination of the collusion-proof constraints and the limited communication constraints which triggers the superiority of delegation (while limited communication alone is not enough).

When the delegated agent is risk-averse, delegation introduces a new transaction cost with respect to centralization with a risk-neutral principal, since the risk associated with the incentive-compatible contract of the bottom agent must be borne by the delegated agent who requests a risk premium.

These insights clarify the problem of delegation in government when interest groups can form. They open up an avenue of research about the optimal structuring of delegation in more complex environments than those considered here. In particular, all the questions we have explored in Part I can be revisited with this new notion of transaction costs adapted to soft information. In addition, these questions can be embedded in a model of partisan politics as in Part II.

10

Concluding Remarks

> 'Without commitment to a paradigm, there could be no normal science.'
>
> Thomas Kuhn (1962), p. 100.

Economic activities as described in the Arrow–Debreu world require a political and judicial system which are left outside economic analysis. However, when public goods are introduced, the need for collective decision making, which is more than defining and enforcing a judicial system, becomes blatantly clear. We have argued that such a collective decision process needs intermediaries who are agents of the people, either for learning more about the issues than what ordinary people can do, or for deciding in the case of unanticipated circumstances.

The people must delegate to these intermediaries, called politicians, the dual roles of supervision and residual decision making. This delegation raises incentive issues which can be analyzed at two levels.

Assuming first that the Constitution attempts to maximize a well-defined notion of social welfare, the first difficulty comes from the private information of politicians which enables them to further their own private interests and to be captured by interest groups. Information here is the determinant of their power and one must study the design of governmental institutions including the selection of politicians to mitigate the costs of delegation.

Part I and Part III of the book followed this line of research. Chapter 2 showed how the Constitution must distort economic activities to avoid the capture of politicians by the economic interest groups they control. Incentives for politicians and bureaucrats must be put in place and decision making must be bureaucratized to limit the stakes of collusion at levels compatible with those incentives. Chapter 3 explored the extent to which the separation of powers can raise the transaction costs of collusion and thereby facilitate the fight against capture. Chapter 4 studied how the design of communication channels between governmental bodies must be structured and contributed to an analysis of checks and balances which stresses the dangers of reciprocal favors. All along, the modeling of collusion itself was a central question. Part I was based on Tirole's collusion model with verifiable (hard) information which can cover only a limited set of circumstances. This is why in Part III we returned to the central question of group incentives by proposing in Chapter 8 a new methodology for characterizing the optimal constitutional responses to the activities of interest groups when their private information is soft and cannot be verified by a third party. Chapter 9 used the same framework to question the costs and benefits of delegation in the realistic case where the Constitution must restrict its communications to those with the politicians. These two chapters open up new avenues of research in political economy, organization theory or sociology, because they provide a general constructive approach to ascertain the economic costs of group behavior based on private information.

Part II recognized that the Constitution was quite limited for controlling the politicians' discretion and incorporated the democratic selection of politicians in the analysis. The foundation for the use of crude majority games to determine which politician becomes the residual decision maker is the complexity of the real world and the incapacity of constitutional rules to anticipate all states of nature. The framers of the Constitution are then faced with the dilemma of endowing politicians with many policy instruments, which favors *ex post* efficiency, at the risk of seeing them extensively pursue their private agendas, or of drastically limiting their discretion and creating a lot of *ex post* inefficiencies. Chapters 4 and 5 explored this trade-off in the context of the regulation of natural monopolies, while Chapter 6 did the same for environmental policy.

All along, information economics has been very useful to formalize a number of ideas which are central to political economy: the various roles of politicians as informed supervisors or residual decision makers, the pros and cons of the separation of powers, the dangers of reciprocal favors, the trade-offs between discretion and flexibility in government, the institutional responses to collusion and corruption, etc.

The models used in this book are still much too simple to account for the richness of political institutions, and many readers will think that political economy is something else. Indeed, the political science literature seems quite far from our models, for two reasons. First, it has focused on distributional conflicts modeled as zero-sum games; and, second, it has exploited the institutional details to model much more carefully the decision-making process within a government.

This is fine, but political economy is more than this. It is the study of the interaction between the working of the economy and the political decision processes. By taking into account the decentralization of information in society, we have obtained a mapping of the political decisions into the determination and the distribution of the information rents—a mapping from politics to economics. Simultaneously, the distribution of these rents defines the stakes of collusive behavior and governs the formation of interest groups which interact on the political scene and determine the political choices—the mapping from economics to politics. We then have all the ingredients for a new political economy, which in the future should be able to better integrate the recent advances of political science.

Appendix. Translations of Passages Quoted in French

p. 3 n. 2

In a popular state, one mechanism more is necessary, namely virtue.

p. 22 n. 6

The great advantage of representatives is their capacity of discussing public affairs. For this the people collectively are extremely unfit.

p. 46 n. 1

There would be an end of everything, were the same man or the same body [of leading men], whether of the nobles or of the people, to exercise those three powers, that of enacting the laws, that of executing the public resolutions, and that of trying the crimes or disputes of individuals.

p. 75 n. 2

But if the legislative power in a free state should have no right to stay the executive, it has the right, and ought to have the means, of examining in what manner the laws it has made have been executed ...

Though in general the judiciary power ought not to be united with any part of the legislative, yet this is liable to three exceptions ...

The executive power ought to have a share in the legislature by the power of rejecting.

p. 78 n. 3

The suffrage by lot is natural to democracy

p. 95 main text

I should be glad to inquire into the distribution of the three powers in all the moderate governments we are acquainted with, in order to calculate from that the degrees of liberty which each may enjoy. But we should not always exhaust a subject so as to leave no work at all for the reader. My business is not to make people read, but to make them think.

p. 129, epigraph

The best tariff of all would be one that made those who travel along a route of communication pay a toll proportionate to the benefit they derive from their travel . . .

It is obvious that the effect of such a tariff would be, first to allow as many people to travel as if there were no charge—hence no loss of benefit to society—and second, to yield a revenue that always sufficed to permit a useful (public) work to be carried out.

I need not say that I do not believe in the possibility of imposing such a voluntary tariff; it would meet with an insurmountable objection in the universal dishonesty of travellers, but it is to that type that one must seek to approximate by means of a compulsory tariff.

p. 130 n. 1

The utility of a route of communication is at its maximum when the toll is nil.

Naturally, in order for the single question, whether tolls should or should not be imposed, to be considered in this manner, it would be necessary to examine what (new) tax or tax increase ought to replace them and what effects these taxes would have.

p. 131 main text

The State will intervene either to exercise the monopoly itself or to organize it in such a way as to be exercised without benefit or loss.

The railway monopoly ought to be exercised purely and simply either by the State or on its behalf, at cost price.

p. 132 n. 3

The construction costs of a canal, even the unavoidable ones, may be such that navigation rights are not enough to pay the interest on the initial outlay, even if the benefits that would accrue from it were far higher than the latter. In that case the nation will have to bear the costs of building it interest-free if it wishes to enjoy the goods that may result from it.

References

Aghion, P. and P. Bolton, (1994), 'Government Domestic Debt and the Risk of Default: A Political-Economic Model of the Strategic Role of Debt', Ch. 11 in *Public Debt Management: Theory and History*, R. Dornbusch and M. Draghy (eds.), Cambridge University Press, Cambridge, England.

Aghion, P. and P. Bolton, (1997), 'Incomplete Social Contracts', mimeo.

Auriol, E. and J.J. Laffont, (1992), 'Regulation by Duopoly', *Journal of Economics and Management Strategy*, 1, 503–533.

Baiman, S., (1982), 'Agency Research in Managerial Accounting: A Survey', *Journal of Accounting Literature*, 1, 154–213.

Balliga, S. and T. Sjostrom, (1996), 'Decentralization and Collusion', mimeo, Harvard University.

Banerjee, A.V., Besley T. and T.W. Guinnane, (1992), 'Thy Neighbor's Keeper: The Design of a Credit Cooperative with Theory and Test', *Quarterly Journal of Economics*, 46, 491–517.

Barnett, A. H., (1980), 'The Pigouvian Tax Rule Under Monopoly', *American Economic Review*, 70 (5), 1037–1041.

Baron, D., (1985a), 'Regulation of Prices and Pollution under Incomplete Information', *Journal of Public Economics*, 28, 211–231.

Baron, D., (1985b), 'Noncooperative Regulation of a Nonlocalized Externality,' *Rand Journal of Economics*, 16, 553–568.

Baron, D. and D. Besanko, (1992), 'Information, Control and Organizational Structure', *Journal of Economics and Management Strategy*, 1, 237–275.

Baron, D. and D. Besanko, (1995), 'Informational Alliances', mimeo, Stanford University.

Baumol, W. and D. Bradford, (1970), 'Optimal Departures From Marginal Cost Pricing', *American Economic Review*, 60, 265–283.

Becker, G., (1976), 'Comment', *Journal of Law and Economics*, 19, 245–248.

Becker, G., (1983), 'A Theory of Competition Among Pressure

Groups for Political Influence', *Quarterly Journal of Economics*, 98, 371–400.

Becker, G., (1985), 'Public Policies, Pressure Groups, and Deadweight Costs', *Journal of Public Economics*, 28, 329–347.

Bentley, A., (1908), *The Process of Government*, University of Chicago Press, Chicago.

Bernstein, M.S., (1955), *Regulating Business by Independent Commission*, Princeton University Press, Princeton.

Besley, T. and S. Coate, (1995), 'Group Lending, Repayment Incentives and Social Collateral', *Journal of Development Economics*, 46, 1–18.

Bohm, P. , (1981), *Deposit-Refund Systems: Theory and Applications to Environmental, Conservation, and Consumer Policy*, Johns Hopkins University Press for Resources for the Future, Baltimore.

Boyer, M., (1979), 'Les effets de la réglementation', *Canadian Public Policy/Analyse de Politiques*, 469–474.

Boyer, M. and J.J. Laffont, (1996), 'Environmental Protection, Producer Insolvency and Lender Liability', Ch. 1 (pp. 1–29) in *Economic Policy for the Environment and Natural Resources*, A. Xepapadeas (ed.), Edward Elgar Publishing, Aldershot.

Boyer, M. and J.J. Laffont, (1997), 'Environmental Risks and Bank Liability', *European Economic Review*, 41, 1427–1459.

Bramhall, D.F. and E.S. Mills, (1966), 'A Note on the Asymmetry between Fees and Payments', *Water Resources Research*, 2, 615–616.

Brennan, G. and J. Buchanan, (1977), 'Towards a Tax Constitution for Leviathan', *Journal of Public Economics*, 8, 255–273.

Breyer, W.S., (1992), *Breaking the Vicious Circle: Toward Effective Risk Regulation*, Harvard University Press, Cambridge, MA.

Buchanan, J., (1969), 'External Diseconomies, Corrective Taxes and Market Structure', *American Economic Review*, 59, 174–176.

Buchanan, J., (1987), 'The Constitution of Economic Policy', *American Economic Review*, 77(3), 243–250.

Buchanan, J.M. and G. Tullock, (1965), *The Calculus of Consent*, The University of Michigan Press, Ann Arbor.

Buchanan, J.M. and G. Tullock, (1975), 'Polluters' Profits and Political Response: Direct Control versus Taxes', *American Economic Review*, 65, 139–147.

Casper, G., (1997), *Separating Power: Essays on the Founding Period*, Harvard University Press, Cambridge, MA.

CEPR (1993), *Making Sense of Subsidiarity: How Much Centralization for Europe?*, CEPR, London.

Coase, R.H., (1946), 'The Marginal-Cost Controversy', *Economica*, 13, 169.

Coate, S. and S. Morris, (1995), 'On the Form of Transfers in Special Interests', *Journal of Political Economy*, 103, 1210–1235.

Coelho, P. , (1976), 'Polluters' Profits and Political Response: Direct Control versus Taxes: Comment', *American Economic Review*, 66, 976–978.

Collier, P. and A. Hoeffler, (1998), 'On Economic Causes of Wars', *Oxford Economic Papers*, 50, 563–573.

Congleton, R., (1984), 'Committees and Rent-Seeking Effort', *Journal of Public Economics*, 25, 197–209.

Crémer, J., (1996), 'Manipulation of Groves Mechanisms', *Games and Economic Behavior*, 13, 39–73.

Crémer, J. and R. McLean, (1988), 'Full Extraction of the Surplus in Bayesian and Dominant Strategy Auctions', *Econometrica*, 56, 1247–1258.

Crémer, J. and M. Riordan, (1987), 'On Governing Multilateral Transactions with Bilateral Contracts', *Rand Journal of Economics*, 16, 553–568.

Crocker, T., (1966), 'The Structuring of Atmospheric Pollution Control Systems', in *The Economics of Air Pollution*, H. Wolozin (ed.), W.W. Norton, New York.

Cropper, M. and W. Oates, (1992), 'Environmental Economics: A Survey', *The Journal of Economic Literature*, 30, 675–740.

Crozier, M., (1963), *Le Phénomène Bureaucratique*, Editions du Seuil, Paris. Translated as *The Bureaucratic Phenomenon*, University of Chicago Press, Chicago (1967).

Cukierman, A. and Y. Spiegel, (1998), 'When Do Representative and Direct Democracies Lead to Similar Policy Choices?', mimeo, Tel Aviv.

Dales, J.H., (1968a), 'Land, Water and Ownership', *Canadian Journal of Economics*, 1, 797–804.

Dales, J.H., (1968b), *Pollution, Property and Prices*, Toronto University Press, Toronto.

Dalton, M., (1959), *Men Who Manage*, reprinted as Ch. 13 in *The Sociology of Economic Life*, M. Granovetter and R. Swedberg (eds.), pp. 314–344, Westview Press, Boulder.

Dasgupta, P. , P. Hammond and E. Maskin, (1980), 'A Note on the

Imperfect Information and Optimal Pollution Control', *Review of Economic Studies*, 47, 857–860.

Deb, A., (1963), *Foremanship*, Asia Publishing House, New York.

Dewees, D.N., (1983), 'Instrument Choice in Environmental Policy', *Economic Inquiry*, 21, 53–71.

Dewees, D.N. and W.A. Sims, (1976), 'The Symmetry of Effluent Charges and Subsidies for Pollution Control', *Canadian Journal of Economics*, 9, 323–331.

Dixit, A., (1996), *The Making of Economic Policy: A Transaction Cost Politics Perspective*, Munich Lectures in Economics, The MIT Press, Cambridge, MA.

Downs, A., (1957), *An Economic Theory of Democracy*, Harper and Row, New York.

Dupuit, J., (1844), 'De la Mesure de l'Utilité des Travaux Publics', *Annales des Ponts et Chaussées*.

Dupuit, J., (1849), 'De l'Influence des Péages sur l'Utilité des Voies de Communication', *Annales des Ponts et Chaussées*.

Dye, R., (1985), 'Costly Contract Contingencies', *International Economic Review*, 26, 233–250.

Edgeworth, F.Y., (1913), 'Contributions to the Theory of Railways', *Economic Journal*.

Ekelund, R.B., (1968), 'Jules Dupuit and the Early Theory of Marginal Cost Pricing', *Journal of Political Economy*, 76, 462–71.

Faure-Grimaud, A. and D. Martimort, (1999), 'Political Stabilization by an Independent Bureaucracy', mimeo, IDEI.

Faure-Grimaud, A., J.J. Laffont and D. Martimort, (1998), 'A Theory of Supervision with Endogenous Transaction Costs', mimeo, IDEI.

Fershtmann, C., K. Judd and E. Kalai, (1991), 'Observable Contracts: Strategic Delegation and Cooperation', *International Economic Review*, 32, 551–559.

Frisch, R., (1939), 'The Dupuit Taxation Theorem', *Econometrica*, 7, 145–150.

Frisch, R., (1970), Nobel Lecture, The Nobel Foundation.

Gibbard, A., (1973), 'Manipulation for Voting Schemes', *Econometrica*, 41, 587–601.

Gouldner, A., (1954), *Patterns of Industrial Bureaucracy*, Free Press, New York.

Green, J. and J.J. Laffont, (1977), 'Characterization of Satisfactory

Mechanisms for the Revelation of Preferences for Public Goods', *Econometrica*, 45, 427–438.

Green, J. and J.J. Laffont, (1979), 'On Coalition Incentive Compatibility', *Review of Economic Studies*, 46, 243–254.

Green, J. and J.J. Laffont, (1982), 'Limited Communication and Incentive Constraints', Ch. 11 in *Information, Incentives and Economic Mechanisms*, T. Groves, R. Radner and S. Reiter (eds.), University of Minnesota Press, Minneapolis.

Green, J. and J.J. Laffont, (1986), 'Incentive Theory with Data Compression', Ch. 10, Vol. III, in *Uncertainty, Information and Communication*, W. Heller, R. Starr and R. Radner (eds.), Cambridge University Press, Cambridge, England.

Grossman, G. and E. Helpman, (1996), 'Electoral Competition and Special Interest Politics', *Review of Economic Studies*, 63, 265–286.

Guesnerie, R. and J.J. Laffont, (1984), 'A Complete Solution to a Class of Principal-Agent Problems with an Application to the Control of a Self-Managed Firm', *Journal of Public Economics*, 25, 329–369.

Gul F., H. Sonnenschein and R. Wilson, (1985), 'Foundations of Dynamic Monopoly and the Coase Conjecture', *Journal of Economic Theory*, 39, 155–190.

Gupta, S., Van Houtven, G. and M. Cropper, (1996), 'Paying for Permanence: An Analysis of EPA's Cleanup Decisions at Superfund Sites', *Rand Journal of Economics*, 27, 563–582.

Hahn, R.W., (1990), 'The Political Economy of Environmental Regulation: Towards a Unifying Framework', *Public Choice*, 65, 21–47.

Hahn, R.W. and A.M. McGartland, (1989), 'The Political Economy of Instrument Choice: An Examination of the U.S. Role in Implementing the Montreal Protocol', *Northwestern University Law Review*, 83, 592–611.

Handlin, O. and M. Handlin, eds. (1966), *The Popular Sources of Political Authority; Documents on the Massachusetts Constitution of 1780*, Belknap Press of Harvard University Press.

Holmström, B. and P. Milgrom, (1989), 'Regulating Trade Among Agents', *Journal of Institutional and Theoretical Economics*, 146, 85–105.

Holmström, B. and P. Milgrom, (1991), 'Multi-task Principal Agent Analysis: Incentive Contracts, Asset Ownership, and Job Design', *Journal of Law, Economics and Organization*, 7, 24–52.

Hotelling, H., (1938), 'The General Welfare in Relation to Problems of Taxation and of Railway and Utility Rates', *Econometrica*, 6, 242–269.

Hotelling, H., (1939), 'The Relation of Prices to Marginal Costs in an Optimum System', *Econometrica*, 7, 151–155.

Itoh, H., (1993), 'Collusion, Incentives, and Risk Sharing', *Journal of Economic Theory*, 60, 410–427.

Jeon, D.S. and J.J. Laffont, (1999), 'The Efficient Mechanism for Downsizing the Public Sector', forthcoming in *World Bank Economic Review*, The World Bank, Washington DC.

Jones, L.P., P. Tandon and I. Vogelsang, (1990), *Selling Public Enterprises*, MIT Press, Cambridge, MA.

Jullien, B., (1997), 'Participation Constraints in Adverse Selection Models', mimeo, IDEI.

Kahn, R.F., (1935), 'Some Notes on Ideal Output', *Economic Journal*, March.

Kamien, M.L., N.L. Schwartz and F.T. Dolbear, (1966), 'Asymmetry between Bribes and Charges', *Water Resources Research*, 2, 147–157.

Kaufman, H., (1961), 'Why Organizations Behave as They do: An Outline of a Theory', *Administrative Theory*, 37–72.

Khalil, F. and J. Lawarrée, (1994), 'On Commitment and Collusion in Auditing', mimeo, University of Washington.

Kiewiet, D.R. and M.D. McCubbins, (1991), *The Logic of Delegation*, The University of Chicago Press, Chicago.

Kneese, A.V. and B.T. Bower, (1968), *Managing Water Quality: Economics, Technology, Institutions*, Johns Hopkins University Press for Resources for the Future, Baltimore.

Kofman, F. and J. Lawarrée, (1993), 'Collusion in Hierarchical Agency', *Econometrica*, 61, 629–656.

Kofman, F. and J. Lawarrée, (1996a), 'A Prisoner's Dilemma Model of Collusion Deterrence', *Journal of Public Economics*, 40, 117–136.

Kofman, F. and J. Lawarrée, (1996b), 'On the Optimality of Allowing Collusion', *Journal of Public Economics*, 61, 383–407.

Kramnick, I., (1987), *The Federalist Papers*, Introduction, Penguin Books, London.

Kuhn, T., (1962), *The Structure of Scientific Revolutions*, The University of Chicago Press, Chicago.

Laffont, J.J., (1990), 'Analysis of Hidden Gaming in a Three Level

Hierarchy', *Journal of Law, Economics and Organization*, 6, 301–324.

Laffont, J.J., (1994), 'Regulation of Pollution with Asymmetric Information', Ch. 2 in *Nonpoint Source Pollution Regulation: Issues and Analysis*, C. Dosi and T. Tomasi (eds.), Kluwer Academic Publishers, Dordrecht.

Laffont, J.J. and D. Martimort, (1999), 'Separation of Regulators Against Collusive Behavior', *Rand Journal of Economics*, 30, 232–262.

Laffont, J.J. and D. Martimort, (1997), 'Collusion under Asymmetric Information', *Econometrica*, 65, 875–911.

Laffont, J.J. and D. Martimort, (1998), 'Collusion and Delegation', *Rand Journal of Economics*, 29, 280–305.

Laffont, J.J. and D. Martimort, (1999), 'Mechanism Design under Collusion and Correlation', forthcoming *Econometrica.*

Laffont, J.J. and E. Maskin, (1979), 'A Differentiable Approach to Expected Utility Maximizing Mechanisms', in *Aggregation and Revelation of Preferences*, J.J. Laffont (ed.), North-Holland, Amsterdam.

Laffont, J.J. and E. Maskin, (1980), 'A Differential Approach to Dominant Strategy Mechanisms', *Econometrica*, 48, 1507–1520.

Laffont, J.J. and T.T. N'Guessan, (1998), 'Competition and Corruption in an Agency Relationship', to appear in *Journal of Development Economics.*

Laffont, J.J. and T.T. N'Guessan, (1999), 'Group Lending with Adverse Selection', to appear in *European Economic Review.*

Laffont, J.J. and J. Tirole, (1987), 'Auctioning Incentive Contracts', *Journal of Political Economy*, 95, 921–937.

Laffont, J.J. and J. Tirole, (1993), *A Theory of Incentives in Procurement and Regulation*, MIT Press, Cambridge, MA.

Laffont, J.J. and J. Tirole, (1996), 'Creating Competition through Interconnection: Theory and Practice', *Journal of Regulatory Economics*, 10, 227–256.

Lane, J.E., (1996), *Constitutions and Political Theory*, Manchester University Press, Manchester and New York.

Lange, O. and F. Taylor, (1938), *On the Economic Theory of Socialism*, University of Minnesota Press, Minneapolis.

Launhardt, W., (1885), *Mathematische Begründung der Volkswirtschaftslehre.*

Lee, D.R., (1975), 'Efficiency of Pollution Taxation and Market

Structure', *Journal of Environmental Economic Management*, 2, 69–72.

Lerner, A., (1937), 'Statics and Dynamics in Socialist Economics', *Economic Journal*, June.

Lewis, T., (1997), 'Protecting the Environment when Costs and Benefits are Privately Known', *Rand Journal of Economics*, 27, 819–847.

Lewis, T. and D. Sappington, (1989), 'Countervailing Incentives in Agency Problems', *Journal of Economic Theory*, 49, 294–313.

Maggi, G. and A. Rodriguez, (1995), 'On Countervailing Incentives', *Journal of Economic Theory*, 66, 238–263.

Mailath, G. and A. Postlewaite, (1990), 'Asymmetric Information Bargaining Problems with Many Agents', *Review of Economic Studies*, 57, 351–368.

Marshall, A., (1890), *Principles of Economics*, Macmillan, London.

Martimort, D., (1995), 'Multiprincipals Regulatory Charter as a Safeguard Against Opportunism', mimeo, INRA, Toulouse.

Martimort, D., (1997), 'The Life Cycle of Regulatory Agencies: Dynamic Capture and Transaction Costs', forthcoming in *Review of Economic Studies*.

Maskin, E., (1999), 'Nash Implementation and Welfare Optimality', *Review of Economic Studies*, 66, 23–38.

Maskin, E., (1979), 'Implementation and Strong–Nash Equilibrium', Ch. 23 in *Aggregation and Revelation of Preferences*, J.J. Laffont (ed.), North-Holland, Amsterdam.

Maskin, E. and J. Tirole, (1990), 'The Principal-Agent Relationship with an Informed Principal 1: Private Values', *Econometrica*, 58, 379–410.

Maskin, E. and J. Tirole, (1999), 'Unforeseen Contingencies and Incomplete Contracts', *Review of Economic Studies*, 66, 83–114.

Mauro, P. , (1995), 'Corruption and Growth', *Quarterly Journal of Economics*, 110, 681–712.

McAfee, P. and J. McMillan, (1995), 'Organizational Diseconomies of Scope', *Journal of Economics and Management Strategy*, 4, 399–426.

McAfee, P. and P. Reny, (1991), 'Correlated Information and Mechanism Design', *Econometrica*, 60, 395–421.

Melumad, N., D. Mookherjee and S. Reichelstein, (1995), 'Hierarchical Decentralization of Incentive Contracts', *Rand Journal of Economics*, 26, 654–692.

Mintzberg, H., (1979), *The Structuring of Organizations*, Prentice Hall, New York.

Mirrlees, J., (1971), 'An Exploration of the Theory of Optimum Income Taxation', *Review of Economic Studies*, 38, 175–208.

Moe, T., (1986), 'Interests, Institutions, and Positive Theory: The Politics of the NLRB', *Studies in American Political Development*, 2.

Montesquieu, (1748), *De l'Esprit des Lois*, in Oeuvres Complètes, Editions du Seuil, (ed. 1964), Paris.

Montinola G., Y. Qian and B. Weingast, (1993), 'Federalism, Chinese Style: The Political Gains of Economic Success of China', mimeo, Hoover Institution, Stanford.

Mookherjee, D. and S. Reichelstein, (1992), 'Dominant Strategy Implementation of Bayesian Incentive Compatible Rules', *Journal of Economic Theory*, 56, 378–399.

Moore, J., (1992), 'Implementation, Contracts and Renegotiation in Environments with Complete Information', Ch. 5 in *Advances in Economic Theory, 6th World Congress of the Econometric Society*, J.J. Laffont (ed.), Cambridge University Press, Cambridge, England.

Mueller, D., (1997), *Constitutional Democracy*, Oxford University Press, Oxford.

Myerson, R., (1979), 'Incentive Compatibility and the Bargaining Problem', *Econometrica*, 47, 61–73.

Myerson, R., (1982), 'Optimal Coordination Mechanisms in Generalized Principal-Agent Problems', *Journal of Mathematical Economics*, 10, 67–81.

Myerson, R. and M. Satterthwaite, (1983), 'Efficient Mechanisms for Bilateral Trading', *Journal of Economic Theory*, 28, 265–281.

Neven, D., (1994), 'The Political Economy of State Aid in the European Community: Some Econometric Evidence', Deep, Lausanne.

Neven D., R. Nuttall and P. Seabright, (1993), 'Regulatory Capture and The Design of European Merger Policy', in *Merger in Daylight*, D. Neven, R. Nutall and P. Seabright (eds.), CEPR Press, London.

Niskanen, W., (1971), *Bureaucracy and Representative Government*, Aldine-Atherton, Chicago.

Noll, R., (1983), 'The Political Foundations of Regulatory Policy', *Journal of Institutional and Theoretical Economics*, 139, 377–404.

Noll, R., (1989), 'Economic Perspectives on the Politics of

Regulation', pp. 1253–1287 in R. Schmalensee and R. Willig (eds.), *Handbook of Industrial Organization*, North-Holland, Amsterdam.

North, D.C., (1990), 'A Transaction Cost Theory of Politics', *Journal of Theoretical Politics*, 2, 355–367.

Olsen, T. and G. Torsvick, (1993), 'The Ratchet Effect in Common Agency: Implication for Regulation and Privatization', *Journal of Law, Economics and Organization*, 9, 136–158.

Olson, M., (1965), *The Logic of Collective Action*, Harvard University Press, Cambridge, MA.

Pelzman, S., (1976), 'Toward a More General Theory of Regulation', *Journal of Law and Economics*, 19, 211–240.

Persson, T., (1997), 'Economic Policy and Special Interest Politics', *Frank Paish Lecture*, mimeo.

Persson, T. and G. Tabellini, (1996), 'Federal Fiscal Constitutions, Risk Sharing and Moral Hazard', *Econometrica*, 59, 689–701.

Persson, T., G. Roland and G. Tabellini, (1997), 'Separation of Powers and Political Accountability', *Quarterly Journal of Economics*, 112, 1163–1202.

Pigou, A.C., (1952), The Economics of Welfare, Macmillan, London (reprint of the 4th (1932) edition).

Plato, (1941), *The Republic of Plato*, translated by F. M. Cornford, Oxford University Press, Oxford.

Pollak, R.A., (1995), 'Regulating Risks', *Journal of Economic Literature*, 33, 179–191.

Porter, R. and D. Zona, (1993), 'Detection of Bid Rigging in Procurement Auctions', *Journal of Political Economy*, 101(3), 518–538.

Posner, R., (1974), 'Theories of Economic Regulation', *Bell Journal of Economics*, 5, 335–358.

Repullo, R., (1986), 'The Revelation Principle under Complete and Incomplete Information', in *Economic Organizations as Games*, K. Binmore and P. Dasgupta (eds.), Basic Blackwell, Oxford.

Riker, W.H., (1962), *The Theory of Political Coalitions*, Yale University Press, New Haven and London.

Riordan, M. and D. Sappington, (1988), 'Optimal Contracts with Ex Post Information', *Journal of Economic Theory*, 45, 189–199.

Roberts, M.J. and M. Spence, (1976), 'Effluent Charges and Licenses Under Uncertainty', *Journal of Public Economy*, 84, 193–208.

Robinson, J., (1934) 'The Economics of Hyperinflation', *Economic Journal*, September.

Robinson, M., (1985), 'Collusion and the Choice of Auction', *Rand Journal of Economics*, 16, 141–145.

Rogoff, K., (1985), 'The Optimal Degree of Commitment to an Intermediate Monetary Target', *Quarterly Journal of Economics*, 100, 1169–1189.

Rose-Ackerman, S., (1978), *Corruption: A Study in Political Economy*, Academic Press, New York.

Rousseau, J.J., (1948), *The Social Contract*, Hafner Publishing Company, New York.

Say, J.B., (1840), *Cours d'Economie Politique*, 7ème partie, Ch. XXIII.

Schumpeter, J., (1954), *History of Economic Analysis*, Oxford University Press, New York.

Seabright, P., (1996), 'Accountability and Decentralization in Government: An Incomplete Contracts Model', *European Economic Review*, 40, 61–90.

Segerson, K., (1995), 'Liability and Penalty Structures in Policy Design', in *Handbook of Environmental Economics*, D.W. Bromley (ed.), Basil Blackwell, Oxford.

Segerson, K., (1996), 'Issues in the Choice of Environmental Policy Instruments', Ch. 6 (pp. 149–174) in *Environmental Policy with Political and Economic Integration*, J.B. Braden, H. Folmer and T.S. Ulen (eds.), Edward Elgar, Aldershot.

Shleifer, A., (1985), 'A Theory of Yardstick Competition', *Rand Journal of Economics*, 16, 319–327.

Shleifer, A. and R. Vishny, (1993), 'Corruption', *Quarterly Journal of Economics*, 109, 599–617.

Smith, A., (1776), *The Wealth of Nations*, The Modern Library, New York (1937 edition).

Spulber, D. and D. Besanko, (1992), 'Delegation, Commitment, and the Regulatory Mandate', *Journal of Law, Economics and Organization*, 8, 126–154.

Starrett, D., (1972), 'Fundamental Non Convexities in the Theory of Externalities', *Journal of Economic Theory*, 4, 180–199.

Stigler, G., (1971), 'The Economic Theory of Regulation', *Bell Journal of Economics*, 2, 3–21.

Stigler, G., (1982), 'Economists and Public Policy', *Regulation*, 6, 13–17.

Stiglitz, J., (1990), 'Peer Monitoring and Credit Markets', *World Bank Economic Review*, 4, 351–366.

Strausz, R., (1997), 'Collusion and Renegotiation in a Principal-Supervisor-Agent Relationship', *The Scandinavian Journal of Economics*, 99, 497–518.

Tirole, J., (1986), 'Hierarchies and Bureaucracies: On the Role of Collusion in Organizations', *Journal of Law, Economics and Organization*, 2, 181–214.

Tirole, J., (1992), 'Collusion and the Theory of Organizations', in *Advances in Economic Theory, Sixth World Congress Vol. 2*, J.J. Laffont (ed.), Cambridge University Press, Cambridge, England.

Tirole, J. (1994), 'The Internal Organization of the Government', *Oxford Economic Papers*, 46, 1–29.

Tollison, R. (1989), 'Rent Seeking', Ch. 23 in *Perspectives on Public Choice*, D. Mueller (ed.), Cambridge University Press, Cambridge, England.

Truman, D., (1951), *The Government Process*, Knopf, New York.

Tullock, G., (1983), *Economics of Income Redistribution*, Kluwer-Nyhoff, Boston.

Vickrey, W., (1945), 'Measuring Marginal Utility by Reactions to Risk', *Econometrica*, 13, 319–333.

Vickrey, W., (1948), 'Some Objections to Marginal-Cost Pricing', *Journal of Political Economy*, 56, 218–38.

Vickrey, W., (1987), 'Marginal – and Average – Cost Pricing', *The New Palgrave*, J. Eatwell *et al.* (eds), Vol. III, 311–318, Macmillan, London.

Walras, L., (1897), 'L'Etat et les chemins de fer', *Revue du Droit Public et de la Science Politique*, mai–juin et juillet–août, reprinted in *August et Leon Walras Oeuvres Economiques Complètes*, Vol. X, *Economica*, 1992, Paris.

Weitzman, M.L., (1974), 'Prices vs Quantities,' *Review of Economic Studies*, 41, 477–91.

Williamson, O.F., (1989), 'Transaction Cost Economics', in *Handbook of Industrial Organization*, Vol. I, R. Schmalensee and R. Willig (eds.), North-Holland, Amsterdam.

Wilson, J., (1980), 'The Politics of Regulation', in *The Politics of Regulation*, J. Wilson (ed.), Basic Books, New York.

Wittman, D., (1989), 'Why Democracies Produce Efficient Results', *Journal of Political Economy*, 97, 1395–1424.

Yohe, G., (1976), 'Polluter's Profits and Political Response: Direct Control versus Taxes: Comment', *American Economic Review*, 66, 981–982.

Index

Lightning Source UK Ltd.
Milton Keynes UK
UKHW010255131021
392123UK00001B/11

9 780198 294245